MW00325263

DOING THE RIGHT THING

Doing the Right Thing

How Colleges and Universities Can Undo Systemic Racism in Faculty Hiring

Marybeth Gasman

PRINCETON UNIVERSITY PRESS

PRINCETON & OXFORD

Copyright © 2022 by Princeton University Press

Princeton University Press is committed to the protection of copyright and the intellectual property our authors entrust to us. Copyright promotes the progress and integrity of knowledge. Thank you for supporting free speech and the global exchange of ideas by purchasing an authorized edition of this book. If you wish to reproduce or distribute any part of it in any form, please obtain permission.

Requests for permission to reproduce material from this work should be sent to permissions@press.princeton.edu

Published by Princeton University Press
41 William Street, Princeton, New Jersey 08540
6 Oxford Street, Woodstock, Oxfordshire OX20 1TR

press.princeton.edu

All Rights Reserved

Library of Congress Cataloging-in-Publication Data

Names: Gasman, Marybeth, author.
Title: Doing the right thing : how colleges and universities can undo systemic racism in faculty hiring / Marybeth Gasman.
Description: Princeton : Princeton University Press, 2022. | Includes bibliographical references and index.
Identifiers: LCCN 2021039410 (print) | LCCN 2021039411 (ebook) | ISBN 9780691193076 (hardback) | ISBN 9780691229447 (ebook)
Subjects: LCSH: Minority college teachers—Selection and appointment—United States. | Minority college teachers—Recruiting—United States. | Racism in higher education—United States. | Faculty integration—United States. | BISAC: EDUCATION / Higher | EDUCATION / Leadership
Classification: LCC LB2332.72 .G37 2022 (print) | LCC LB2332.72 (ebook) | DDC 3378.1/2089—dc23
LC record available at https://lccn.loc.gov/2021039410
LC ebook record available at https://lccn.loc.gov/2021039411

British Library Cataloging-in-Publication Data is available

Editorial: Peter Dougherty & Alena Chekanov
Production Editorial: Ali Parrington
Production: Erin Suydam
Publicity: Maria Whelan & Kathryn Stevens
Copyeditor: Molan Goldstein

Jacket illustration by Liam Eisenberg, Marlena Agency

This book has been composed in Adobe Text and Gotham.

Printed on acid-free paper. ∞

Printed in the United States of America

10 9 8 7 6 5 4 3 2 1

For Chloë, who is the sole evidence I have that there is a God. She walks by my side as we ascend the peaks of life and lifts me up in the valleys.

I think we've been . . . really focused [on] hiring from the Ivies, we've got to get the thoroughbred, and that has also precluded us from looking more broadly at candidates in terms of race, ethnicity, or other aspects of diversity. Now there is some talk of extending beyond, but I will wait to see how much the departments actually will end up doing it, because we want to be like Harvard.

—AAU UNIVERSITY DEAN

CONTENTS

List of Tables   xi

Preface   xiii

1 Let's Lay the Cards on the Table   1

2 What Does Faculty Diversity Look Like?   15

3 "We Care about Diversity, but What about Quality?"   59

4 What about the Pipeline?   93

5 Where Are the Leaders?   132

6 Do Search Committees Know What They Are Doing?   150

7 Should We Require a Diversity Statement?   185

8 Exceptions? No! Excuses? Yes!   194

9 Dismantling and Reforming the System:
A Call to Action   210

Appendix A. Approach to the Study   231

Appendix B. A Deeper Look at Law Schools   235

Acknowledgments   241

References   245

Supplementary Bibliography   257

Index   265

TABLES

1. AAU Universities by Region and Public/Private Status   21

2. Faculty Racial and Ethnic Diversity at AAU
   Institutions (Tenured and Tenure-Track)   26

3. Faculty Racial and Ethnic Diversity at AAU
   Institutions (Tenured)   36

4. AAU Institutions with ADVANCE Grants   43

5a. Racial/Ethnic Breakdown of Tenure-Track and
   Tenured Women Faculty at AAU Institutions   46

5b. Racial/Ethnic Breakdown of Tenure-Track and
   Tenured Women Faculty at AAU Institutions   52

6. PhD Conferrals by Race/Ethnicity in Select Fields,
   2011–2018 (All Institutions)   96

7. Black/African American PhD Conferrals by Select
   Fields and Institutional Type, 2011–2018   102

8. Hispanic PhD Conferrals by Select Fields and
   Institutional Type, 2011–2018   104

9. Asian American PhD Conferrals by Select Fields and
   Institutional Type, 2011–2018   106

10. American Indian/Alaska Native PhD Conferrals
   by Select Fields and Institutional Type, 2011–2018   110

11. Native Hawaiian or Other Pacific Islander PhD
   Conferrals by Select Fields and Institutional Type,
   2011–2018   112

12. White PhD Conferrals by Select Fields and
    Institutional Type, 2011–2018   114

13. Nonresident PhD Conferrals by Select Fields and
    Institutional Type, 2011–2018   116

14. Non-AAU Very High Research Institutions   126

15. Non-AAU High Research Institutions   128

16. AAU Provosts Gender and Race   148

17. Full-time T14 Law Students by Race/Ethnicity,
    Fall 2016 (Percentages)   238

PREFACE

The United States is in the midst of a reckoning; it is being judged by its citizens for the world to see. Its institutions and organizations, which have been touting their commitment to racial and ethnic diversity, have been confronted overtly. Hollow statements that have long masked missing representation, and failed inclusion efforts, are no longer believed or accepted. People from all racial and ethnic backgrounds are challenging the efforts and commitments of those in power in corporations, the military, the police, the government, arts organizations, entertainment, the legal system, publishing, media, education, and many other areas. They are asking for movement, action, and proof that our nation's institutions are serious about embracing racial justice and dismantling systemic racism. Colleges and universities are not immune to this criticism and call to action. In fact, like all of our institutions, they are responsible for clinging to sameness and creating and upholding systems that perpetuate the status quo and fail to foster equity. Given their commitment to diversity and "academic excellence," they must lead the way to racial justice and equity instead of being dragged along kicking and screaming as they hold tightly to the past.

Marybeth Gasman
July 25, 2020

DOING THE RIGHT THING

1

Let's Lay the Cards on the Table

> A lot of these myths that are out there—"Oh, we don't have the pipeline," or "We can't get them to move to our town," or "The research areas don't match up with what we are looking for"—all of these myths are just created to sustain the situation that we have. The key is to recognize that falling back on all of these old myths is a barrier to making progress.
> —AAU UNIVERSITY PROVOST

Colleges and universities in the United States are admired around the world for their research, innovation, and academic excellence. In recent years, many institutions of higher education have even been lauded for their increased diversity in enrollment at the undergraduate level. To the dismay of some who believe diversity waters down institutional quality and academic excellence, between 1975 and 2016, the population of college undergraduates changed significantly, with increases across most racial and ethnic groups. Hispanic student enrollment has increased from 4% to 18%, Black student enrollment from 10% to 14%, Asian American and Pacific Islander enrollment from 2% to 7%, and Native American enrollment from 0.7% to 0.8% (National Center for Educational Statistics, 2019). At some of the nation's most selective institutions, the percentage of undergraduate students of color has increased substantially, and high standards of quality have remained intact. For example, as I am writing this book, Columbia University, New York University, and Stanford University have student bodies that consist of 66% students of color. Even more impressive, UCLA and UC-Berkeley boast undergraduate populations that consist of 73% students of color. And in the middle of the country, both Northwestern University and the University of Chicago have student bodies consisting of nearly 55% students of color.[1] Racial and ethnic diversification has advanced in undergraduate student populations across the country and even at the nation's most prestigious institutions.

Yet these colleges and universities—which boldly proclaim a dedication to overall diversity and excellence in their public statements, strategic plans, and on their websites—fail at achieving diversity (and thus excellence) among their faculty. Of all full-time, tenure-track, and tenured faculty in degree-granting postsecondary institutions in 2017, 41% were White men; 35% were White women; 6% were Asian/Pacific Islander men; 5% were Asian/Pacific Islander women; and 3% each were Black men, Black women, Hispanic men, and Hispanic women. Those who were American Indian/Alaska Native and those who were of two or more races each made up 1% or less of full-time faculty (National Center for Educational Statistics, 2019).

At the same time that colleges and universities are criticized by some for sacrificing excellence for the sake of diversity across various aspects of their institutions, in reality they are not aggressively pursuing racial and ethnic diversity among their faculty, nor are these ideas at the core of their definitions or understandings of excellence. Yes, colleges and universities call for "inclusive excellence," but typically this phrase is in place to assure critics that the only way that

---

1. Of note, the majority of the students of color at all of these research universities are from middle- and upper-income families. Pell Grant–eligible student percentages range from 13% to 21%. Forty percent of undergraduate students receive Pell Grants overall. For comparison's sake, at Historically Black Colleges and Universities, 71% of students are Pell Grant eligible. Student body information for research universities mentioned was drawn from institutional websites.

diversity will be pursued is if that diversity adheres to the criteria and pedigree deemed acceptable by those in power, namely Whites.

Colleges and universities—as well as their faculty—that purport to be the best in the world, that brag about their *U.S. News and World Report* rankings, and that hold fast to the belief that they truly want racial and ethnic diversity across all aspects of the academy must follow through on their promises. To date, they have not been genuine in terms of diversifying the faculty and eliminating the idea that Whiteness means excellence. Individuals from all racial and ethnic backgrounds are essential to creating knowledge and should have the opportunity to do so in an environment that appreciates, affirms, and supports them.

What would happen if the very definition of excellence were broadened to be more inclusive? What if universities reconceived their notions of academic excellence to have meaning only if racial and ethnic diversity are centered in these definitions? What would happen if faculties used the power that is linked to their shared governance voice—their contributions to university decision making—to foster justice and equity with regard to their ranks? What would result if faculties realized that diversifying their ranks is their responsibility and that not doing so is evidence that they don't support and are intellectually lazy about issues of equity? And how would the academy change if faculties realized, acknowledged, and grappled with the role that they play in upholding systemic racism in the academy, and especially within the faculty hiring process? These questions and more are at the center of my evidence and arguments in this book, and I aim to convince readers that faculties have the power to change this system that privileges Whiteness and rewards measures of excellence rooted in systemic racism.

Let me share a story to get to the heart of my argument. A professor asked me the following question:

Architects are in the business of producing buildings. Plausibly, what's most important is that we have the best producers of buildings, not that the producers be diverse. Plausibly, professors are in the business of producing knowledge. Why not care about having the best producers of knowledge, and if they happen to be White, so be it?[2]

I responded by saying, "I would argue that we won't know our potential for producing the best buildings, the most beautiful and impressive buildings, unless we are inclusive about who has the opportunity to produces these buildings. If we are more inclusive, we may even expand our definitions and understandings of 'the best,' the most beautiful, and impressive buildings. Likewise, I would argue that we don't truly know who the best producers of knowledge are if we aren't inclusive about who has the opportunity to produce knowledge. If we are more inclusive, we may even expand our definitions of 'the best' in terms of the production of knowledge"[3]

The Origin of an Idea

While I was on stage at the *New York Times* Higher Education Forum in 2016, the MacArthur Fellow and award-winning journalist Nikole Hannah-Jones asked me a question pertaining to the lack of faculty of color at most colleges and universities, but especially at highly selective institutions. Having been a professor for fifteen years at an Ivy League university, my response was frank: "The reason we don't have more people of color among college faculty is that we do not want them. We simply don't want them." Those in the audience were surprised by my candor.

At a cocktail party after the forum, an editor from the *Hechinger Report*, Lawrie Mifflin, approached me, asking if I'd be willing to put my comments in writing for her publication. I said yes. I was tired of watching as faculty colleagues throughout the nation constantly

---

2. This question was asked of me by Jacob Velasquez, an assistant professor at Cosumnes River College in Sacramento, California.

3. For an interesting discussion of the lack of diversity in architecture and its impact, see James S. Russell, "Confronting Architecture's Complicity with Racism," Bloomberg CityLab (March 25, 2021), https://www.bloomberg.com/news/features/2021-03-25/envisioning-an-architecture-of-blackness-at-moma.

brought up quality issues the minute diversity was raised as a goal, feigning a commitment to diversity but doing very little to achieve it. The *Hechinger Report* essay was later picked up by the *Washington Post*. The essay that appeared in both publications provided more context for my on-stage statement, more data, and concrete solutions to the lack of faculty diversity on college campuses. I pointed to the growing diversity of various academic disciplinary pipelines without corresponding growth in the professoriate. For example, between 2006 and 2016, there was a 32% increase in the number of doctorates awarded to African Americans, and during the same period, there was a 67% increase in doctorates earned by Latinos (National Science Foundation, 2018). Yet, we aren't seeing a substantial increase in the total number of professors of color.[4]

I also mentioned the wide-scale use of narrow, pedigree-driven definitions of quality and merit (an ideal principle when all things are equal, however, all things are not equal within the academy nor outside of it). I discussed the exceptions that are made for White candidates on a regular basis and the failure of universities to train search committees and hold them accountable. Lastly, I commented on the lack of innovation on the part of universities to diversify their faculty despite decades of research and practical recommendations by scholars. The *Washington Post* editor titled my essay "An Ivy League Professor on Why Colleges Don't Hire More Faculty of Color: 'We don't want them,'" which created an incredible buzz around the article. The national newspaper capitalized on my status at Penn, one of the nation's most prestigious universities, a member of the Ivy League, and a place, like other Ivy League institutions, that proudly chases "the best" at both the faculty and student levels.

I received more than 7,000 messages after *The Washington Post* (2016) published my essay. Most of the messages were from people of color telling me their stories of being rejected over and over by

---

4. Of note, one could argue that systemic racism is not the only reason for the low percentage of faculty of color being hired (i.e., proportional increases are based on already small numbers of faculty in the first place.)

faculty search committees; many of the stories were gut-wrenching and sad. One African American woman wrote, "despite having terrific credentials and applying for over 200 faculty positions, I have been denied for a faculty position over and over, making me wonder if pursuing a PhD was worth it. . . . I wonder if I should discourage other African Americans from doing so." A Latina wrote, "I wept when I read your essay because I have always suspected what you wrote but didn't know for sure. I am glad you revealed the truth but to hear it was hard, almost devastating." Over 100 people sent me their CVs and asked if I knew of institutions that were seriously seeking a diverse faculty, and people continue to send CVs whenever the article gets reposted on social media. An African American woman asked, "Can you introduce me to colleagues who will value me and help me grow as a professional? Can you offer advice on my resume?" Others wrote about the many times they were "told privately that [they] didn't fit in by a member of a search committee" or that they "weren't good enough to join the faculty" at various institutions "due to their institutional pedigree." A Latino man confessed that he was told his pedigree wasn't good enough for a faculty engineering position even though he attended the flagship university in his state. "I have several published articles in top journals. What more can I do to be qualified in a field with hardly any Latino professors?" One African American man expressed with hope, "I'm actually optimistic that if people read your essay and reflect, perhaps they will change. Sometimes it takes being shamed to change your ways and to see the world from the perspectives of others." Although my comments in the *Washington Post* were not new—others had written about these issues long before me, including many people of color whom I will discuss in the pages that follow—what stood out, and what made people take notice, was my position as a White woman at an Ivy League institution. Why? First, when someone with the "appropriate" credentials and who looks like those maintaining systemic racism speaks out, people are more likely to listen and believe them. And second, many people of color took notice because they aren't used to White people in the academy being honest and speaking in a forthright manner about racial inequity. How do I know? People told me.

The stories sent to me by people of color were not new to me. I have witnessed these experiences with my own students and with students throughout the nation, as I often sit on dissertation committees for students of color across various disciplines and at other universities.[5] Most recently, I had a mentee, a Black man, who applied for over 100 faculty positions at colleges and universities in the United States and Canada. He has a superb background, having attended some of the most prestigious institutions in France, the United States, and Canada. Despite these accomplishments, a strong dissertation, and ten first-author publications, he has not been able to secure a faculty position for the past six years. As I wrote this book, I was still sending out letters of recommendation for him.

I also received countless messages from White people telling me that they have seen or experienced most—or everything—I wrote about in the essay at their own institutions. A White man told me, "We did the same things you described in your essay to [White] women in my chemistry department for years. We questioned their qualifications to keep them out." Some White people told me about their stories of fighting for justice and becoming "unpopular or targeted" because of the fight. It is important to acknowledge that if one speaks out against racism and injustice, there are very real possibilities that there will be retaliation, marginalization, and ostracism as

5. As I was responding to suggestions from my editor at Princeton University Press, two African American women–Joy Melody Woods and Shardé Davis–started a hashtag on Twitter—#BlackintheIvory—which generated thousands of accounts of racism experienced by students, staff, and faculty within academe. As I scrolled through these tweets, I saw they were very similar in tone and experiences to the emails I received in 2016. For more information on the movement created by Woods and Davis, see Nidhi Subbaraman (2020), How #BlackInTheIvory put a spotlight on racism in academe, *Nature*, https://www.nature.com/articles/d41586 -020-01741-7; and Francie Diep (2020), "I was fed up": How #BlackInTheIvory got started, and what its founders want to see next, *Chronicle of Higher Education*, https://www.chronicle.com/article/I-Was-Fed-Up-How/248955. You can also follow the hashtag on Twitter to learn more.

a result (Duffy and Sperry, 2014; Hollis, 2015). I have experienced all of these firsthand.

Others who wrote to me divulged that they had remained silent all too often, that my essay inspired them to act, and that they were "committed to challenging their colleagues' racism even if it means being marginalized." Still others admitted that they were guilty of many of the actions I pointed out in my essay and regretted their behavior. One White man characterized himself as a "recovering racist fighting the good fight now after realizing how much fear and hatred I had about the changing landscape of higher education." These faculty members had seen substantial change over the course of their careers in the curriculum, and often in the student body, due to protests, sit-ins, and efforts—large and small—to make campuses more inclusive (Andrews and Biggs, 2006; Morgan and Davies, 2012; Polletta, 1998; Turner, González, and Wood, 2008; Williamson-Lott, 2018). Many of them had been supportive of these efforts but admitted to being quiet and complacent when it came to diversifying their own ranks and breaking down the systems that perpetuate sameness in the professoriate.

I also received many messages that attempted to justify racism and hate. The most interesting observation from a review of all the messages received (over 7,000) was that although I wrote the essay about faculty of color more generally, the negative and hateful comments were entirely about African Americans. Let me provide an example from one of the many emails that illustrates my point. According to a White man and professor at an Ivy League university, "Too often the Black professorial caucuses are militant agitators. At [my institution] they've just about wrecked the place. They've gotten the Black students so fired up they (the students) are demanding separate lodging, separate dining halls, and separate student centers. They have also forced colleges to institute extreme curtailments on freedom of speech and thought. It is ironic that at [my institution], the militants who hate the place so much will leave school with no student loan debt in accordance with the school's financial aid policy. There's gratitude for you. Integration on the college campus is just not working I'm sorry to say. I wish it would. But facts are facts." The mere presence of African Americans makes this White man uncomfortable. He is just one of many individuals who wrote similar comments to me and is also representative of the systemic behavior that scholars have pointed to for decades—behavior that serves as a roadblock to equity, inclusivity, and justice in the professoriate (Matthew, 2016a, 2016b; Posselt, 2016; Smith, 2015; Turner, González, and Wood, 2008).

Consulting an Expert

Daryl Smith, professor emeritus at the Claremont Graduate School, has inspired me for decades—since I was a PhD student at Indiana University. I read of her work in many of my classes. Given that she has written extensively on issues of faculty diversity, I wanted to interview her for this book—to bolster the overall context. I'm glad that I engaged her for numerous reasons, as her voice adds substantially to the book; I have drawn upon her knowledge throughout when appropriate. I was particularly interested in her perspective on why universities and faculty, more specifically, don't move in meaningful ways on issues of diversity in hiring, as that has been my experience. Smith is forthright, and when I asked her this question, she noted that she disagreed with my notion about the lack of faculty diversity—that "We don't want them." In fact, she thinks institutions want to bring in more diversity, but "they don't want to do what it takes to get it done." I think she and I actually agree. If you truly want something, you work to make it happen; if you don't put in the work to diversify the faculty, you really don't want to diversify the faculty.

Smith told me a story that she uses to help people understand the reasons why these kinds of changes don't happen or are slow to happen. She relayed, "I tell this little story. It puts a context [in place] for institutional change. And the context is my own humility about the fact that I could teach a doctoral seminar on adult development in which I could demonstrate why exercise is critical to healthy aging— all the research [says so], I know it, I believe it—but at four o'clock in the afternoon, I can't get myself up to go exercise. And I say, if I can't get myself to do what I absolutely know is essential, why do I think institutional change will be simple?"

She continued, explaining to me that she purposefully used technology as an example in her book on faculty diversity—*Diversity's Promise for Higher Education*, because it provides an instance of how institutional change happened in a fairly rapid manner. According to Smith, "we understood technology was an imperative. We didn't care that some faculty members stood up and said libraries would close and books would go away. And you know, they stood up. We all sat there, waited [un]til they finished their tirade and sat down." However, she explained, "With diversity, that's not what we do. Two people stand up and say something, and we stop." The language around diversity in faculty hiring has been framed around social justice, affirmative action, and a variety of other ways, but Smith thinks that it has to be framed around the idea that "diversity is imperative for your [institutional] mission" and explains that diversity is increasingly becoming an "imperative for excellence in almost every industry" (Chang, Milem, and Antonio, 2005; Sensoy and DiAngelo, 2017; Smith, Turner, et al., 2004; Turner, González, and Wood, 2008). I build on Smith's ideas and assert that racial and ethnic equity, in particular, need to be centered in our definitions of academic excellence or we are in no way excellent.

Over many years, what I have found consistent across institutions that I visited and, more recently, across people I talked with for this book is that the need to connect excellence to diversity is essential for leaders. Why? Because racism engenders immediate questions around quality the very moment that diversity is put forward as a goal. However, this idea of "excellence" is different from what Daryl Smith is talking about above. She thinks that in order to achieve excellence as an organization, diversity must exist, and she works hard to demonstrate, using data, how important diversity is in the life of an organization and its ability to grow, thrive, and innovate (Page, 2019). When "excellence" is mentioned in faculty hiring discussions (or student admissions, for that matter), it is raised when people fear that diversity will lead to the erosion of quality. They often do not see how important and essential diversity is to achieving excellence in an organization. They attach excellence to diversity as a way to quell the fears of those who harbor racist notions around the inclusion of those from underrepresented racial and ethnic groups. Instead, I believe they should expand the definition of excellence to include greater racial and ethnic diversity and a commitment to equity.

In this book, I argue that our definitions of excellence are flawed and that excellence in higher education can only exist when diversity is present. There cannot and should not be a trade-off—meaning that we forgo diversity for excellence. This kind of trade-off is rendered impossible as excellence within our faculty candidate pools, departments, colleges, schools, and universities cannot exist without diversity—both broadly defined and with racial and ethnic diversity firmly at the center. To have the best scholars and the best ideas, and to achieve the excellence that we so greatly desire, we must have the voices, perspectives, and presence of a highly diverse group of individuals. It is the role of faculty to safeguard the excellence of institutions of higher education, and thus we cannot forgo our responsibilities and act in intellectually lazy ways around issues of equity and systemic racism.

Past Research on Faculty Recruitment

There have been very few books written about the faculty hiring process despite its importance. Caroline Sotello Turner and Samuel Meyers (1999) published *Faculty of Color in Academe: Bittersweet Success*, which chronicles the experiences of faculty of color and covers discrimination issues in the faculty hiring process. Turner followed up this book with *Diversifying the Faculty: A Guidebook for Search Committees* (2002), which is a very helpful step-by-step guidebook for search committees but does not pull from national data or interviews or tackle the issues that make faculty hiring so thorny. These books are twenty years old at this point. Additionally, JoAnn Moody wrote a handbook in 2004 (updated in 2012), similar to Turner's, that includes some attention to faculty recruitment, but the majority of the book is focused on retention and mentoring.[6]

---

6. There are additional books that provide practical skills around various aspects of faculty hiring. These include: Jeffrey Buller (2017), *Best Practices for*

Gabriella Muhs, Yolanda Niemann, Carmen González, and Angela Harris covered the same kinds of incidents as Turner and Meyers in their book *Presumed Incompetent: The Intersections of Race and Class for Women in Academia* (2012). Likewise, Patricia Matthew chronicled first-person narratives of discrimination experienced by faculty in her edited book *Written/Unwritten: Diversity and the Hidden Truths of Tenure* (2016b). Although Matthew's collection of essays focuses on tenure, it follows various individuals of color from the faculty hiring process through tenure, detailing their experiences. And as mentioned, Daryl Smith's book, updated in 2020, *Diversity's Promise for Higher Education* uses extensive data and explores issues of faculty diversity and implicit bias within the larger framework of institutional diversity.

Many researchers have produced peer-reviewed work pertaining to various aspects of the faculty hiring process, examining bias, pipelines, process, gender, and race. I have drawn upon and built upon their work throughout this book. To date, however, there has not been a book that takes on the issue of systemic racism in faculty hiring on a large scale, drawing on multiple data sources and providing concrete solutions and pathways for change. That is my goal.

The Purpose of This Book

In this book, I draw on wide-scale data from the National Center for Educational Statistics, the National Science Foundation's Survey of Earned Doctorates, interviews with those involved in the faculty recruiting process across American Association of Universities (AAU) institutions, and a variety of other sources. A detailed description of my research approach and data sources can be found in Appendix A. I have written this book in a conversational tone

---

Faculty Search Committees: How to Review Applications and Interview Candidates. Jossey-Bass; and Christopher Lee (2014). *Search Committees: A Comprehensive Guide to Successful Faculty, Staff, and Administrative Searchers.* Stylus Press. In addition, there are books that look at the career choices of "high-achieving minority students" and their interest or lack of interest in faculty careers (e.g. Stephen Cole and Elinor Barber (2003). *Increasing Faculty Diversity: The Occupational Choices of High-Achieving Minority Students.* Harvard University Press.)

and in a way that is intended to appeal to a more general audience of faculty, administrators, and students across academic disciplines as well as the larger public interested in higher education.

With this book, I aim to persuade the reader of the many ways that universities—and their faculties—reinforce and perpetuate systemic racism in faculty hiring. I also hope to change behavior. I know that it will be difficult to convince some readers. However, I hope to make progress with those readers who play a role in faculty hiring, purport to believe in equity and justice for people of color, and claim to want to remove systemic racism from our institutions, yet cannot—as Daryl Smith says—get off the couch and move. I aim to convince these faculty members and administrators that regardless of their disciplines and intellectual expertise, it is their role—part of their shared governance obligations—to become educated about the ways that pedigree and Whiteness undergird systemic racism in faculty hiring. Moreover, if we know that we have problems in the pipeline, in the hiring process, and as a result of our personal biases, I aim to push faculties to stop merely acknowledging the problems but to work to concretely change the overall system that only works for a few, and not for justice. The system that, in effect, limits knowledge by limiting who produces it.

The final chapter of this book offers a series of data-driven, practical ideas and strategies for challenging ourselves and for dismantling and rebuilding faculty hiring processes. Although I do believe that bias and injustice are pervasive in the academy, I also believe that we have the ability to make substantial and deeply meaningful change if we want to, but only if we truly want to. I am an optimist in the fight for justice.

Lastly, I wrote this book with the premise that diversity is important in faculties and that equity is essential. These facts are not up for debate with me. Not only is there ample research that shows that racial and ethnic diversity is important to student learning, student interactions, and student socialization (Bayer and Rouse, 2016; Gurin et al., 2004; Springer, 2006), but there is also much evidence to show that more racial and ethnic diversity makes organizations stronger and encourages better ideas (Bayer and Rouse, 2016; Chapple and Humphrey, 2014; Gurin et al., 2004; Hafsi and Turgut, 2013;

Ifill, 2000; Ottaviano and Peri, 2006; Taylor et al., 2010). In addition, we are in the midst of a rapidly changing college student population across the nation. Let's be clear: we should have diverse faculties regardless of what our student bodies look like; however, increasing the diversity of our faculties has become an absolute necessity at this point. It has become clear over the last decade—with various protests and calls to action on the part of students—that our current faculties are not prepared to teach a diverse nation (Conrad and Gasman, 2015). We need to bring in new ideas, voices, and perspectives across various forms of diversity. In this book, I discuss racial and ethnic diversity, as those are my particular areas of expertise; however, I hope that others will build on this research and choose to explore issues of gender, religion, sexuality, ability, and political perspective in the future.

If, as a reader, you still aren't convinced that having a diverse faculty is essential, consider this example from Professor Daryl Smith:

> I was [at a] hospital giving a talk, and the person who invited me was a cardiologist and she said, "There's going to be one of our doctors who's only interested in science. He's not interested in diversity. He's interested in good science." I said, "Oh good." And she said, "He's going to follow you around all day." I said, "Oh, good, because as far as I'm concerned [diversity] is about good knowledge and good research." So I used Ambien as one example. Since just last year, we discovered that women were being double dosed. The healthy dose stayed in women's systems on average much longer than in men's. So women were driving under the effects of Ambien—not good science. Why did that happen? Because nobody disaggregated the data by gender. We have also learned that there was a very common heart drug that was being given to men, except it looked like it was dangerous for Black men. [The reason that we have bad science] is that there weren't enough Black men in the clinical trials. When you frame diversity in this way, you find that people go, "Oh."

For some, it takes evidence that goes well beyond justice to embrace diversifying the professoriate.

2

What Does Faculty Diversity Look Like?

The fastest growing populations are international faculty
and White women [faculty]. It's not okay to have no [White]
women, but we need to bring in a richer diversity.
—DARYL SMITH, 2019

Diversity is a nebulous word within the academy.[1] Institutions call for it and express their commitment to it in speeches, strategic plans, public statements, and on their websites. Some college and university constituents embrace diversity in all its forms; others, in specific or selective forms; still others object to the idea of diversity and don't see the value. Some people think our notions of diversity are watered down and that the word has become mere lip service to a cause. The fact is that calls for more diversity and stated commitments to diversity are both out of synch with and contradict the reality of faculty

1. For the purposes of this book, I am interested in racial and ethnic diversity (often as they intersect with gender), although I value diversity across the board in higher education—including diversity of thought. I believe in academic freedom even for ideas that I don't agree with and find objectionable.

hiring practices. This problem renders true diversity, which must include racial and ethnic diversity, in the higher education context a myth. Why? Because racial and ethnic diversity conflict with traditional (White) definitions of academic excellence instead of serving as the foundation for such excellence.

Issues of faculty diversity are most concerning at the nation's highly selective research universities; hence, I focused on the universities that are members of the American Association of Universities (AAU) throughout this book. Founded in 1900, the AAU is composed of sixty-five public and private research universities in the United States and Canada. Membership is by invitation only, and historically it was based on doctoral education and sponsored research. This arrangement makes it different from membership in the American Council on Education (ACE)[2] and the American Association of Colleges and Universities (AAC&U)[3] (Thelin, 2011). In the words of the historian John Thelin, "One unexpected consequence of the concentration of research power in a relatively small circle of elite universities was that it promoted, rather than discouraged, institutional aspirations across the higher-education landscape" (p. 106). Thelin also adds that most institutions in the South were initially left out of the AAU, as "the South had long been dismissed as an academically underdeveloped higher education environment" (p. 106). However, in the post–World War II period, institutions such as Emory University, Texas A&M University, and the University of Florida joined the

2. Membership in the American Council on Education is open to degree-granting accredited colleges and universities in the United States and its territories; higher education–focused nonprofit associations in the United States and its territories; degree-granting colleges and universities based outside the United States; and higher education associations based outside the United States. For more information, see https://www.acenet.edu/Membership-Advancement/Pages/Membership/Membership.aspx.

3. Membership in the Association of American Colleges & Universities is open to regionally accredited institutions of higher education, college and university system offices, and higher education associations in the United States. Higher education institutions that are authorized by their national governments are also eligible for membership. For more information, see https://www.aacu.org/join-aacu.

few southern institutions that had been invited to the AAU earlier in the twentieth century (Thelin, 2011).

I will focus on the sixty institutions that are in the United States.[4] Selection as an AAU institution is based on a number of factors, including competitively funded federal research support; faculty membership in the national academies; faculty awards, fellowships, memberships, and citations; federal, state, and industrial research funding; doctoral education and degree granting; postdoctoral appointees; and quality of undergraduate education (Association of American Universities, 2012). Diversity of the student body and faculty are not considered as part of the criteria for membership in the AAU.

Despite a lack of stated commitment to or requirement for faculty diversity for membership, the AAU and its member institutions are widely admired across the world, representing a highly successful group of institutions by most traditional measures. These institutions are committed to the pursuit of groundbreaking, rigorous research, high-quality teaching, and community engagement. Yet, the AAU institutions (as well as others) cannot be truly excellent until they expand their notions of excellence to include an enacted commitment to diversity among the faculty, staff, and students.

The majority of AAU institutions talk about the importance of "inclusive excellence" or "diversity" in their missions and on their websites. For example, the University of Pennsylvania claims, "Penn is committed to creating a community of students, scholars, and staff that reflects the diversity of the world we live in."[5] Or, the University of Michigan, which boasts that "The University of Michigan cannot be excellent without being diverse in the broadest sense of that word. We also must ensure that our community allows all

4. At the time that I was researching this book, there were sixty US AAU institutions. On November 7, 2019, after my data collection was complete and nearly all of the writing for this book was complete, three new US universities joined the AAU: Dartmouth College, the University of California–Santa Cruz, and the University of Utah. See Ellis (2019).

5. See the University of Pennsylvania's website at www.upenn.edu for more information.

individuals an equal opportunity to thrive."[6] Despite these individual proclamations, diversity does not manifest in the AAU's mission, which states: "Our member universities earn the majority of competitively-awarded federal funding for research that improves public health, seeks to address national challenges, and contributes significantly to our economic strength, while educating and training tomorrow's visionary leaders and innovators. AAU member universities collectively help shape policy for higher education, science, and innovation; promote best practices in undergraduate and graduate education; and strengthen the contributions of leading research universities to American society."[7] The factors mentioned above, upon which membership is decided, fail to include diversity. I wonder what would happen if membership were also contingent on faculty and student diversity? Who would lose membership? Who would gain membership? How would prestige be defined in higher education overall, given the aspirational notion of the AAU (Thelin, 2011)? What if diversity were the cornerstone of prestige in higher education?[8]

6. See the University of Michigan's website at diversity.umich.edu for more information.

7. Even when one delves deeper into the AAU website, into the key issues area, diversity is not listed. The key issues include: accreditation and accountability, campus climate [in relation to Title IX] and safety, federal budget, higher education legislation, higher education regulation, humanities, immigration, innovation and competitiveness, intellectual property, research administration and regulation, science and security, and taxation and finance. See https://www.aau.edu/key-issues.

8. Of note, although there is no noticeable mention of diversity on the AAU website nor in the organization's description of what makes for an AAU institution, through a Google search, I was able to find a 1997 statement on diversity (https://www.aau.edu/sites/default/files/AAU-Files/AAU-diversity-statement-4-17-97.pdf) and a 2015 statement (https://www.aau.edu/newsroom/press-releases/statement-diversity-board-directors-association-american-universities). I also found a press release related to eight AAU institutions coming together to increase PhD diversity. This press release was issued on September 12, 2019 (https://www.aau.edu/newsroom/press-releases/aau-launches-phd-initiative-pilot-eight-universities). As I was doing revisions for the book at the request of my editor at Princeton University Press, the nation was in the midst of large protests sparked by the May 25, 2020, murder of George Floyd by a Minneapolis police officer. The

Throughout this book, I'll reference various AAU institutions through interviews (without detailing the specific names of the institutions),[9] the use of national data, and materials acquired from websites (see appendix A for details). These AAU institutions are central to discussions of faculty diversity in hiring and issues of systemic racism, as many of their ideas are emulated and held up as best practices by other institutions throughout the United States (Waymer and VanSlette, 2016). The AAU institutions in the United States include Boston University, Brandeis University, Brown University, California Institute of Technology (Cal Tech), Carnegie Mellon University, Case Western Reserve University, Columbia University, Cornell University, Duke University, Emory University, Georgia Institute of Technology (Georgia Tech), Harvard University, Indiana University, Iowa State University, Johns Hopkins University, Massachusetts Institute of Technology (MIT), Michigan State University, New York University (NYU), Northwestern University, Ohio State University, Pennsylvania State University, Princeton University, Purdue University, Rice University, Rutgers University, Stanford University, Stony Brook University, Texas A&M University, Tulane University, University of Arizona, University of Buffalo, University

---

AAU did not issue a statement condemning systemic racism or police brutality during this time as so many other organizations did (as of June 12, 2020). The American Council on Education, for example, issued a statement on June 2, 2020 (https:// www.acenet.edu/News-Room/Pages/Statement-by-ACE-President-Ted-Mitchell -on-Racial-Violence-and-Injustice.aspx). The AAU did issue statements pertaining to President Trump's vile treatment of international students (https://www .aau.edu/newsroom/press-releases/aau-president-welcomes-reversal-misguided -ice-policy-international-students) and DACA students (https://www.aau.edu /newsroom/press-releases/aau-president-thanks-scotus-urges-legislative-action -protect-daca)—issues that were prominent during the same time as the large-scale protests against racism in the United States in spring and summer of 2020.

9. All of the individuals and institutions that I interviewed for this book are disguised. However, there may be times that I discuss AAU institutions based on publicly available data. Because the group of AAU institutions in the United States is small (n = 63; n = 60 as I wrote this book), I have not identified which AAU institutions participated and which ones did not participate in this study; this information would violate the universities' confidentiality and the confines of my Institutional Review Board (IRB) process at the University of Pennsylvania.

of California (UC)–Davis, UC-Berkeley, UC-Irvine, UCLA, UC–San Diego, UC–Santa Barbara, University of Chicago, University of Colorado–Boulder, University of Florida, University of Illinois, University of Iowa, University of Kansas, University of Maryland, University of Michigan, University of Minnesota, University of Missouri, University of North Carolina–Chapel Hill, University of Oregon, University of Pennsylvania, University of Pittsburgh, University of Rochester, University of Southern California, University of Texas at Austin, University of Virginia, University of Washington, University of Wisconsin, Vanderbilt University, Washington University in St. Louis, and Yale University. As I discuss the AAU institutions, I refer to them by their region of the country as well as their public or private status (see table 1).[10]

Faculty Diversity at AAU Institutions

To have a deeper understanding of faculty diversity at the institutions in the AAU, I drew upon 2017 data from the US Department of Education's National Center for Educational Statistics (NCES).[11] To appreciate the challenges around faculty hiring, it is key to see the full landscape of the institutions.

The AAU members with the highest percentages of Black tenured and tenure-track faculty are the University of North Carolina (5.7%), University of Illinois (4.8%), Brown University and Emory University (both 4.7%), and Johns Hopkins University and University of Virginia (both 4.6%) (see table 2). When examining these universities, I noticed that most of them are in the South, where there are larger concentrations of African Americans. However, Brown University is also on the list. Of interest, Brown launched a purposeful faculty hiring and diversity initiative after Ruth Simmons, the first African American president of an Ivy League institution,

---

10. The starred institutions in table 1—the University of Utah, Dartmouth College, and UC–Santa Cruz—were not members of the AAU when I conducted the research for this book.

11. Data from 2017 were the latest available as I wrote this book.

Table 1	AAU Universities by Region and Public/Private Status		
Northeast	**South**	**West**	**Midwest**
Boston University (private)	Duke University (private)	Cal Tech (private)	Carnegie Mellon University (private)
Brandeis University (private)	Emory University (private)	Stanford University (private)	Case Western Reserve University (private)
Brown University (private)	Georgia Tech University (public)	University of Arizona (public)	Indiana University (public)
Columbia University (private)	Johns Hopkins University (private)	UC-Davis (public)	Iowa State University (public)
Cornell University (private)	Rice University (private)	UC-Berkeley (public)	Michigan State University (public)
Dartmouth College* (private)	Texas A&M University (public)	UC-Irvine (public)	Northwestern University (private)
Harvard University (private)	Tulane University (private)	UCLA (public)	Ohio State University (public)
MIT (private)	University of Florida (public)	UC-San Diego (public)	Pennsylvania State University (public)
New York University (private)	University of Maryland (public)	UC-Santa Barbara (public)	Purdue University (public)
Princeton University (private)	University of North Carolina (public)	UC-Santa Cruz* (public)	University of Chicago (private)
Rutgers University (public)	University of Texas at Austin (public)	University of Colorado–Boulder (public)	University of Illinois (public)
Stony Brook University (public)	University of Virginia (public)	University of Oregon (public)	University of Iowa (public)
University of Buffalo (public)	Vanderbilt University (private)	University of Southern California (private)	University of Kansas (public)
University of Pennsylvania (private)		University of Utah* (public)	University of Michigan (public)
University of Rochester (private)		University of Washington (public)	University of Minnesota (public)
Yale University (private)			University of Missouri (public)
			University of Pittsburgh (public)
			University of Wisconsin (public)
			Washington University in St. Louis (private)

*Was not a member when research for this book was conducted.
Source: Association of American Universities, https://www.aau.edu.

commenced a three-year examination of the institution's history of involvement in slavery (Brown University Steering Committee on Slavery and Justice, 2006). Likewise, the University of Illinois, also on the list, has key African American faculty who have been intentional in hiring large numbers of faculty of color. For example, James D. Anderson, the dean of the education school at Illinois, has worked with colleagues William Trent, a professor of sociology, and Chris Span, associate dean in the school of education, to change the racial and ethnic makeup of the school, and these African American men have also been outspoken advocates across the university as a whole (Span, 2016). Bringing issues of racial inequity out into the open is essential to making change on college and university campuses.

The AAU institutions with the five lowest percentages of Black faculty are Cal Tech (0.7%), Carnegie Mellon University (1.3%), Brandeis University (1.6%), University of Colorado–Boulder (1.8%), and University of Washington (1.9%) (see table 2). Although faculty searches are national, often international, in scope, there are those who argue that location is a deterrent to hiring African Americans. In the case of these institutions with very low percentages of Black faculty, the Black populations vary across the cities where they are located. Cal Tech is located in Pasadena, CA, where Black people make up 17% of the population. Likewise, Carnegie Mellon University and Brandeis University are located in Pittsburgh (23% Black) and Boston (28% Black), respectively. The University of Washington is located in Seattle, where 7% of the population is Black. Of all these institutions, the University of Colorado–Boulder is located in the city with the lowest percentage of African Americans (1.2%), yet still has more Black faculty than Cal Tech, Carnegie Mellon, and Brandeis (World Population Review, 2020). Perhaps we should put to rest the argument that an institution can't attract African Americans without a critical mass of Black people in the surrounding area. Yes, a diverse population is a draw, but African Americans are willing to relocate to secure faculty positions in their fields, regardless of the racial makeup of the local population.

Faculty diversity for Hispanics[12] presents a different picture, with concentrations in parts of the nation where large numbers of Latinos live—such as California, Arizona, Florida, and Texas—and dire representation in other parts of the country. Still, some AAU institutions manage to attract respectable numbers even in areas of the United States that don't boast a significant Latino population (see table 2). The institutions with the five highest percentages of Hispanic tenured and tenure-track faculty are the University of Arizona (7.3%), UC–Santa Barbara (6.9%), University of Texas at Austin (6.8%), UCLA (6.7%), and UC–San Diego and Rice University (both 6.6%). Many of the universities with higher percentages of Hispanic faculty have low numbers of Black faculty. Only three institutions boasted above 4.5% Black and Hispanic faculty: the University of North Carolina–Chapel Hill, University of Illinois, and Brown University (see table 2). Of note, all three have long-standing, comprehensive efforts focused on diversifying the faculty at their institutions. I mentioned Brown University and the University of Illinois previously in this chapter, but the University of North Carolina has also done considerable work.[13] Since 1983, the institution has sponsored the Carolina Post-Doctoral Program, which is directly focused on diversifying the institution by engaging a highly talented and diverse group of postdoctoral candidates.[14]

12. Federal data sets are organized using the term "Hispanic." For more information on the origins of the term, see Mora (2014).

13. After this book went into production, Nikole Hannah-Jones was denied a tenured position at the University of North Carolina–Chapel Hill. Although Hannah-Jones's case is not a typical tenure case—she is a journalist appointed to an endowed chair that is traditionally given to nonacademics, yet comes with tenure— her case drew national attention to the discontent among African American faculty and students on the campus and caused some African American faculty to leave the institution. The research and writing for this book was done before the Hannah-Jones tenure question surfaced. Of note, Nikole Hannah-Jones was offered tenure at UNC–Chapel Hill on June 30, 2021. She turned down the position and took a post at Howard University, an Historically Black Institution in Washington, DC.

14. For more information on the Carolina Post-Doctoral Program, see https://research.unc.edu/carolina-postdocs/about.

Many of the over 185 participants in this program have gone on to join the faculty at the University of North Carolina.

Most of the AAU institutions have strong percentages (over 10%) of Asian American tenured and tenure-track faculty. However, data reported to the National Center for Educational Statistics is not disaggregated, and thus it is difficult to know if this percentage contains underrepresented Asian American groups (Vietnamese, Hmong, Laotian, etc.) (see table 2). Research by Ann Tiao (2006), Robert Teranishi (2013), Teranishi, Nguyen, and Alcantar (2020), and Frank Wu (2003) has shown that when data pertaining to Asian Americans is disaggregated, there are large educational and opportunity disparities that surface. The AAU institutions with the five largest percentages of Asian American tenure-track and tenured faculty are Johns Hopkins University (19.9%), Purdue University (19.7%), Case Western Reserve University (18.5%), UC-Irvine (18.4%), and University of Pittsburgh (18.3%). Only Brandeis University, Princeton University, University of North Carolina, University of Oregon, University of Virginia, and Vanderbilt University have percentages of Asian American faculty under 10%, with Vanderbilt having fewer Asian American faculty members than any other AAU institution at 6.6% (see table 2). The majority of the Asian American scholars across the AAU institutions are in the sciences; Asian American representation is lower in the humanities and social sciences, falling behind African Americans and Latinos (American Academy of Arts & Sciences, 2019).

Given that Native Hawaiians and Pacific Islanders (NHPI) make up only 0.4% of the US population, this group is also severely underrepresented across the faculty of the AAU institutions, with the greatest percentage being at the University of Colorado–Boulder at 0.3% (see table 2). The NHPI population is almost nonexistent among higher education faculty. Only Yale University, UCLA, University of Pittsburgh, UC-Irvine, and Michigan State University have at least 0.2% NHPI faculty (see table 2). Likewise, the American Indian and Alaska Native (AIAN) population is underrepresented within the AAU institutions. The AAU institution with the greatest percentage of AIAN faculty is UC–Santa Barbara (0.8%), and only seven additional AAU institutions have over 0.5% AIAN faculty. It is important to point out that the NHPI and AIAN populations are sparse overall in higher education at both the faculty and student level (Shotton et al., 2013). However, lack of representation could be addressed with more outreach, recruitment, and support for these populations. If we identify a problem, we need to work to solve it, including investing in pipeline programs from the K–12 system.

In terms of White tenured and tenure-track faculty, the AAU institutions with the five largest percentages of White tenure-track and tenured faculty are Cal Tech (80.1%), Duke University (78.3%), University of Rochester (77.8%), University of Virginia (77.6%), and Indiana University (77.4%). The AAU institutions with the five lowest percentages of White tenure-track and tenured faculty are Georgia Tech (49.9%[15]/57.9%), Rutgers University (62.5%), UC-Berkeley (63.9%), University of Maryland (64.6%), and Pennsylvania State University (65.2%). Georgia Tech boasts the most diverse faculty in terms of US racial and ethnic groups of any AAU university (see table 2). Cal Tech is the least diverse AAU university (and the smallest), having a faculty of 292 that is over 80% White. Given Cal Tech's emphasis on science and technology, and the vast inequities across these fields in the production of students and faculty, the low percentage is indicative of overall systemic inequity (see table 2). However, as we will see in chapter 4, there are people of color being produced across the PhD ranks, including the sciences (National Science Foundation, 2018).

Unfortunately, data are not collected on the percentage of White tenure-track and tenured faculty who come from low-income families or are first-generation college graduates, or both, so it is not possible to examine the progress or lack of progress made by AAU institutions or other universities around socioeconomic diversity among

15. According to NCES data, only 49.9% of Georgia Tech's faculty is White. However, 32.8% of its faculty are nonresidents—the largest percentage of any AAU institution by a significant amount—and this population's racial and ethnic makeup is not reported. I used data on the institution's website to provide a more accurate percentage and so that the institution makes sense in relation to other institutions in the AAU.

Table 2 — Faculty Racial and Ethnic Diversity at AAU Institutions (Tenured and Tenure-Track)

Institution	Total Faculty	% AIAN	% Asian	% Black	% Hispanic
Boston University	905	0.0	10.3	2.9	3.5
Brandeis University	244	0.0	9.0	1.6	2.5
Brown University	675	0.1	11.1	4.7	4.6
California Institute of Technology	292	0.0	14.0	0.7	3.8
Carnegie Mellon University	697	0.0	12.5	1.3	2.4
Case Western Reserve University	751	0.3	18.5	3.3	2.4
Columbia University	1,656	0.1	14.9	4.3	3.3
Cornell University	1,398	0.4	11.1	4.1	4.0
Duke University	1,647	0.1	13.9	4.0	3.2
Emory University	1,006	0.4	15.1	4.7	2.1
Georgia Institute of Technology	829	0.0	10.9	3.0	2.8
Harvard University	1,494	0.0	11.5	4.1	3.5
Indiana University–Bloomington	1,379	0.1	12.3	4.1	4.8
Iowa State University	1,259	0.2	18.2	2.4	3.3
Johns Hopkins University	3,035	0.2	19.9	4.6	3.2
Massachusetts Institute of Technology	1,015	0.0	11.5	3.0	4.0
Michigan State University	1,870	0.6	14.9	4.1	4.9
New York University	1,946	0.1	12.9	3.9	4.5
Northwestern University	1,345	0.1	12.4	4.2	4.4
Ohio State University	2,455	0.1	14.1	3.8	3.7

Source: National Center for Educational Statistics, Integrated Postsecondary Education Data System, 2017.

% NHPI	% White	% +2	% Unknown	% Nonresident	% Male	% Female
0.0	77.2	1.1	0.0	5.0	66.7	33.3
0.0	73.0	0.4	9.4	4.1	61.1	38.9
0.0	72.7	1.3	1.3	4.0	70.2	29.8
0.0	80.1	0.0	0.0	1.4	78.8	21.2
0.0	70.3	0.9	3.7	8.9	76.0	24.0
0.0	73.1	0.1	0.1	2.1	68.8	31.2
0.1	67.3	0.7	2.7	6.7	69.0	31.0
0.0	74.5	0.6	0.2	5.1	68.4	31.6
0.1	78.3	0.4	0.0	0.0	71.0	29.0
0.0	73.4	0.5	0.1	3.8	65.8	34.2
0.0	49.9	0.2	0.4	32.8	77.0	23.0
0.0	73.8	0.9	0.0	6.3	70.5	29.5
0.0	77.4	1.1	0.1	0.1	65.8	34.2
0.1	70.5	0.5	0.0	4.8	67.6	32.4
0.1	68.1	0.0	0.0	3.8	60.9	39.1
0.0	67.4	1.3	9.9	3.0	77.6	22.4
0.2	71.3	0.4	0.0	3.7	63.8	36.2
0.1	74.1	0.5	0.2	3.7	64.6	35.4
0.0	73.2	1.0	1.4	3.3	69.3	30.7
0.0	67.1	0.9	4.7	5.5	63.0	37.0

Institution	Total Faculty	% AIAN	% Asian	% Black	% Hispanic
Pennsylvania State University	1,744	0.4	13.9	4.0	3.7
Princeton University	776	0.0	9.1	3.7	3.9
Purdue University	1,688	0.1	19.7	3.0	3.9
Rice University	519	0.0	12.9	2.3	6.6
Rutgers University–New Brunswick	1,698	0.1	13.0	3.2	3.8
Stanford University	1,469	0.1	12.3	2.1	3.7
Stony Brook University	1,000	0.1	14.9	2.8	3.5
Texas A&M University–College Station	2,011	0.3	17.9	3.6	5.9
University at Buffalo	1,098	0.5	18.2	2.4	2.4
University of Arizona	1,503	0.7	11.1	2.1	7.3
University of California–Berkeley	1,361	0.2	13.2	3.8	6.2
University of California–Davis	1,508	0.4	15.2	2.0	6.4
University of California–Irvine	1,221	0.3	18.4	3.1	6.1
University of California–Los Angeles	1,724	0.6	17.7	4.2	6.7
University of California–San Diego	1,333	0.2	16.7	2.3	6.6
University of California–Santa Barbara	853	0.8	10.3	2.3	6.9
University of Chicago	1,126	0.1	13.0	2.8	3.5
University of Colorado–Boulder	1,180	0.6	10.9	1.8	5.4
University of Florida	2,010	0.1	13.2	3.1	6.1
University of Illinois at Urbana-Champaign	1,762	0.3	17.0	4.8	5.6
University of Iowa	1,348	0.2	12.8	2.1	4.2

% NHPI	% White	% +2	% Unknown	% Nonresident	% Male	% Female
0.0	65.2	0.6	6.7	5.6	67.0	33.0
0.0	74.9	0.5	2.1	5.8	69.7	30.3
0.1	66.9	1.1	0.2	5.1	70.6	29.4
0.0	74.2	1.0	0.0	3.1	73.0	27.0
0.0	62.5	0.6	10.8	6.1	63.1	36.9
0.0	65.6	1.0	4.2	11.1	73.0	27.0
0.0	66.8	0.4	4.3	7.2	68.8	31.2
0.0	66.5	0.7	1.7	3.4	71.1	28.9
0.1	70.1	0.5	0.0	5.9	67.9	32.1
0.0	66.2	0.9	8.5	3.3	64.8	35.2
0.1	63.9	1.2	8.7	2.5	68.0	32.0
0.0	67.2	0.3	4.1	4.4	63.6	36.4
0.2	65.4	0.7	2.4	3.4	62.7	37.3
0.2	65.5	0.2	1.8	3.1	67.5	32.5
0.0	67.9	0.1	0.9	5.4	71.4	28.6
0.0	67.5	0.6	5.2	6.3	63.8	36.2
0.0	72.8	1.0	3.5	3.4	72.6	27.4
0.3	68.8	0.9	8.0	3.3	65.4	34.6
0.0	72.8	1.2	0.3	3.2	69.8	30.2
0.0	65.9	1.1	1.2	4.1	66.1	33.9
0.0	75.6	0.6	1.6	2.9	67.2	32.8

Institution	Total Faculty	% AIAN	% Asian	% Black	% Hispanic
University of Kansas	1,214	0.6	14.4	3.3	3.6
University of Maryland–College Park	1,396	0.1	15.8	4.5	4.4
University of Michigan–Ann Arbor	2,790	0.4	15.5	4.5	4.1
University of Minnesota–Twin Cities	2,171	0.6	13.2	2.7	2.9
University of Missouri–Columbia	973	0.4	15.5	4.2	4.3
University of North Carolina–Chapel Hill	1,333	0.5	9.2	5.7	4.5
University of Oregon	759	0.4	9.1	2.2	5.5
University of Pennsylvania	1,613	0.1	13.3	3.4	4.0
University of Pittsburgh	1,602	0.0	18.3	2.9	3.1
University of Rochester	1,265	0.0	13.4	2.2	2.2
University of Southern California	1,493	0.2	16.7	2.5	4.1
University of Texas at Austin	1,840	0.2	10.5	4.0	6.8
Tulane University of Louisiana	616	0.5	12.0	3.6	4.1
University of Virginia	1,460	0.0	9.9	4.6	2.9
University of Washington	1,617	0.6	13.1	1.9	4.1
University of Wisconsin–Madison	1,924	0.3	12.6	2.4	3.5
Vanderbilt University	768	0.1	6.6	4.4	4.7
Washington University in St Louis	1,310	0.1	15.1	4.3	2.8
Yale University	2,132	0.1	13.6	3.3	3.0
Grand total	**83,106**	**0.3**	**14.1**	**3.4**	**4.3**

% NHPI	% White	% +2	% Unknown	% Nonresident	% Male	% Female
0.0	74.2	1.4	0.3	2.1	65.8	34.2
0.1	64.6	0.7	6.9	2.8	66.5	33.5
0.1	70.9	1.1	1.1	2.3	66.1	33.9
0.1	73.5	1.4	1.6	3.9	64.2	35.8
0.1	70.8	0.3	1.2	3.1	66.1	33.9
0.0	73.3	0.7	2.8	3.4	61.1	38.9
0.0	70.2	1.3	8.0	3.2	60.6	39.4
0.0	75.9	0.9	0.0	2.4	69.9	30.1
0.2	71.7	0.4	0.7	2.7	68.5	31.5
0.0	77.8	0.6	0.0	3.8	65.3	34.7
0.0	68.1	1.7	3.1	3.6	70.6	29.4
0.0	73.8	1.0	0.0	3.6	66.7	33.3
0.0	72.4	1.3	1.1	5.0	66.9	33.1
0.1	77.6	0.9	0.0	4.0	69.3	30.7
0.1	70.2	1.8	5.4	2.8	61.5	38.5
0.1	74.4	1.1	3.2	2.5	65.2	34.8
0.1	74.0	0.7	6.6	2.7	68.4	31.6
0.1	76.9	0.6	0.0	0.2	72.1	27.9
0.2	68.4	1.5	5.7	4.2	64.0	36.0
0.1	**70.4**	**0.8**	**2.5**	**4.2**	**67.1**	**32.9**

White faculty or faculty of color. There have been three extensive research studies examining how socioeconomic background has an impact on the experiences of faculty. Only one of the studies focused specifically on faculty from low-income backgrounds, detailing their experiences and the feeling of not belonging (Lee, 2017). The others included broad cross sections of faculty and found that among their samples, the majority of faculty came from middle-class and upper-middle-class backgrounds (Grimes and Morris, 1997; Haney, 2015). Moreover, the researchers found resistance among faculty from more upper-middle-class and affluent backgrounds to understanding the differences and experiences of faculty and students from low-income homes. Although expanding the representation of faculty from low-income White families is essential, it cannot be done at the expense of hiring more faculty of color. As Daryl Smith shared, colleges and universities have made progress with international faculty and White women but have remained resistant to large-scale hiring of faculty of color.

Tenured AAU Faculty

If we delve a bit deeper and examine tenured faculty alone, the landscape looks sparser as most of the gains for people of color are in the assistant professor ranks. Increased diversity in faculty hiring across racial and ethnic groups is relatively recent. The AAU institutions with the five highest percentages of Black tenured faculty are the University of North Carolina–Chapel Hill (5%), University of Virginia (4.6%), Vanderbilt University (4.4%), University of Illinois (4.3%), and University of Michigan (4.2%) (see table 3). All but nine AAU institutions have less than 4% Black tenured faculty members. Of note, the institutions with the highest percentage of Black tenured faculty are located in the South, where there are significant Black communities in terms of numbers. However, this group also includes two AAU institutions in the Midwest with sparser Black communities than in the South: Champaign-Urbana, Illinois, where the University of Illinois is located, is 11.4% Black; and Ann Arbor, the home of the University of Michigan, is only 6.5% Black.

The AAU institutions with the five lowest percentages of tenured African American faculty are Cal Tech (0.8%), University of Oregon (1.1%), Carnegie Mellon University (1.3%), UC-Davis and University of Rochester (both 1.5%), and University of Arizona and University of Colorado–Boulder (both 1.6%). The southern university with the lowest percentage of tenured African American faculty is Rice University in Houston, Texas, at 2.2%. If we believe the most common excuse for lack of faculty diversity—location and geography—Rice University should be able to attract a significant African American faculty, as the city of Houston boasts a 22.5% African American population, with a significant and active African American middle class, and has since the 1800s (World Population Review, 2019; see table 3).

The AAU institutions with the five highest percentages of Latino tenured faculty members are the University of Arizona (7.1%), UC–Santa Barbara (6.9%), UCLA (6.5%), Texas A&M University (6.2%), and UC–San Diego (6.2%) (see table 3). Tenured Latino faculty are in states with large numbers of Latinos—including Texas, California, and Florida. They are also in states with rapidly growing Latino populations such as Oregon, which has had a 75% increase in its Hispanic population in recent years, and Illinois, which is home to 4% of the nation's Hispanic population and 17% of the state's citizens identifying as Latino (Pew Research Center, 2019).

The AAU institutions with the five lowest percentages of tenured Latino faculty members are the University of Rochester (1%), Case Western Reserve University (1.7%), Emory University (1.9%), Yale University (2.1%), and Carnegie Mellon University and Washington University in St. Louis (both 2.3%) (see table 3).

When I looked more closely at data related to those faculty who are tenured and those who are on the tenure-track, I saw some institutions, such as Johns Hopkins University, that have significantly increased the number of Black and Latino faculty into tenure-track positions in recent years, demonstrating their commitment to diversity in real numbers. Of note, Johns Hopkins has a comprehensive approach to faculty diversity—including the review of pipeline data, implicit bias training, postdoctoral programs, targets of opportunity,

diversity advocates, clear search-committee protocols, data transparency, dedicated funding, and outspoken and committed leadership. They are employing all of the practices that are known to
increase faculty diversity, and more importantly, when they identified a long-term problem in faculty hiring, they began to work on it
rather than merely wishing it would go away.[16] Each of the strategies
used by Johns Hopkins and others are discussed in this book from
various perspectives.

Although data from the National Center for Education Statistics are not disaggregated for Asian Americans, making it hard
for us to see the presence of underrepresented groups within the
racial category, within the tenured ranks of faculty, Asian Americans account for significant numbers. The top five AAU institutions
with the largest percentage of Asian American tenured faculty are
Purdue University (20.2%), Iowa State University (18.8%), UCLA
(18.6%), University of Buffalo (18.5%), and UC-Irvine (18.4%). The
AAU institutions with Asian American tenured faculty below 10%
are Boston University (9.6%), Brandeis University (7.1%), Harvard
University (9.9%), Indiana University (9%), Princeton University
(9%), University of North Carolina–Chapel Hill (9.2%), University
of Oregon (9.9%), University of Rochester (9.6%), University of
Virginia (8.5%), Vanderbilt University (6.4%), and Yale University
(9.8%). Vanderbilt University has the lowest percentage of tenured
Asian American faculty (see table 3).

The American Indian and Alaska Native (AIAN) representation
among tenured faculty in the AAU institutions is almost nonexistent, with only Cornell University, Michigan State University, Tulane
University, University of Buffalo, University of Arizona, UCLA,
UC–Santa Barbara, University of Colorado–Boulder, University of
Kansas, and University of Washington having at least 0.5% AIAN
on the faculty (see table 3). Most of these institutions are the same
as those that have more significant percentages of tenure-track

16. For more information on the work of Johns Hopkins University, see https://
hub.jhu.edu/2015/11/30/faculty-diversity-initiative/.

AIAN faculty. With regard to Native Hawaiian and Pacific Islander (NHPI) tenured faculty, only one AAU institution has more than 0.1%—the University of Pittsburgh at 0.3% (see table 3).

When examining the tenured faculty members only at AAU institutions, they are overwhelmingly White, with 88% of the institutions having a tenured faculty that is at least 70% White. A stated commitment to diversity has not manifested into a diverse reality among tenure-track and tenured faculty. Yes, since 1993, there has been a 10% decrease in White faculty across all colleges and universities and all faculty ranks. However, most gains in diversity in the faculty have been in the non-tenure-track ranks. For example, non-tenure-track faculty make up 12% of faculty of all racial and ethnic backgrounds but 17% of faculty of underrepresented minorities (Finkelstein, Conley, and Schuster, 2016).

A Closer Look at Gender

As women of color face a double bind—one in which they must contend with both racism and sexism (Espinosa et al., 2019; Griffin, 2019; Johnson, 2007; Malcom and Malcom, 2011; Ong et al., 2011), it is important to pay close attention to their representation in the academy. When I interviewed Daryl Smith for this book, she told me "The fastest-growing populations are international faculty and White women [faculty]. It's not okay to have no [White] women, but we need to bring in a richer diversity." Beginning in 2001, the National Science Foundation (NSF) worked hard to diversify the science, technology, engineering, and math (STEM) fields around gender with the allocation of their ADVANCE grants. The grants are focused on enhancing "the systemic factors that support equity and inclusion and to mitigate the systemic factors that create inequities in the academic profession and workplaces" (National Science Foundation, 2019). The program was originally focused on gender equity but has come to also address racial equity (see table 4) (Armstrong and Jovanovic, 2017; Blackwell, Snyder, and Mavriplis, 2009; Cozzens et al., 2012; Meyerson and Tompkins, 2007;

Table 3

Faculty Racial and Ethnic Diversity at AAU Institutions (Tenured)

Institution	Total Faculty	% AIAN	% Asian	% Black	% Hispanic
Boston University	684	0.0	9.6	2.3	2.8
Brandeis University	197	0.0	7.1	2.0	2.5
Brown University	532	0.0	11.1	3.8	3.4
California Institute of Technology	245	0.0	11.8	0.8	3.7
Carnegie Mellon University	472	0.0	12.5	1.3	2.3
Case Western Reserve University	589	0.3	17.3	2.9	1.7
Columbia University	1,123	0.2	14.3	3.7	2.4
Cornell University	1,071	0.5	10.4	3.7	3.3
Duke University	1,300	0.1	12.7	3.7	2.7
Emory University	753	0.4	13.3	4.1	1.9
Georgia Institute of Technology	654	0.0	10.9	3.1	3.1
Harvard University	1,107	0.0	9.9	3.8	3.1
Indiana University–Bloomington	1,011	0.1	9.0	3.4	3.5
Iowa State University	877	0.2	18.8	2.2	3.0
Johns Hopkins University	1,071	0.2	12.7	2.1	2.9
Massachusetts Institute of Technology	770	0.0	12.1	3.2	3.2
Michigan State University	1,415	0.7	14.0	3.8	3.7
New York University	1,515	0.0	11.5	3.9	4.2
Northwestern University	1,023	0.1	12.4	4.0	4.3

Source: National Center for Educational Statistics, Integrated Postsecondary Education Data System, 2017.

% NHPI	% White	% +2	% Unknown	% Nonresident	Male	Female
0.0	83.0	1.2	0.0	1.0	70.2	29.8
0.0	79.2	0.5	8.1	0.5	64.0	36.0
0.0	78.0	0.9	0.8	2.1	72.4	27.6
0.0	83.3	0.0	0.0	0.4	80.4	19.6
0.0	79.9	0.6	2.3	1.1	78.2	21.8
0.0	77.6	0.0	0.2	0.0	72.3	27.7
0.0	75.9	0.3	2.0	1.3	72.7	27.3
0.0	80.3	0.4	0.2	1.3	70.1	29.9
0.1	80.7	0.1	0.0	0.0	74.2	25.8
0.0	79.4	0.3	0.1	0.5	69.1	30.9
0.0	52.0	0.2	0.2	30.7	79.2	20.8
0.0	79.9	0.5	0.0	2.8	74.7	25.3
0.0	82.9	1.2	0.0	0.0	67.5	32.5
0.1	74.9	0.1	0.0	0.7	72.3	27.7
0.0	81.4	0.0	0.0	0.7	75.1	24.9
0.0	73.4	1.3	6.2	0.5	79.9	20.1
0.1	76.9	0.5	0.0	0.2	67.8	32.2
0.1	79.2	0.2	0.1	0.9	67.6	32.4
0.0	77.3	0.5	1.0	0.4	72.5	27.5

Institution	Total Faculty	% AIAN	% Asian	% Black	% Hispanic
Ohio State University	1,824	0.1	13.7	3.5	3.4
Pennsylvania State University	1,313	0.3	13.9	3.8	3.8
Princeton University	581	0.0	9.0	3.4	2.9
Purdue University	1,227	0.1	20.2	2.9	4.1
Rice University	413	0.0	12.3	2.2	5.6
Rutgers University–New Brunswick	1,335	0.1	13.1	2.9	3.9
Stanford University	1,127	0.1	11.4	2.3	3.1
Stony Brook University	709	0.1	13.7	2.5	3.5
Texas A&M University–College Station	1,591	0.3	17.7	3.5	6.2
Tulane University of Louisiana	444	0.5	11.0	2.7	4.3
University at Buffalo	807	0.6	18.5	2.2	2.6
University of Arizona	1,091	0.6	10.0	1.6	7.1
University of California–Berkeley	1,126	0.1	13.5	3.7	6.0
University of California–Davis	1,201	0.4	16.2	1.5	5.6
University of California–Irvine	998	0.4	18.4	2.5	5.5
University of California–Los Angeles	1,480	0.5	18.6	4.1	6.5
University of California–San Diego	1,066	0.1	17.1	2.2	6.2
University of California–Santa Barbara	697	0.7	10.2	2.3	6.9
University of Chicago	852	0.1	12.7	3.2	2.9
University of Colorado–Boulder	869	0.6	10.7	1.6	5.6
University of Florida	1,524	0.0	12.9	3.0	5.6

% NHPI	% White	% +2	% Unknown	% Nonresident	% Male	% Female
0.0	71.9	0.8	3.6	3.1	65.8	34.2
0.0	71.3	0.6	5.5	0.8	70.1	29.9
0.0	82.4	0.2	0.9	1.2	72.8	27.2
0.1	71.6	0.9	0.1	0.1	74.6	25.4
0.0	79.4	0.2	0.0	0.2	75.3	24.7
0.0	71.3	0.4	4.9	3.4	65.7	34.3
0.0	69.8	0.8	3.3	9.1	76.9	23.1
0.0	74.3	0.1	2.8	2.8	71.7	28.3
0.0	69.6	0.4	1.5	0.8	74.2	25.8
0.0	78.6	1.1	0.5	1.4	71.2	28.8
0.0	75.7	0.2	0.0	0.1	69.5	30.5
0.0	73.2	0.4	6.8	0.3	67.5	32.5
0.1	68.7	0.8	6.3	0.7	69.1	30.9
0.0	71.6	0.1	3.7	0.9	66.1	33.9
0.1	69.4	0.3	1.9	1.4	66.2	33.8
0.1	68.7	0.1	0.9	0.5	69.3	30.7
0.0	71.1	0.0	0.8	2.6	75.0	25.0
0.0	74.3	0.3	2.0	3.3	65.4	34.6
0.0	77.3	0.8	2.0	0.9	74.3	25.7
0.1	75.4	0.6	4.4	1.0	67.3	32.7
0.0	77.0	1.1	0.1	0.3	72.7	27.3

Institution	Total Faculty	% AIAN	% Asian	% Black	% Hispanic
University of Illinois at Urbana-Champaign	1,282	0.2	17.5	4.3	5.7
University of Iowa	1,017	0.3	12.1	2.3	4.0
University of Kansas	945	0.6	14.0	2.8	3.6
University of Maryland–College Park	1,108	0.1	16.3	3.6	4.1
University of Michigan–Ann Arbor	2,140	0.4	14.6	4.2	4.3
University of Minnesota–Twin Cities	1,678	0.4	13.9	2.3	2.5
University of Missouri–Columbia	735	0.4	15.5	1.9	3.5
University of North Carolina–Chapel Hill	1,032	0.4	9.2	5.0	3.6
University of Oregon	566	0.4	9.9	1.1	5.7
University of Pennsylvania	1,228	0.1	12.7	3.1	2.9
University of Pittsburgh	1,152	0.0	17.5	1.9	2.9
University of Rochester	586	0.0	9.6	1.5	1.0
University of Southern California	1,199	0.2	15.8	2.6	3.9
University of Texas at Austin	1,514	0.3	10.2	4.0	5.9
University of Virginia	1,048	0.0	8.5	4.6	2.8
University of Washington	1,299	0.7	13.2	1.9	4.0
University of Wisconsin–Madison	1,496	0.3	12.1	1.8	3.2
Vanderbilt University	597	0.2	6.4	4.4	2.8
Washington University in St Louis	958	0.1	12.6	3.7	2.3
Yale University	1,046	0.2	9.8	2.6	2.1
Grand total	**61,310**	**0.2**	**13.4**	**3.1**	**4.0**

% NHPI	% White	% +2	% Unknown	% Nonresident	% Male	% Female
0.0	70.7	0.8	0.7	0.2	69.0	31.0
0.0	79.2	0.5	1.4	0.3	70.1	29.9
0.0	77.6	1.3	0.2	0.0	67.6	32.4
0.0	70.4	0.6	4.3	0.5	71.1	28.9
0.1	74.2	0.9	0.7	0.4	69.7	30.3
0.1	78.8	1.1	0.3	0.6	66.6	33.4
0.1	76.7	0.3	1.2	0.3	69.7	30.3
0.0	80.1	0.7	0.5	0.5	63.3	36.7
0.0	74.7	0.5	7.6	0.2	62.9	37.1
0.0	80.2	0.6	0.0	0.4	74.4	25.6
0.3	77.0	0.2	0.2	0.1	71.6	28.4
0.0	86.9	0.5	0.0	0.5	74.4	25.6
0.0	74.5	1.6	1.3	0.1	73.2	26.8
0.0	77.8	0.9	0.0	0.9	68.6	31.4
0.0	82.3	0.9	0.0	1.0	72.2	27.8
0.0	73.9	1.9	4.0	0.4	63.7	36.3
0.1	79.8	0.9	1.5	0.4	67.6	32.4
0.0	79.4	0.3	4.7	1.8	72.0	28.0
0.0	80.8	0.5	0.0	0.0	75.8	24.2
0.1	79.9	1.2	2.7	1.3	73.2	26.8
0.0	**75.8**	**0.6**	**1.6**	**1.3**	**70.6**	**29.4**

Morimoto et al., 2013; Stepan-Norris and Kerrissey, 2016; Zippel and Ferree, 2019).[17] However, the main benefactors of these grants and the subsequent initiatives were White women (Ceci and Williams, 2011; Johnson, 2007; Moss-Racusin et al., 2012). It took NSF a considerable amount of time to embed women of color in the ADVANCE grants (Hunt et al., 2012). According to Daryl Smith, "It's distressing when I see women—White women—pushing the gender thing, but not understanding women of color in this fight." Whenever Smith works with campuses on their diversity efforts, she asks for data disaggregated by both race and gender. She notes that most campuses have seen an increase in women, but this increase is the result of White women being hired and not women of color. We see growth for White women, but we don't regularly see these same White women advocating for intersectionality, which is the interconnectedness of identities, including race, class, and gender and the interdependent systems of disadvantage and discrimination that results from these intersections (Cooper, 1892; Crenshaw, 1989; Evans, 2007; Extra, 2018). More bluntly, we don't see White women insisting that women of color be hired. During our conversation, Smith also reminded me of an important book I had read earlier in my career—a book that tells the story of the lack of intersectionality in higher education—*"But Some of Us Are Brave": All the Women Are White, All the Blacks Are Men.* The book is an anthology by Gloria T. Hull, Patricia Bell Scott, and Barbara Smith published in 1993. Those interested in making advances in the faculty in terms of gender and race would benefit from reading this work.

When I examined national data related to women overall, they make up a mere 32.9% of tenure-track and tenured faculty at AAU institutions. Black women account for 4.9%, Hispanic women for 4.8%, Asian American women for 13.3%, American Indians and

17. Since its inception in 2001, the program has awarded 70 Institutional Transformation awards, 37 IT-Catalyst awards, 31 Leadership awards, 81 Partnership awards, 8 Adaptation awards, and 43 ADVANCE Fellowship awards. Twenty-four of the AAU institutions have received transformation grants between 2001 and 2018. For more information, see https://www.nsf.gov/crssprgm/advance/awards.jsp.

Table 4	AAU Institutions with ADVANCE Grants	
Boston University	Princeton University	University of Illinois
Brown University	Purdue University	University of Maryland
Cal Tech	Rice University	University of Michigan
Case Western Reserve University	Rutgers University	University of Minnesota
Columbia University	Stanford University	University of Missouri
Cornell University	Texas A&M University	University of North Carolina
Duke University	Tulane University	University of Oregon
Georgia Tech	UC-Davis	University of Pennsylvania
Indiana University	UC-Irvine	University of Pittsburgh
Iowa State University	UC–San Diego	University of Southern California
Johns Hopkins University	UC–Santa Barbara	University of Virginia
Michigan State University	UC–Santa Cruz	University of Washington
New York University	University of Arizona	University of Wisconsin
Ohio State University	University of Colorado–Boulder	Yale University
Pennsylvania State University	University of Florida	

Source: National Science Foundation, https://www.nsf.gov/funding/pgm_summ.jsp?pims_id=5383.

Alaska Natives for 0.3%, and Native Hawaiians and Pacific Islanders for 0.1%. White women account for 68.4% of women at AAU institutions in tenure-track and tenured positions (see tables 5a and 5b).

Of interest, the five AAU institutions with the largest representation of Black women in tenured and tenure-track positions are University of North Carolina–Chapel Hill (8.7%), Washington University in St. Louis (7.9%), Johns Hopkins University (7.5%),

Vanderbilt University (7.4%), and Emory University (7.3%)—all institutions located in southern states (see tables 5a and 5b). The top five AAU institutions with the largest numbers of Hispanic women in the tenured and tenure-track faculty ranks are University of Arizona (9.5%), University of Texas at Austin (9.3%), UC–Santa Barbara (8.1%), UC-Davis (8.0%), and UC–San Diego (7.3%)—all institutions in areas with large concentrations of Latinos (10% of the local population or more).

Asian American women are represented across the tenured and tenure-track faculty ranks at AAU institutions. However, as mentioned, data are not disaggregated, and thus we can't see traditionally underrepresented Asian American groups in these data. The AAU institutions with the five largest percentages of Asian American tenure-track or tenured women faculty are Johns Hopkins University (21%), UC-Irvine (18.6%), Purdue University and UCLA (both 17.3%), University of Pittsburg (18.8%), and UC-Davis (16%).

UCLA and Yale University at 0.5% and 0.4% respectively have the largest percentages of Native Hawaiian and Pacific Islander women tenured and tenure-track faculty in the AAU. UC–Santa Barbara (1.9%) and the University of Washington, University of Buffalo, and University of Arizona (all 1.1%) have the highest percentages of American Indian and Alaska Native tenured and tenure-track women faculty. Tables 5a and 5b provide detail about women of color in the AAU, noting their underrepresentation across most institutions.

Benchmarking Faculty Diversity

During my conversation with Daryl Smith, she mentioned that the AAU institutions typically benchmark against each other; much like most institutions, they look at the work of "peer" universities. Her concern with this approach is that most of the AAU institutions are not doing well in terms of faculty diversity, so if they benchmark against other AAU institutions, they don't appear to be doing as terribly with regard to their diversity efforts. In her words, "If you are doing a touch better [than another AAU institution], you'll feel good." Benchmarking is "terrible," according to Smith, and when she visits campuses she wants to see progress over time at the institutions rather than benchmarking results. Much like Smith, I also found that the AAU institutions that I engaged with only benchmarked against other AAU institutions, and in many cases, only a few of them (5–9 institutions typically). As long as they were on par or doing better than their main competition, most AAU administrators in this study felt that they were "at least" making progress.

All but three of the universities belonging to the AAU,[18] arguably the most selective, prestigious, and wealthy institutions in the nation, express a commitment to diversity in their strategic plans. For example, Indiana University's strategic plan includes discussions of diversity around faculty hiring, student enrollment, freedom of thought, and global engagement.[19] At Rutgers University, the strategic plan includes language about removing obstacles that stand in the way of learning and belonging on campus for all individuals. The institution also embraces diversity across the board among students, staff, and faculty—noting that its commitment to diversity is active rather than passive."[20] Compared with the other AAU institutions, Brown University had the most comprehensive coverage of diversity in its strategic plan. The university, rather than having a sentence here and there about diversity scattered throughout the strategic plan, includes large sections about its commitment to diversity in

18. These institutions include Cal Tech, New York University, and Yale University. Cal Tech does not have a public strategic plan and does not include statistics related to race or ethnicity of students or faculty on its website. Yale University lists academic priorities and a strategic sustainability plan for public consumption, but neither of the documents is focused on race, equity, or diversity. NYU's strategic plan makes no mention or race, diversity, or equity. Of note, another group of institutions only mentioned diversity, inclusion, and race one time. I reviewed strategic plans in September and October of 2019.

19. For Indiana University strategic plan, see https://provost.indiana.edu/doc/IUB-Bicentennial-Strategic-Plan.pdf.

20. For the Rutgers strategic plan, see https://ucmweb.rutgers.edu/strategicplan/UniversityStrategicPlan.pdf.

Racial/Ethnic Breakdown of Tenure-Track and Tenured Women Faculty at AAU Institutions

Institution	Total Women	AIAN Women	% AIAN	Asian Women
Boston University	301	0	0.0	33
Brandeis University	95	0	0.0	14
Brown University	201	1	0.5	26
California Institute of Technology	62	0	0.0	8
Carnegie Mellon University	167	0	0.0	18
Case Western Reserve University	234	0	0.0	36
Columbia University	514	1	0.2	73
Cornell University	442	3	0.7	49
Duke University	477	0	0.0	67
Emory University	344	1	0.3	50
Georgia Institute of Technology	191	0	0.0	21
Harvard University	440	0	0.0	53
Indiana University–Bloomington	471	0	0.0	64
Iowa State University	408	0	0.0	55
Johns Hopkins University	1,188	3	0.3	250
Massachusetts Institute of Technology	227	0	0.0	22
Michigan State University	677	3	0.4	96
New York University	689	1	0.1	100
Northwestern University	413	1	0.2	45

Source: National Center for Educational Statistics, Integrated Postsecondary Education Data System, 2017.

% Asian	Black Women	% Black	Hispanic Women	% Hispanic
11.0	11	3.7	8	2.7
14.7	2	2.1	2	2.1
12.9	12	6.0	8	4.0
12.9	0	0.0	2	3.2
10.8	3	1.8	3	1.8
15.4	10	4.3	5	2.1
14.2	33	6.4	22	4.3
11.1	29	6.6	23	5.2
14.0	27	5.7	17	3.6
14.5	25	7.3	4	1.2
11.0	9	4.7	7	3.7
12.0	28	6.4	20	4.5
13.6	22	4.7	22	4.7
13.5	11	2.7	18	4.4
21.0	89	7.5	32	2.7
9.7	8	3.5	7	3.1
14.2	31	4.6	38	5.6
14.5	34	4.9	34	4.9
10.9	28	6.8	21	5.1

Institution	Total Women	AIAN Women	% AIAN	Asian Women
Ohio State University	909	2	0.2	100
Pennsylvania State University	575	0	0.0	61
Princeton University	235	0	0.0	26
Purdue University	497	1	0.2	86
Rice University	140	0	0.0	23
Rutgers University–New Brunswick	627	0	0.0	62
Stanford University	396	1	0.3	48
Stony Brook University	312	0	0.0	47
Texas A&M University–College Station	581	3	0.5	82
Tulane University of Louisiana	204	0	0.0	15
University at Buffalo	353	4	1.1	53
University of Arizona	529	6	1.1	49
University of California–Berkeley	435	2	0.5	69
University of California–Davis	549	5	0.9	88
University of California–Irvine	456	2	0.4	85
University of California–Los Angeles	561	6	1.1	97
University of California–San Diego	381	0	0.0	55
University of California–Santa Barbara	309	6	1.9	35
University of Chicago	308	0	0.0	34
University of Colorado–Boulder	408	4	1.0	53
University of Florida	607	2	0.3	72

% Asian	Black Women	% Black	Hispanic Women	% Hispanic
11.0	38	4.2	40	4.4
10.6	35	6.1	25	4.3
11.1	14	6.0	11	4.7
17.3	19	3.8	16	3.2
16.4	3	2.1	6	4.3
9.9	34	5.4	24	3.8
12.1	14	3.5	18	4.5
15.1	15	4.8	12	3.8
14.1	31	5.3	40	6.9
7.4	14	6.9	8	3.9
15.0	12	3.4	10	2.8
9.3	12	2.3	50	9.5
15.9	18	4.1	30	6.9
16.0	20	3.6	44	8.0
18.6	16	3.5	35	7.7
17.3	32	5.7	37	6.6
14.4	22	5.8	28	7.3
11.3	9	2.9	25	8.1
11.0	11	3.6	12	3.9
13.0	7	1.7	21	5.1
11.9	30	4.9	35	5.8

Institution	Total Women	AIAN Women	% AIAN	Asian Women
University of Illinois at Urbana-Champaign	598	3	0.5	94
University of Iowa	442	2	0.5	43
University of Kansas	415	2	0.5	56
University of Maryland–College Park	467	1	0.2	71
University of Michigan–Ann Arbor	947	3	0.3	135
University of Minnesota–Twin Cities	778	7	0.9	84
University of Missouri–Columbia	330	1	0.3	35
University of North Carolina–Chapel Hill	518	3	0.6	44
University of Oregon	299	1	0.3	25
University of Pennsylvania	486	1	0.2	65
University of Pittsburgh	505	0	0.0	85
University of Rochester	439	0	0.0	68
University of Southern California	439	1	0.2	70
University of Texas at Austin	612	3	0.5	57
University of Virginia	448	0	0.0	47
University of Washington	623	7	1.1	73
University of Wisconsin–Madison	670	2	0.3	81
Vanderbilt University	243	0	0.0	16
Washington University in St. Louis	366	0	0.0	51
Yale University	768	0	0.0	117
Grand total	**27,306**	**95**	**0.3**	**3,637**

% Asian	Black Women	% Black	Hispanic Women	% Hispanic
15.7	41	6.9	38	6.4
9.7	13	2.9	19	4.3
13.5	22	5.3	15	3.6
15.2	31	6.6	29	6.2
14.3	51	5.4	44	4.6
10.8	30	3.9	29	3.7
10.6	16	4.8	21	6.4
8.5	45	8.7	28	5.4
8.4	9	3.0	18	6.0
13.4	29	6.0	20	4.1
16.8	21	4.2	18	3.6
15.5	10	2.3	12	2.7
15.9	16	3.6	25	5.7
9.3	32	5.2	57	9.3
10.5	28	6.3	15	3.3
11.7	20	3.2	25	4.0
12.1	27	4.0	29	4.3
6.6	18	7.4	12	4.9
13.9	29	7.9	10	2.7
15.2	35	4.6	26	3.4
13.3	**1,341**	**4.9**	**1,310**	**4.8**

Table 5b — Racial/Ethnic Breakdown of Tenure-Track and Tenured Women Faculty at AAU Institutions

Institution	NHPI Women	% NHPI	White Women	% White
Boston University	0	0.0	227	75.4
Brandeis University	0	0.0	63	66.3
Brown University	0	0.0	141	70.1
California Institute of Technology	0	0.0	52	83.9
Carnegie Mellon University	0	0.0	123	73.7
Case Western Reserve University	0	0.0	177	75.6
Columbia University	1	0.2	333	64.8
Cornell University	0	0.0	308	69.7
Duke University	0	0.0	364	76.3
Emory University	0	0.0	247	71.8
Georgia Institute of Technology	0	0.0	85	44.5
Harvard University	0	0.0	308	70.0
Indiana University–Bloomington	0	0.0	358	76.0
Iowa State University	0	0.0	296	72.5
Johns Hopkins University	3	0.3	777	65.4
Massachusetts Institute of Technology	0	0.0	144	63.4
Michigan State University	1	0.1	478	70.6
New York University	1	0.1	487	70.7
Northwestern University	0	0.0	286	69.2

Source: National Center for Educational Statistics, Integrated Postsecondary Education Data System, 2017.

2+ Women	% 2+	Unknown Women	% Unknown	Nonresident Women	% Nonresident
3	1.0	0	0.0	19	6.3
0	0.0	8	8.4	6	6.3
5	2.5	2	1.0	6	3.0
0	0.0	0	0.0	0	0.0
1	0.6	2	1.2	17	10.2
0	0.0	0	0.0	6	2.6
6	1.2	14	2.7	31	6.0
6	1.4	2	0.5	22	5.0
2	0.4	0	0.0	0	0.0
2	0.6	0	0.0	15	4.4
0	0.0	1	0.5	68	35.6
2	0.5	0	0.0	29	6.6
4	0.8	1	0.2	0	0.0
3	0.7	0	0.0	25	6.1
0	0.0	0	0.0	34	2.9
4	1.8	31	13.7	11	4.8
6	0.9	0	0.0	24	3.5
4	0.6	0	0.0	28	4.1
9	2.2	6	1.5	17	4.1

Institution	NHPI Women	% NHPI	White Women	% White
Ohio State University	0	0.0	619	68.1
Pennsylvania State University	0	0.0	384	66.8
Princeton University	0	0.0	159	67.7
Purdue University	0	0.0	337	67.8
Rice University	0	0.0	100	71.4
Rutgers University–New Brunswick	0	0.0	375	59.8
Stanford University	0	0.0	245	61.9
Stony Brook University	0	0.0	192	61.5
Texas A&M University–College Station	0	0.0	392	67.5
Tulane University of Louisiana	0	0.0	152	74.5
University at Buffalo	0	0.0	246	69.7
University of Arizona	0	0.0	337	63.7
University of California–Berkeley	0	0.0	264	60.7
University of California–Davis	0	0.0	346	63.0
University of California–Irvine	0	0.0	280	61.4
University of California–Los Angeles	3	0.5	348	62.0
University of California–San Diego	0	0.0	255	66.9
University of California–Santa Barbara	0	0.0	198	64.1
University of Chicago	0	0.0	227	73.7
University of Colorado–Boulder	1	0.2	262	64.2
University of Florida	0	0.0	446	73.5

2+ Women	% 2+	Unknown Women	% Unknown	Nonresident Women	% Nonresident
13	1.4	54	5.9	43	4.7
4	0.7	37	6.4	29	5.0
1	0.4	7	3.0	17	7.2
10	2.0	3	0.6	25	5.0
3	2.1	0	0.0	5	3.6
5	0.8	87	13.9	40	6.4
10	2.5	11	2.8	49	12.4
0	0.0	21	6.7	25	8.0
5	0.9	9	1.5	19	3.3
5	2.5	3	1.5	7	3.4
3	0.8	0	0.0	25	7.1
9	1.7	51	9.6	15	2.8
10	2.3	32	7.4	10	2.3
2	0.4	19	3.5	25	4.6
3	0.7	17	3.7	18	3.9
3	0.5	13	2.3	22	3.9
1	0.3	2	0.5	18	4.7
4	1.3	14	4.5	18	5.8
4	1.3	8	2.6	12	3.9
8	2.0	36	8.8	16	3.9
6	1.0	1	0.2	15	2.5

Institution	NHPI Women	% NHPI	White Women	% White
University of Illinois at Urbana-Champaign	0	0.0	381	63.7
University of Iowa	0	0.0	342	77.4
University of Kansas	0	0.0	300	72.3
University of Maryland–College Park	1	0.2	274	58.7
University of Michigan-Ann Arbor	2	0.2	661	69.8
University of Minnesota-Twin Cities	1	0.1	574	73.8
University of Missouri–Columbia	0	0.0	240	72.7
University of North Carolina–Chapel Hill	0	0.0	364	70.3
University of Oregon	0	0.0	206	68.9
University of Pennsylvania	0	0.0	354	72.8
University of Pittsburgh	1	0.2	361	71.5
University of Rochester	0	0.0	332	75.6
University of Southern California	0	0.0	285	64.9
University of Texas at Austin	0	0.0	428	69.9
University of Virginia	0	0.0	332	74.1
University of Washington	1	0.2	427	68.5
University of Wisconsin–Madison	2	0.3	480	71.6
Vanderbilt University	0	0.0	166	68.3
Washington University in St. Louis	1	0.3	273	74.6
Yale University	3	0.4	481	62.6
Grand total	**22**	**0.1**	**18,679**	**68.4**

2+ Women	% 2+	Unknown Women	% Unknown	Nonresident Women	% Nonresident
10	1.7	8	1.3	23	3.8
5	1.1	6	1.4	12	2.7
11	2.7	3	0.7	6	1.4
5	1.1	39	8.4	16	3.4
10	1.1	13	1.4	28	3.0
13	1.7	10	1.3	30	3.9
1	0.3	5	1.5	11	3.3
5	1.0	15	2.9	14	2.7
6	2.0	22	7.4	12	4.0
5	1.0	0	0.0	12	2.5
2	0.4	6	1.2	11	2.2
1	0.2	0	0.0	16	3.6
8	1.8	18	4.1	16	3.6
10	1.6	0	0.0	25	4.1
7	1.6	0	0.0	19	4.2
19	3.0	33	5.3	18	2.9
10	1.5	24	3.6	15	2.2
0	0.0	24	9.9	7	2.9
2	0.5	0	0.0	0	0.0
18	2.3	55	7.2	33	4.3
314	**1.1**	**773**	**2.8**	**1,135**	**4.2**

myriad areas.[21] One cannot help but wonder if having an African American president—Ruth Simmons—has left a legacy at the institution around its commitment to diversity. My assumption is that her influence was far and wide.

Much like their strategic plans, AAU presidents and provosts regularly espouse how they value diversity in the student body as well as within the faculty. Often the arguments for diversity are tied to the educational environment and the need for diverse perspectives rather than the notions of equity and justice. Despite proclamations about diversity in faculty hiring, the AAU institutions have some of the least diverse faculties, even as their student bodies are becoming increasingly more diverse. In effect, all of the talk about diversity has not manifested in faculty hiring. In the next chapters, I will delve into some of the reasons behind the lack of faculty diversity, which are systemic in nature, and I will call for and outline changes that are aimed at achieving equity.

21. For Brown University's strategic plan, see https://www.brown.edu/web /documents/Revised_BOD_Operational_Plan_2018.09.04.

3

"We Care about Diversity, but What about Quality?"

> In academia, you are purposefully vague so you
> can't be held accountable to anything.
> —AAU UNIVERSITY DEAN

The word "quality," or merit, is often used by Whites to dismiss people of color who are otherwise competitive for faculty positions and other opportunities (Guinier, 2015; Rivera, 2015; Smith, 2000; Turner and Myers, 1999).[1] Even those faculty on search committees who appear to be dedicated to access and equity in their research or speech will often point to "quality" or lack of "quality" as a reason for not hiring a person of color who is in reality just as qualified as the White candidates. Typically, questioning "quality" means that

1. I will be using the words "quality" and "merit" interchangeably, as they were used in this way during my interviews and they are also used in this way in the literature on the faculty hiring. Of note, quality is defined as "the standard of something as measured against other things of a similar kind; the degree of excellence of something" and merit is defined as "the quality of being particularly good or worthy, especially so as to deserve praise or reward" (Dictionary.com). These words are regularly listed as synonyms for each other.

the candidate does not have the right pedigree. They did not go to one of a few "elite" or highly selective institutions for their PhD or they were not mentored by a prominent person in their field—someone known by members of the search committee and highly respected by those on the committee (Clauset, Arbesman, and Larremore, 2015; Cyranoski et al., 2011). These prominent people are typically White men, and occasionally White women, but rarely people of color. What we forget is that attending an elite institution and being mentored by a prominent person is linked to social capital, and systemic racism guarantees that people of color have less of it (Clauset, Arbesman, and Larremore, 2015; Rivera, 2015; Morgan et al., 2021). Although having the "right" pedigree may seem like a vestige of discrimination in the past, given the importance of an AAU pedigree today and the lack of people of color on track to earn this pedigree (see chapter 4), having the "right" pedigree— and gatekeeping against those who don't have one—is a current and important issue. Using these measures to assess quality ensures that most people of color are not given full consideration in the faculty recruitment process and that privilege is perpetuated (Smith, 2000; Turner and Myers, 1999; Gasman, 2016a; 2016b). In this chapter, I will explore the ways that "quality" is used in faculty recruiting and hiring at AAU institutions and more generally.

Although most faculty and institutions cling to traditional notions of "quality," which are highly subjective, and typically include where the candidate's PhD came from and who has mentored the candidate, some scholars have urged us to think about quality in much more wide reaching ways, including types of publications alongside placement and quantity, teaching skills and observed teaching, demonstrated commitment to students, alignment with the institutional mission, commitment to a diverse student body, and willingness to engage the community (Amir and Knauff, 2008; Clauset, Arbesman, and Larremore, 2015; Fowler, Grofman, and Masuoka, 2007; Griffin, 2020; Hanneman, 2001; Henrich and Gil-White, 2001; Katz et al., 2011; Miller, Glick, and Cardinal, 2005; Morgan et al., 2021; Myers, Mucha, and Porter, 2011; Schmidt and Chingos, 2007; Tomlinson and Freeman, 2018; Wakelee and Cordeiro, 2006). Nevertheless,

these recommendations have not been actualized or institutionalized at most AAU institutions. The lack of action is linked to higher
education's competitive nature (i.e., rankings and accolades that
solidify legitimacy) and habit of mimicking other institutions or
being homogeneous in its actions and policies in an effort to gain
legitimacy (i.e., institutional isomorphism) (Clauset, Arbesman,
and Larremore, 2015; DiMaggio and Powell, 1983; Geiger, 2004;
Musselin, 2018).

Unfortunately, many search committees operate under the
assumption and practice that their desired qualifications are neutral and nondiscriminatory. In fact, those desired qualifications can
be discriminatory because they are an indication of an individual's
economic and social status, rather than the potential of a candidate
(Morgan et al., 2021; Rivera, 2015). For example, the people who
mentor a student can be directly linked to the student's socioeconomic background and access to social capital. Often in order to
get the most well-known and respected professors to serve as an
advisor, a student must come from a narrow set of undergraduate
institutions. These institutions typically include Ivy League universities, elite small private liberal arts colleges, and a few public flagship
universities. Sociologist Eduardo Bonilla-Silva (2009) gets to the
root of the issue in his book *Racism without Racists*. He explains that
institutions established in Whiteness and led by Whites reproduce
Whiteness across their culture, symbols, curricula, and traditions
while pretending to be race-neutral environments free of racialized
decision making and policies. They may claim to want to change,
often recognizing how systemic racism curtails opportunity, but
they will continue to resist change (Sensoy and DiAngelo, 2017).

In a powerful study funded by the Ewing Marion Kauffman
Foundation, Aaron Clauset, Samuel Arbesman, and Daniel Larremore (2015) used network analysis to explore systematic inequality
and hierarchy in faculty hiring. Examining the distinctly different
disciplines of computer science, history, and business across 461
departments at colleges and universities (n = 19,000 tenured and
tenure-track professors), they found that "faculty hiring follows a
common and steeply hierarchical structure that reflects profound

social inequality" (n.p.). Moreover, their results show that the institutional prestige of one's doctoral program leads to better faculty placement, increased faculty productivity, and a more influential position within the discipline. Of particularly grave concern, 25% of doctorate-granting institutions produced 71–86% (depending on the discipline) of all tenure-track and tenured faculty in the sample of 19,000. And, a mere 9–14% (depending on the discipline) of faculty have secured a faculty position at an institution that is more prestigious than the institution from which they earned their doctoral degree. Although the authors examined gender, finding that women fare much worse than men in terms of their ability to secure prestigious faculty positions even when holding degrees from the most elite institutions, they did not examine race and ethnicity. At the end of the report, Clauset, Arbesman, and Larremore issue a call for additional research, stating that the "specific mechanisms that produce and maintain these hierarchies remain unclear. A better understanding of their nature would facilitate the disentanglement of genuine merit from mere social status within prestige hierarchies, and shed new light on the operation of current faculty markets" (n.p.). I hope that this book is an answer to the authors' call for research and makes clear the "specific mechanisms that produce and maintain these hierarchies" and, thus, the inequities in faculty hiring.

Within the academy, merit and quality are, in fact, intertwined, with quality defining merit in ambiguous ways. According to Lauren Rivera (2015) in the book *Pedigree*, "Constructions of merit are not value neutral. They are couched within broader power struggles in a society." She adds an example, noting:

> As sociologist Jerome Karabel shows, prior to the 1920s, admission to Harvard, Princeton, and Yale was based largely on subject tests and demonstrated intellectualism. Yet as Jewish enrollments grew and anti-Semitism increased, definitions of merit shifted. To exclude Jewish students and secure advantages for white Anglo-Saxon Protestants, the emphasis on intellectual prowess gave way to a focus on personal "character" as demonstrated by [an] applicant's involvement in sports, extracurricular activities, and perceived "manliness." (p. 9)

Rivera warns that "Merit is an ever-evolving, moving target that simultaneously shapes and is shaped by power relations in a given society" (p. 9). However, she cautions that "One constant . . . is that definitions of merit at any given time and place tend to reflect the values and qualities of elites. Elites generally control society's gate-keeping institutions and thus have the power to shape what merit is and how it is to be measured in a given domain" (p. 9).

Rivera warns us that "Elites may rig these criteria in their favor to preserve privileges for themselves and their children; they also may do so to keep out members of groups they consider threatening" (p. 9). And much like those who are cautioning faculty search committees about unconscious bias in hiring (see chapter 6), Rivera tells us: "There are also critical unconscious psychological processes at play. In nearly every domain of social life, we tend to define merit in our own image" (p. 9). She urges us to "Ask anyone—regardless of social class—what constitutes a good student, parent, or even driver, and typically the response will be a description of the type of student, parent, or driver *they are*" (p. 9). When all- or majority-White search committees define what constitutes quality, it is typically a definition that reflects who they are. Lastly, Rivera shares that "Since elites usually set the rules of the game, it is not surprising that in whatever manner merit is defined and measured in society's gatekeeping institutions, elites seem to have more of it" (p. 9). Thus, when the pool of faculty candidates comes from a narrow group of PhD-granting institutions, those in places of privilege, mainly Whites, continue to prevail in hiring processes.

One way that pedigree manifests is a faculty member's socioeconomic status growing up and the education levels of their parents. In 2021, Allison Morgan and colleagues published an article on the socioeconomic roots of academic faculty that sheds additional light on our discussion of pedigree, sameness, and the perpetuation of Whiteness. Morgan and her team found—using a survey of 7,218 professors in academic departments across eight disciplines, including STEM, social sciences, and the humanities—that the "estimated median childhood household income among faculty is 23.7% higher than the general public, and faculty are 25 times more likely to have a parent with a PhD" (p. 1). And, of even more importance for our discussion herein, "the proportion of faculty with PhD parents nearly doubles at more prestigious universities," and this statistic has been stable over the past fifty years (p. 1). They conclude that the professoriate is and has been "accessible to the mainly socioeconomically privileged" (p. 1). Morgan and her colleagues note that this type of privileging ensures that Black and Hispanic scholars will continue to be underrepresented. More specifically, they claim, "These results have direct implications for efforts to increase the racial and geographic diversity of the professoriate, particularly at the prestige-seeking institutions that train most future professors, as Black and Hispanic adults are less likely to hold graduate degrees compared to White adults, and are less likely to have grown up in wealthy neighborhoods" (p. 6).[2] Of course, Morgan and her colleagues are not suggesting that those individuals from higher socioeconomic homes with PhD-holding parents should not be hired into faculty positions; however, they are making it clear that these individuals are disproportionally privileged and that when we fail to acknowledge this privilege, we work against our commitments to diversifying the faculty and we perpetuate sameness—and given the current makeup of the academy, we perpetuate Whiteness at the expense of diversity.

Looking to the Past to See Ourselves

Before Lauren Rivera's work, historian James D. Anderson tackled the issue of merit and quality. He did this both in his presidential address at the annual meeting of the History of Education Society in 1992 and in his published speech, in the *History of Education Quarterly* as "Race, Meritocracy, and the American Academy during the Immediate Post–World War II Era" in 1993. Anderson's article

---

2. Of note, Morgan and her colleagues also speak to inequities in intellectual ideas in their article: "The higher-prestige placement of faculty from wealthier socioeconomic backgrounds also represents a structural barrier to the visibility of the ideas of lower socioeconomic status faculty, because scientific discoveries made at most prestigious universities are more likely to spread throughout academia" (2021, p. 6).

should be assigned reading for all faculty search committees as it clearly explains, with ample evidence, how systemic racism manifests in ways that continue today. I have assigned this article in my History of Higher Education course since I began teaching it in 2003. In the article, Anderson helps us understand the relationship of race and meritocracy in US higher education. Although the example he uses is from the postwar period, it is still entirely salient today, and the responses from campus administrators that Anderson examined are far too similar to those that I received after the *Washington Post* published my opinion essay (Anderson, 1993).

Anderson (1993) tells the story of a group of highly qualified Black scholars and their employment experiences at historically White colleges and universities in the North. Through this story, which I will elaborate on below, Anderson is able to "explore the usefulness of the social science concept of institutional racism for framing and explaining the formation and development of specific types of racial exclusion or discrimination in educational systems that operate with explicitly race-neutral or 'color-blind' laws, procedures, and policies" (p. 151). He defines institutional or systemic racism as "a form of ethnic discrimination and exclusion through routine organizational policies and procedures that do not use ethnicity or color as the rationale for discrimination, but instead rely on nonracist rationales to effectively exclude members of ethnic minority groups" (p. 151).

Anderson introduces the example mentioned above by making sure that the reader knows that in 1940, there was no southern or northern White university that employed an African American in a "regular academic appointment" (p. 153). He notes that most readers would understand why African Americans were not on the faculty at southern universities, as the racial discrimination was overt and "manifested in frequently hostile interactions between whites and blacks, and generally [was] prescribed by law" (p. 153). On the other hand, many readers might assume that northern White universities were different from their southern counterparts. As Anderson states, "In northern white universities racial discrimination was customary, but it was not prescribed by law, and [by World War II] meritocratic principles specifically rejected race and ethnicity as criteria for determining the qualifications of scholars for faculty appointments" (p. 153). Regardless of these principles, Anderson shows that northern White institutions were just as discriminatory as southern White institutions.

Anderson explains that while most scholars attributed the exclusion of African Americans from southern White universities to racism, they attributed the exclusion from northern White universities to "nonracist" causes such as publishing requirements, lack of advanced degrees, too much focus on teaching, and individual choice (the desire to teach at Black colleges in the South) as the reasons why African Americans were not on the faculties at northern White universities (Anderson, 1993). However, until 1942, Anderson demonstrates with evidence, "no African American scholar, no matter how qualified, how many degrees he or she had earned, or how many excellent articles and books he or she had published, was hired in a permanent faculty position at any predominantly white university in America" (p. 154). The first African American scholar hired into a full-time position was William Boyd Allison Davis, an anthropologist, at the University of Chicago.[3]

In his article, Anderson, through the use of a study by the Julius Rosenwald Fund in 1945, demonstrates the ways that institutional racism and color-blind policies perpetuate inequity. In 1945, Fred Wale, the director of education for the Rosenwald Fund,[4] sent letters to nearly six hundred college and university presidents asking if their institutions would be willing to hire "high quality" African American scholars. Wale had a list of roughly 150 Black scholars with impeccable qualifications, and he mailed that list to the same

3. Anderson notes that most scholars think that the first full-time faculty member hired at a White majority university was Julian H. Lewis at the University of Chicago. However Lewis was listed as an "associate member" of the faculty. In addition, although Anderson states that William Boyd Allison Davis held the faculty post beginning in 1941, the University of Chicago states that he began as a professor in 1942, shortly after earning his PhD at the institution.

4. The Julius Rosenwald Fund focused on "the well-being of mankind" but was most interested in the education of Blacks in the South. For more information, see Ascoli (2015).

group of presidents. Over the course of a month about a third of the presidents replied. Interestingly, 400 of the presidents never replied to Wale at all (Anderson, 1993).

Among the two hundred or so presidents that Wale corresponded with, "virtually none" saw the "complete absence of African American scholars" from their faculties as an indication of "racially discriminatory hiring practices" (p. 158). The president of the University of California–Berkeley, Monroe Deutsch, wrote, "I assure you that the university has steadily sought to choose its faculty, and its students as well, solely on the basis of their qualifications and without regard to race, ancestry, religion, or color" (p. 158). Deutsch added, "It is true that we have no Negro on our faculty, but I believe in all sincerity that there has been no prejudice against Negroes" (p. 158). Likewise, Alvin Eurich, the president of Stanford University, claimed, "For each position we fill at Stanford we are concerned with the matter of appointing the most competent person we can find; we have placed no restrictions on race, creed, or color" (p. 158). Anderson provides quote after quote from the correspondence between Wale and the presidents of northern White universities and summarizes all of the correspondence with "Whether it was a small religious college in Iowa, a major state university in Pennsylvania, or a prestigious private university in California, throughout the northern states the presidents of colleges and universities maintained strongly that qualified scholars were not excluded because of race, color, religion or national origins" (p. 159). Yet, none of the two hundred institutions that replied to Wale, nor the four hundred that did not, employed an African American in a full-time faculty position.

Intriguingly, according to Anderson (1993), Wale's initial correspondence could be considered a question in the abstract. However, once he sent the presidents the list of qualified African American scholars who were willing and interested in faculty positions at northern White universities, "the presidents' commitment to meritocratic principles" was challenged in a "much more direct manner" (p. 160). Wale engaged the presidents in detailed and extensive correspondence on issues of race and meritocracy. Worth mentioning, the list of African American scholars that Wale had generated spread across all major disciplines, and the academics on the list had earned their PhDs from the most prestigious institutions in the nation, including the University of Chicago (a full 20 African American scholars), Harvard University (15), Columbia University (10), University of Michigan (6), University of Pennsylvania (5), Massachusetts Institute of Technology (1), Brown University (1), and University of Wisconsin (1) (Anderson, 1993). Of interest, these universities were all members of the AAU. Wale provided a list of African American faculty whose credentials were on par with the faculties at the most prestigious colleges and universities in the United States. All of the individuals were also well published in the most prestigious journal in their fields, held associate editorships with major journals, presented at national conferences, and worked with national organizations in leadership and service roles related to their fields.

Upon learning of the impressive credentials of the African American scholars on Wale's list, the presidents "affirmed their belief in meritocratic principles and hiring procedures, and then searched for reasons unrelated to race to account for the long-standing exclusion of such outstanding African American scholars from colleges and universities (Anderson, 1993, p. 166). The president of the University of California system, Robert Sproul, wrote, "To the best of my knowledge there is no group prejudice against Negroes on the staff of the University. We have employed a Negro for a part-time coaching position with the football team for many years" (p. 166).[5] According to Anderson, the presidents of the colleges and universities in the North "maintained strongly that in selecting faculty there was no discrimination on the basis of race, color, religion, or national origins" (p. 167). He added, "There were virtually no exceptions to this pattern of self-denial, and even the complete absence of African American scholars from their faculties did little to shake their faith in the mythical color-blind meritocracy. They could always point

---

5. Boasting about the presence of African Americans in sports to extol a commitment to diversity continues to take place at colleges and universities. See Hruby (2016).

to what they believed to be nonracist rationales for the exclusion of African American scholars" (p. 167).

Anderson provides a poignant example in Virginia Gildersleeve, the president of Barnard College. In her correspondence with Fred Wale, she "boasted of her commitment to a racially neutral hiring policy" (p. 168) and as such, Wale went to visit her to see if there were candidates of interest on his list. However, Wale realized quickly that Gildersleeve was, "wittingly or unwittingly, engaged in meritocratic rhetoric, which camouflaged traditional institutionalized practices of racial discrimination and exclusion" (p. 168). Gildersleeve prided herself on not seeing color and told Wale she was not even sure what a "Negro" was. As Anderson puts it, the presidents of the northern White universities possessed a commitment to meritocratic principles "with a religiosity that was disconnected from practice" (p. 168). Other presidents communicated their admiration for the stellar scholars on Wale's list but explained that these African Americans would be better off at universities with more "Negro companions" (p. 169). Much like members of search committees today who decide not to interview a candidate of color because "they will probably leave" or "there is nothing for them culturally in the community," these presidents decided that the impressive candidates would be better off elsewhere.

Of substance, some of the presidents claimed that their "Negro friends" cautioned them against hiring African Americans because they might not have positive experiences at the universities. Deciding whether or not a candidate of color will want a faculty position or stay at an institution for them continues to be an issue today. And referring to information from "Black friends" as a way to justify not hiring African American faculty continues to happen and is just as questionable today because those who use this excuse are typically seeking to "get a pass" at racism (Berchini, 2016). Other presidents foreshadowed anti-affirmative-action arguments, according to Anderson, claiming that hiring African Americans from the list could be considered discrimination against White applicants (Anderson, 1993). Even though none of the institutions employed any African Americans in full-time faculty positions, presidents argued that they could not engage in "reverse discrimination" by hiring scholars from Wale's list. "Reverse discrimination" is often used as a dog whistle for some faculty members who are opposed to target-of-opportunity hires.

Anderson notes that the majority of presidents simply acknowledged the list upon receipt and offered to give it consideration but did not. Other presidents were more honest and told Wale, "Our college is not ready for it quite yet," as Clarence Josephson, president of Heidelberg College wrote (p. 170). Anderson concluded that, in essence, there were no "opportunities for highly qualified African American scholars in northern white colleges and universities at midcentury" (p. 170). He also concluded through deep analysis of the presidential letters sent to Wale that a typical approach to "reconciling meritocratic principles with traditional patterns of racial discrimination was threefold: first, affirm one's commitment to a color-blind hiring policy; second, ignore the request to hire African American scholars; and third, focus on what was being done for African Americans in nonacademic areas" (p. 171). Various presidents told Wale that although they didn't have African Americans on the faculty, they were present in the dining room or tea room, in secretarial positions, and in sports positions.

There was some hope that resulted from Wale's efforts. After several years of going back and forth with college and university presidents about the scholars on his list, a small number of colleges pursued some of them. Institutions such as William Penn College, Southwestern College, Sterling College, and Roosevelt College hired African American faculty on a full-time basis, often writing to Wale to tell him that they had suffered in terms of donations and enrollment because of their choice to hire Black faculty (Anderson, 1993).

Although James D. Anderson wrote about the 1940s, his research and conclusions are still relevant today. In Anderson's words: "Even in today's environment, the question of hiring African American scholars [and other people of color] at traditionally White universities is invariably followed by the questioning of 'qualification' or 'merit.'" Anderson leads me to ask, once again, what would happen if our definitions of quality began with diversity—if diversity itself was the foundation of quality and excellence? What if we truly believed that only the best research and teaching can be done when we have a diverse team, group, faculty doing it?

Defining Quality within AAU Institutions

As I have discussed, quality is a slippery, complicated, sometimes unsavory, and ever-changing concept in academia. It contains a variety of data points—some more or less objective than others—a staunch defense of pedigree, a craving for sameness and all too often Whiteness, and a yearning for prestige (Buris, 2004; Guinier, 2015; Han, 2003). I spent hours talking with various administrators and faculty search committee chairs across the AAU institutions about quality and found it nearly impossible to define the term precisely or with any certainty based on their responses. Yet, the answers to my inquiries around how each institution defined quality had overlap and similarities.

As I broached the topic of quality and how each person or perhaps institution defined it, I was often greeted with a sigh and initial comments about the difficulty or near impossibility of defining the idea at their institution. But, after about a minute, each person would begin to discuss what constituted quality in the faculty search process at their university, discussing the nuances as well as the problems with the definitions from their perspective. Below, I explain how quality unfolds at the AAU institutions. Although I have organized the thoughts into subsections, they overlap as these subsections are connected and muddy.

Variance across Disciplines

When I asked questions about quality, the first answer I would get is that quality varies by discipline. I would let the person I was interviewing know that I was aware of this fact, but that I wanted to learn more about how their institution as a whole defined quality and then perhaps, a few examples of how it has been defined in specific disciplines at their institution. According to deans at both Ivy League and Big Ten universities, quality "varies tremendously" and "a lot by department." For example, a Big Ten university dean shared, "you have disciplines like economics, where quality is often measured by where you went to school and who your advisor was, as opposed to say psychology, where it's really much more defined by the number of papers and the quality of the journals you're [publishing in]." He added that for him personally, "the psychology model is better. The economics model bothers me, but that's what they do (Amir and Knauff, 2008). Your PhD is from one of ten institutions, and your advisor was somebody famous." You're a "quality person" due to your institution and advisor—due to your pedigree, as Lauren Rivera would argue.[6] He elaborated on quality issues by noting that his university has a bias in favor of Big Ten institutions: "That's just who we view as our peers and you're evaluated that way. It's one of those things where institutional quality factors play into hiring decisions. It just works out that way." Although this administrator knows the process at his institution is problematic, narrow, and discriminatory, he accepts it rather than working to challenge it. I'm reminded of Daryl Smith's analogy about exercise—you can know that exercise is good for you intellectually, but do you actually get up and move to make it happen?

When discussing what quality means for his university, a provost from the Midwest told me, "I think research productivity is the main thing people are looking for. That varies across schools." He noted that the medical school is looking for people to "eventually bring in a million and a half a year in NIH money." He added, "But in the academic affairs disciplines, they're looking for strong researchers first and potentially great teachers and just the general kind of philosophical fit with the [department]." When I asked him if search committees are looking for strong teachers, he responded, "I think if the person is an excellent teacher that probably breaks ties. But no, we're looking to [recruit] great scholars first and foremost."

---

6. For a detailed study of pedigree in economics departments, see Amir and Knauff (2008).

A vice provost at a public university on the West Coast shared with me that "the issue of quality essentially remains a black box within the individual departments." It's mysterious and hard to define. He believes it's essential for the disciplinary experts to define quality, but he can help diversify the pool by urging the faculty to think about cluster hires, or a more broadly written job description, or tapping into a postdoctoral diversity program. Often faculty members aren't thinking about these ideas as they are focused on their research. Although there is some variation across disciplines, by and large, the AAU institutions defined quality—even across disciplines in similar ways—in ways that reinforce pedigree and thus sameness.

Use of Objective Data

When I talked to administrators from the AAU institutions, there was much discussion of objective data and the importance of ensuring that search committees have access to such data in order to determine the quality of the candidates. At a midwestern private university, the vice provost mentioned that he likes to push the faculty search committees to focus on more objective data such as what is on the candidate's CV. "This [approach] allows the search committee to gauge productivity, quality of research and teaching and determine how much people are publishing." In addition, his institution uses an equity representative to guide the vetting of CVs in the search committee meetings. A vice provost in the Northeast added that "the quality of journals is very important, the quality of the [book] publishing house, if it is humanities [especially], and the letters of recommendation. And, of course, if possible, the funding."

According to a business school dean in the South, "We are an R1 research school, and so the research is very, very central to our mission. By and large, when we do selection of candidates, we really look through the research output or research potential. If it's an entry-level person, it's research potential, and if it's a person who's been out for a few years, it's research output. I think that's our single mission. I would say these are three things—research, research, research— and then maybe collegiality and their ability to teach." "In the junior market, [we ask] have they done some publishing? Have they done research and published it? Did they have a prestigious postdoc? . . . [We want to know] that they've been able to use this time to get their research out. Do they go to prestigious conferences?" Likewise, a department chair at a university in the South mentioned that she is looking for people with a strong publication record, a strong track record for being a scholar, the ability to bring in a lot of money, and "a good enough teacher because we're emphasizing teaching a lot." She laughed and added, "you know, all that stuff, that same old stuff." And, when referring to new faculty, she stated that they "hire on potential"—"if you are an assistant professor, you can't have a track record. You come in on potential. Well, potential is usually, well, your school and who your advisor was and you know, that same old, very, quite frankly, White-centric stuff." She also admitted that the academy needs to change all of this "stuff," but she thinks most efforts to change are "lip service" because an institution can't truly change when it's "using the same old evaluation criteria." Much like her counterparts, she knows there is an issue and that the criteria reinforce Whiteness, but she doesn't know what to do about it. And, even when discussing the way her institution uses objective data in faculty hiring, she also noted that what really matters is where you earned your PhD and who your advisor was.

As we continued to discuss issues of quality in the hiring process, the department chair brought up the recent "Varsity Blues" scandal, in which wealthy parents were buying their children's way into schools such as the University of Southern California and Stanford University (Golden and Burke, 2019; Teare, 2019). She noted that what happens in faculty hiring is similar to the admissions scandal in that those in academia weren't surprised that parents were buying their way into college—"Everybody's surprised except academia itself. Because we know all this drama happens." She added that everyone knows why we don't have more diversity in faculty hiring. This admission, which was not unique to this individual, demonstrates that universities are aware of their failings around racial and ethnic diversity in faculty hiring, yet they don't move to improve. How can universities boast about academic excellence and claim that diversity is imperative in statements and speeches, but not work to center faculty diversity? Instead of improving, they rely on the privilege-ridden measures of the prestige of the PhD-granting institution and mentor, which reinforce inequity.

Some administrators regularly develop checklists around quality in an attempt to reach objectivity. A law school dean in the West told me that her school uses a checklist, and that she learned this strategy while working at a Minority Serving Institution (MSI) in Texas that had a National Science Foundation ADVANCE grant (discussed in chapter 2). When the law school dean came to her new institution, she suggested that they develop a checklist right away. The checklist is generated by the faculty and can change over time and depending on the search. She added that she wanted to make quality explicit and transparent—what is considered a qualification and what is not? She also wanted to push her faculty to think about qualifications beyond research, such as strong teaching and practical experience that could add to the various roles the faculty plays in the academy.

A dean at a midwestern university told me that issues of quality in faculty hiring can be quite tense. He communicated that his university is looking for excellent researchers, but faculty candidates must also be superb teachers. When interacting with faculty candidates, he tells them, "If you like teaching and you like to engage with undergraduates, we have a great job for you. If you hate that, this is a terrible place; it's like torture." Likewise, a dean at another midwestern university explained, "We tried this year to actually, as a faculty, begin the process of articulating teaching quality. Do you have evidence of teaching quality? Attention to students—how good are they at just interacting? How much do they care about students?" For junior scholars, "We ask for a teaching statement . . . what is their philosophy of teaching? What have they done? What kind of teaching scores might they already have?" As I was talking to administrators from AAU institutions that also held other designations such as being a public university, a land grant university, or a member of the Big Ten, I found that these institutions were less inclined to define quality as being limited to graduates of a few institutions. They were also more likely to value teaching ability and a commitment to service in addition to research expertise among candidates.

Continuing to expand the definition of quality beyond research productivity, but maintaining a commitment to objective data, some institutions were looking for leadership potential and the contributions a candidate could make to the department or school. In the words of a dean on the West Coast, "We think about a future administrator, institutional leaders, and of course, diversity . . . how the different elements of diversity are reflected in the candidate's work, in their background experiences, and thinking about how that could help in terms of mentoring the different segments of our student population." A dean in the Northeast focused on impact: "We look for signs of academic impact . . . what is the impact on your discipline? Where are you publishing? For our school, which is more practical, we also ask, 'Are you having an impact on the social policy areas where you work beyond the academy?' Is this a person who is entrepreneurial . . . someone who is a builder?" In many ways, this dean was expanding the definition of quality for his institution.

Administrators reminded themselves that for junior scholars, "The tricky thing is we all look at recommendation letters. Because of the implicit bias training that we've been doing about how to read some of those letters with a couple ounces of salt. . . . The adjectives that are used for men as opposed to women, for majority White as opposed to minority [candidates]" are very different. According to Sensoy and DiAngelo (2017), all of the extra service work and mentoring that faculty of color do is rarely taken into consideration when reviewing their job applications, and the lack of this work on the part of many White colleagues (especially White men) is rarely seen as a deficit (Matthew, 2016a; Matthew, 2016b). Likewise, even though there is research that shows implicit bias and explicit racism in student course evaluations, rarely are these issues discussed when search committees scrutinize teaching evaluations (Williams, 2007).

Using a variety of objective data is a better process than relying on the privileging of a small group of institutions or the prestige of a candidate's mentor. However, Sensoy and DiAngelo (2017) warn us that no CV is race neutral or truly objective; even with names and affiliations removed, CVs are linked to pedigree. While CVs are an essential and more just source of information than pedigree, we must be vigilant about how inequities can manifest in data deemed objective. Even when approaching the hiring process with the idea of objectivity in mind, the qualifications of candidates of color are often scrutinized in ways that disadvantage them in the search process (Anderson, 1993; Sensoy and DiAngelo, 2017).

It is typical for search committees to organize candidates for a job, using objective metrics such as number of publications, ranking of the journals in which the candidates have published, grant money, and awards. The assumption behind this type of organization is that it will lead to a comparison of candidates that is more equitable. However, these objective data include *quality* of journal articles, *quality* of book presses, *quality* of teaching evaluations, *quality* of letters of recommendations, and *quality* of funding. The issue with labeling these data points as entirely objective is that they are not; they are all inherently subjective and they leave out large swaths of the work done by faculty candidates (Sensoy and DiAngelo, 2017). Of course, being subjective does not mean that these factors are without merit. Taken together and with the understanding that they are laden with subjectivity, these factors can demonstrate the potential of a candidate. However, it is essential to keep in mind that having access to top journals, top book presses, prestigious recommenders, and prominent funding sources can be the result of one's pedigree and social capital and as such are not the only measures of potential for search committees to consider.

Some of the AAU administrators were up front about the problem with ascertaining quality based on objective data, realizing that it can be problematic. However, they didn't want to change their approach. A vice provost in the South told me: "We're going to use proxies [for quality], right? At the end of the day, unless you hire your own students, which of course [brings about] different issues of bias and the difficulties of being objective, you're always relying on proxies for quality and likely productivity and collegiality, right? The opinion of someone who you'd view as credible, training from people who are successful and elite in the field." Processing as she was speaking, she added, "I don't want to remove those proxies. We still want letters from peer AAU institutions in this person's discipline, but nonetheless, how do we try to ensure that we don't simply use those proxies without really deeply diving into evaluating them. The reality is we are fortunate, we have a lot of success in recruiting. We have the great fortune that generally, if we get candidates, there's going to be a candidate in the pool that can satisfy the traditional metrics." With regard to junior hires, she stated, "but are we hiring people straight into a tenure-track position—people who got their doctorate at a non-peer institution? No, I don't think so." She clarified that within the tenured ranks, things change as "we have a lot more data about the person and their work." Sometimes faculties are willing to excuse the quality of a faculty member's institution if they have a track record of "academic star"–level success and they are already tenured.

The Influence of Pedigree

As Lauren Rivera warns, pedigree—in this case, a record of distinguished academic ancestry—is highly valued at "elite" institutions. During my conversations with AAU administrators, it was rare that they didn't hold tightly to the importance of pedigree even when they knew that doing so was exclusionary. Pedigree and its value manifested across every discipline, and every AAU administrator with whom I talked mentioned its importance. A provost at a midwestern university, when discussing one of his departments that is ranked number one in the world, related that quality is highly important and his faculty is looking "for the best in the world." However, he cautioned that the hiring processes in this department are open to "manipulation, or unconscious bias, for sure." As provost, he "rallied" against this type of behavior and wasn't popular because of it. Still, in his words, "I don't know how far the message got out, but they re-did the search and got a much bigger pool." He added, "I never give a speech without talking about how important it is to have a diverse faculty and student body, but especially, we're especially challenged on the faculty. Maybe I shouldn't call it a bully pulpit, but the platform I have as provost to speak [is important]."

A vice chancellor for equity on the West Coast shared with me, "I think there's a de facto privileging of pedigree, and that takes the form, not only of where you [got] your PhD, but, for example, in most STEM fields, you need a postdoc. [In STEM fields] I think the bottom line is the postdoc experience, becomes the de facto feeder of academic tenure-track positions." He added, when I asked him his thoughts on the humanities, "I think for far too long, people have assumed that the humanities and the arts get it, and I would argue that they don't. I think, were you to pull out some of the [departments] that have a focus on racial and ethnic minorities and [White] women, you would see a significant drop in a [school's] overall representation."

A dean in the Northeast shared with me that various questions are proxies for "excellence" and "quality" when people don't have deep expertise in a specific area—noting that people equate quality with "Who have they worked for? Do we know them?" "Where did they do their graduate work or a postdoc?" "Are they publishing in journals I know of?" She also mentioned that she wondered if these are good measures and to what extent bias enters the process. Of greater concern, she added that she worries that departments choose "people they feel comfortable with" over the best candidates for the positions.

A dean at a midwestern university declared, "I do think that we live in a hierarchical [world], so the University of Chicago" is considered better than us. "We know that, but it doesn't mean that every individual connected with [an institution] is better." He also noted that there are departments in various disciplines that are very well known and he would look to those for hires. He would look at candidates from other [non-peer] institutions, but he would look at their materials a lot more closely. Those candidates that aren't coming from the most exclusive institutions are immediately held suspect. It is important to note that at most major universities, regardless of their AAU membership, the majority of decisions are made around considerations of quality and prestige. As Charles Clotfelter demonstrated in his important book *Buying the Best: Cost Escalation in Elite Higher Education* (1996), universities aggressively desire and work to become part of the most elite group of institutions, and faculty hiring (especially of those with elite backgrounds) is one factor in this desire and push. The issue at hand, however, is that in this desire, and all of the decisions that accompany it, is the perpetuation of privilege and pedigree and a very narrow definition of quality (consider, for example, the discussion of faculty hiring hierarchies in Clauset, Arbesman, and Larremore, 2015). Once again, universities strive for academic excellence, but a commitment to racial and ethnic diversity is not centered—prestige is.

A provost in the Midwest shared that his university is more open with regard to which institution the candidates come from. They are much more likely to look at who the advisor is over the institution. He added, "Because we know there are some stellar faculty at those institutions that are maybe not as well-ranked, but they've, for whatever reason, they've stayed at those institutions, but they produce superb research themselves, and they're well known for producing excellent graduate students. . . . [W]e would look at those. The other part we do is we will look at some of the institutions below us and see who their rising stars are." Interestingly, the language of "below us" continues to bear allegiance to pedigree and prestige even when the goal is to be more inclusive.

A vice provost on the West Coast admitted that often departments attempt to "go after their aspirational candidate" but the problem is that everyone is going after this candidate and his own institution is "not ranked high enough to yield [the candidate]." He added, "That's kind of ridiculous, because there's so much opportunity costs that are lost with that strategy, but they sort of feel that this is how we do it." To counter this behavior, he gives some disciplines the opportunity to bring in more people. Search committees have to get permission, but sometimes having a larger short list of candidates brings in more diversity and surprises the search committee. Often the aspirational candidate doesn't turn out to be the candidate of choice when there are more candidates from which to choose. People of color are more apt to be brought in for faculty searches when search committees are able to bring in a larger short list of candidates. The people of color are typically the "extra person" to bring in. Here's a question: what if we brought more candidates to campus regularly? How did three become the norm? Yes, money is a factor, but given how much money is spent on moving faculty from hiring to tenure and how much money universities put into showing how they support diversity, it seems likely that bringing in one or two more additional candidates could lead to a more diverse faculty.

A business school dean in the South responded, when I asked him if his institution focused its hiring of new faculty on a specific set of institutions, as I had heard this from many of the AAU administrators, "I think we are starting to be. I think we've been sort of really focused [on] hiring from the Ivies—we've got to get the thoroughbred—and that has also precluded us from looking more broadly at candidates in terms of race, ethnicity, or other aspects of diversity. Now there is some talk of extending beyond, but I will wait to see how much the departments actually will end up doing it, because we want to be like Harvard." Expanding, he acknowledged, "It's also some sort of reflected glory, you can brag and say we recruited from Stanford this year, versus [recruiting] from Florida International University or some[place like that]." Here we see that institutions are more concerned about being able to brag about where they're recruiting candidates from (prestige) than being inclusive, using objective data, and looking widely for the best candidates for the position and the institutional mission (Clotfelter, 1996).

An Ivy League provost confessed that defining quality in faculty searches is very difficult. He tries to provide guidance from his position but "there is resistance to hiring outside the circle—the Ivy-plus schools." Much like others I talked with at the AAU institutions, he mentioned that "people want to hire people like themselves, the same schools or boarding schools, the same colleges. It's comfortable. We have a hard time pushing through this issue." Imagine for a minute looking at the boarding school that a candidate for a faculty position attended. Also imagine putting one's boarding school on one's CV and how the very act of doing so is riddled with privilege and an acknowledgment of the importance and value of pedigree. This provost also explained that faculties want to hire the best person in their discipline and they want the best person at their institution. They want the number one person, and if that person is a White man, they still want to hire the "best" person and aren't concerned with the lack of diversity in their department or that their definitions of "best" might be limited.

When I asked how this kind of exclusive and exclusionary hiring has an impact on faculty diversity, the provost told me that at his institution, they "pick people of color from other Ivy-plus institutions" but he wondered about the potential candidates from Historically Black Colleges and Universities (HBCUs), Hispanic Serving Institutions (HSIs), or "even state institutions." He added that his university rarely chooses anyone "fresh out of a PhD program" from one of these types of institutions. However, they do hire "more established people who come out of [non-Ivy-plus] institutions, but they have established a career, maybe won a MacArthur 'genius' award." Given how rare it is for faculty members to win MacArthur genius awards, the chances of moving from a non-Ivy-plus institution to this Ivy League university are slim.

Ironically, given her location in the South, a department chair shared with me that she thinks most of her faculty are unaware of the contributions of HBCUs, and if a candidate does come from an HBCU and is strong, her faculty thinks that the candidate is an exception and not the norm. She inferred that her faculty thinks "it's a Black school, right?" and that because it's Black, it must not be as good or as rigorous. People can transfer racism against individuals to racism against institutions that are affiliated with people of color. This has been happening regularly to HBCUs since their establishment in the 1800s—a phenomenon that I have written about extensively in my book *Envisioning Black Colleges* (Gasman, 2007).

Many AAU university administrators discussed wanting to "win" against Harvard. They are fighting for the same candidates as Harvard and expending considerable energy trying to get these candidates on their faculty. Most told me that they rarely ever win in these competitions. Imagine the cost involved in fighting for candidates that you rarely win and how those funds could be used to hire a strong and more diverse faculty. Even when institutions try to stay focused and steer away from chasing the aspirational candidate or whomever Harvard is after, they tend to fall back into the pattern. Below, an administrator speaks to the power of genealogy (or pedigree):

I would say, in general, we really put an emphasis on the quality of the work submitted and the [candidate's] performance on campus, in terms of the research they present. We're a very research-intensive organization, so I think we do tend to put more emphasis on that than we do . . . let's say on teaching, on experience, or other things I think other institutions might. I think if I'm reading between the lines, and maybe I'm reading the wrong lines, I have been at pains to explain to departments that we should not over-invest in let's call it the genealogy of a particular candidate, which program, which advisor they had.

She elaborated: "I think I see a clear pattern in this college, and I'm sure it repeats itself in other places, where faculty members tend to gravitate to their own graduate programs, or to graduate programs that they consider to be in the top ten programs, and that does happen, and that worries me a little bit. I don't have a strong solution for that. You can look at it one way through a lens and say this is very exclusionary. You can look through another lens and . . . [think] these are the best departments and the best candidates, so there is sort of a circularity. I think I just want to ensure that we are attentive to the actual work that the individual brings to the table."

Even when pushing herself to critique the process and naming the exclusion that it manifests, this administrator fell back on the idea that her faculty members are choosing candidates from institutions and departments from which they came because these are the places from which the best candidates come, and not because they want to produce and cling to sameness and Whiteness (Clauset, Arbesman, and Larremore, 2015). Most people hiring at all types of institutions fall back on hiring people like themselves because they are familiar, and they aim to emulate what happens at like institutions. However, colleges and universities boast about their commitment to racial and ethnic diversity and the pursuit of truth and knowledge, making institutional isomorphism even more problematic (DiMaggio and Powell, 1983). These ideals—diversity, truth, and knowledge—must be centered in institutional pursuits of academic excellence or they cannot be achieved with any sincerity.

Ratings and rankings are at the heart of elitism, according to a provost in the Northeast: "There is a kind of elitism or parochialism in connection [to searches] that is in direct relation to the chasing of the rankings crunch that the university has been in. And I think what is worse is that when we bring in faculty only from the top fifty schools, they self-perpetuate (Clauset, Arbesman, and Larremore, 2015). I get a young faculty member who says, 'The best programmers are at Harvard so we only look at Harvard people.' And guess where [he] came from? Of course, he came from Harvard. I find the orientation toward rankings really disappointing and challenging. And I wish that all the Ivies would simply say [to *U.S. News and World Report*], we are no longer playing with you."

This provost also communicated her frustration with her institution trying to "game" the rankings: "People are analyzing the methodology, and then they're gaming the methodology so that they can move up. That's not actually about substantive change in quality on the ground. That's just about mathematics. I find the whole thing really distasteful."

Working to try to make significant change in faculty hiring at one Ivy League institution, the provost's office conducted ten years of analysis on faculty hiring within the department of engineering—an area that many in the current faculty say is difficult to diversify. The analysis showed them that they were good at going from the general pool to a long list of candidates; the long list was diverse in terms of White women and people of color. The long list contained the objective metrics of high-quality people that everyone agreed upon. However, the final candidates that were flown in for campus visits tended to be White men.

During the analysis, the provost's office looked at those people who were considered but not chosen. They located those who had not been chosen to see what happened with their careers. According to the provost, "We were able to find all these [White] women and people of color whom we didn't pick, who then went on to have wonderful careers at our peer institutions or other institutions. We basically used this exercise to say that faculty are actually not really good at [faculty hiring]." He expanded, "We think we're good at picking for what we say is important to us, which is diversity and excellence, and it turns out . . . we lose all these candidates who are great and we don't end up . . . choosing; our short list isn't any better than some random selection of the pool." He also identified the problem, noting that they were narrowing the pool using a "small list of brand-name schools" and "people we know in those schools." They were falling back on pedigree. He added, "By doing that, we're just reinforcing the system because we're just falling into the same networks, as opposed to diversifying the networks."

After realizing the problem, the provost took the findings to departments across the institution so that they would realize how systemic discrimination plays out in faculty hiring; he also became more data-driven in the hiring process as a result of the analysis. Being armed with data helped this provost to make systemic change and shift the mindset of the faculty.

With regard to hiring people like themselves, a dean at a Big Ten university admitted that sometimes his faculty will ask the "dumb question." They will ask candidates, "Did you see the game?" and if the person doesn't "know what game you're talking about," they might think a candidate isn't compatible. However, the dean says he ensures that this kind of judgment doesn't happen on a regular basis.

Another Big Ten dean told me, frustrated, that "unsurprisingly, we end up replicating ourselves, with the difference being that the expectations in terms of productivity prior to appointment are greater now than they were twenty years ago when I was hired." He added, "We see largely the same institutions. [At] most institutions, you try to hire among your peers or among your aspirational peers." Interestingly, he shared that for their special, diversity-related programs and postdocs, they are willing to look at institutions in the West or South and HBCUs. However, most of their hires are from the Midwest and occasionally from the Northeast. In this institution's case, regional bias has racial implications. When I asked him why he thinks that people tend to gravitate to the same institutions, he responded, "I think a little bit of it is comfort. A little bit of it is inertia." Although he admitted that "disciplines are slow to change," he also added that "some of it is legitimate. I think there's more of a falloff in quality and scholarship than people like to admit. What the falloff in quality does not reflect, though, is potential. So we have candidates from R2, R3 institutions, universities outside the AAU. Maybe the nature of the work that they completed in their PhD program is less than what we would normally expect, but often it's used as a predictor of future productivity as well. There's a much greater risk. Everybody's afraid of making a bad choice because you've made an investment that's basically a multi-year investment in somebody, and so that fear of making a mistake is greater, is great enough to nudge search committees to move in a comfortable path." Across the AAU institutions, I heard the sentiment that "lesser" institutions (or non-AAU and less elite AAU institutions) weren't as good, and neither were the PhDs they were producing. Interestingly, these comments were not based on empirical data as they were relayed to me.[7]

A vice provost at a university in the South mentioned that her institution doesn't define quality or provide guidance on quality from the provost's office. She also noted, "I think there are disciplines where individuals, although they've been trained not to do this, they will look at pedigree and will then focus on certain schools where candidates might come from, but we do train search committees not to do this. Do they do it? Yes. Have we told them not to? Yes."

Having listened to many AAU provosts tell me how their institutions recruit from a limited group of universities, I asked a diversity representative in the Northeast if she noticed a preference for individuals from specific universities, in terms of the institution where the PhD was earned. Her response was, "You don't even need to finish the question, yes!" And she elaborated, "There are the usual players and, of course, it depends on the department, right? All the Ivy [League institutions], obviously, you get de facto extra points for

7. I explore these ideas more thoroughly in chapter 4.

that [affiliation]. Big research universities like Michigan and Texas and Chicago [matter]. You know that I mean, the big research institutions with a lot of money. Those are often the de facto preference and where people have gone themselves or maybe their advisors or leaders in the field are." She added, "I've been in spaces where faculty members have said something like 'Oh that person went to that school. I just don't think that they'll be up to the rigor to get tenure at [our institution].' And [I'm thinking] how do you know that? This is a research 1 university as well that you are talking about. Do you work there? [This] is a very standard way of talking about folks. That's the coded way that implicit bias can sneak in and one of the many ways." Again, search committees are judging candidates and the institutions from which they come on a hunch rather than based on empirical data—a practice that runs counter to the rigorous research that faculty members expect from each other. Perhaps the faculty should prepare for and apply the same precision to faculty hiring as it does to its research process.

These perspectives from AAU administrators have held consistent for decades. For example, Smith, Turner, and colleagues (2004) found that candidates with PhDs from the top research institutions were privileged in nearly all hiring cases. Search committees look to a small group of universities for candidates, believing that only specific institutions produce candidates that are good enough for their institutions. These universities tend to be a small group of the AAU institutions. Some search committees even look at where candidates secured their undergraduate degrees despite these candidates holding PhDs. According to University of Southern California professor Julie Posselt,

The perspective that I hear says that some departments are just known in the field for providing good training, and that's understood to be like a sort of human-capital justification for prioritizing applicants from particular institutions, but more often . . . the reasons for privileging applicants from a small set of institutions is that they believe in them on some level. They feel either a personal connection or a personal sense of trust from either the program as a whole, because they know it on some level or it's recognized on some level, or they know the people who are writing letters from those institutions, so this is where closed networks really affect how applications get judged.

The Old Boys' Network

Explaining that definitions of quality are discipline specific, the provost of a midwestern university admitted to me that if you did a survey of the faculty being considered for new tenure-track jobs at his university, you'd find that "everybody hailed from . . . the same twenty-five institutions regardless of discipline." The provost's assumed survey results are consistent with network analysis conducted by Clauset, Arbesman, and Larremore (2015) in that both reveal that a small group of institutions dominates as producers of "qualified" PhDs for faculty positions. When this provost was looking at his own field, he told me that most hiring committees home in on about five to seven schools that they know are the best. He said, "In my field, I could pick, no problem, without hesitation, the seven schools that I would—I'm confessing bias here . . . I know the advisors." He added, "The old boys' network does look a little different than it used to, but it's still a network." Knowing that these insular networks lead to insular hiring, the provost acknowledged, "I say this fully aware of the fact that the pipeline language is a really flawed conception and there's excellence everywhere. And yet, I still know that if I'm looking at an application pool—hell, even if I looked at it blindly, I suspect, like if the person's school and advisors were just kept off [the applications], because the kind of training that these students get in terms of how to look good for an application pool—it would still end up being most of the same institutions." Pedigree manifests even when masking PhD-granting institutions and faculty advisors, as students at the most prestigious institutions often have immediate and continual access to more opportunities that will help them become faculty. And thus, determining faculty preparation for faculty positions is an intensive process that takes training, preparation, precision, and an understanding of how prestige, pedigree, and systemic racism can color our understandings of quality.

A provost in the South explained it this way, "What we have found is, like many places, our faculty operate on what I refer to as the known networks. So when we have an opening in our department, I'm going to let all my friends, who I know through my professional association, . . . know about this open position, [and] tell my graduate students. And we know people tend to know people who are like them. So if we have a predominantly White and male faculty, that's who the faculty know, so how do we think about creating a pool that is the unknown network?"

One of the Big Ten deans who I interviewed also had concerns about the "old boys' network," noting that he is "less fond of" the practice of "members of the search committee or departments [reaching out to] home institutions or other institutions . . . where they have friends, asking for candidates to apply." He added, "I don't think it's particularly equitable" in comparison to advertising widely. When a department is homogeneous in terms of racial, ethnic, and gender makeup, people tend to reach out to people just like them—often White and often male. When departments become more diverse (as well as the PhD programs from which they graduated), reaching out across networks tends to bring about a more diverse pool (see chapter 4 for a discussion of pipeline issues).

An associate provost at a private research institution in the Northeast relayed a story to me about her institution's desire to begin recruiting from only top twenty departments. About a decade ago, under the leadership of a new provost, there was a push to "start recruiting faculty from top twenty institutions in the disciplines. And that was a mandate from the provost and the president." At first the search committees pushed back, but not because they were concerned about growing elitism. Their concern was that they would be unsuccessful recruiting from top twenty departments. According to the associate provost, however, "it absolutely worked. It was a matter of setting an institutional expectation that we would recruit many, many more faculty from those top programs." Interestingly, the institution has now revisited this change. While the recruiters think that the decision was important at one stage of their evolution, "it's too rigid a thumbnail to give to search committees." In the words of the associate provost, "The general message was valuable, which was that we're a lot better than we think we are, and we can be competitive and make competitive offers for people at really top places that we aspire to be. That was a great message, but applying it in some kind of rigid way is counterproductive. And so we're softer on that, but it did a lot of good work for us." The idea of "better" and the methods for becoming "better" are deeply and inherently connected to elitism, pedigree, and the idea of chasing the "best" candidate.

The same associate provost told me later in the conversation, "We have a top five list that a really disproportionate number of our hires come from. And some of that is geographical because there's a lot of people who [earn their PhDs nearby] and they want to stay in the area." She shared that sometimes a search committee will recommend someone from an institution that is not as well known or is different—maybe it is a "different size" or has a "very strong religious flavor." The committee members will argue that "the candidate that [they] want to hire is placed there for a very peculiar reason or [the candidate] is wonderful and [is] underplaced, and sometimes the argument carries the day. But the provost will push back on that when she hears it." Elitism is reinforced by some upper-level administrators when search committees look to expand the pool of institutions from which candidates are chosen.

Some AAU administrators are pushing their faculty to have a wider approach to hiring, making convincing arguments that their narrow scope of institutions is hurting their chances of having a diverse faculty. Interestingly, the AAU institutions where these changes are taking place are typically those that have experienced a scandal related to race or large-scale protests. The dean of an engineering school in the Midwest shared with me that her school does not focus on a specific set of institutions from which to draw candidates. It doesn't want to limit prospects and tries to advertise as widely as possible. Interestingly, this institution is less selective in terms of student admissions compared with many of the other institutions in the AAU. She expressed her frustration that some colleagues assume that candidates of color are less qualified; when the pool of candidates is more diverse, some colleagues assume that the pool is less strong. In her words, "There is a misperception that this is an either-or thing. We've got to really diversify our pool, so that means we have to give on quality a bit. That is so untrue, and that really bothers me. Absolutely, you need to have a diverse pool, but there's never any question that they're the most qualified people as well." Because people hold racial biases that say that people of color are not as good, when they appear in the hiring pool, the pool itself is assumed to be not as good, not as strong. A diverse pool brings about fears that the pool is not of a high quality.

Linking Diversity to Excellence

There is a constant need to link excellence with diversity, as AAU administrators are fearful that if they only stress diversity, they will receive criticism that they are lowering the quality of the candidates and the institution. For example, a provost in the Northeast shared with frustration: "I can't tell you that there is one way that the departments are talking about quality. However, their favorite term is either quality or excellence or rigor. It's all coded stuff . . . and it's so sad because every time we have a conversation about diversity, equity, and inclusion, [I wonder] why there has to be this complementary or this parallel conversation about the quality of the candidate. It's so disturbing and sad."

In the minds of many, diversity or diversifying the faculty immediately leads to questions of reduced quality as faculty members of color are seen as being less qualified. A provost at a midwestern university told me that his "big thing" is that "you can't separate [excellence and diversity] ethically." Interestingly, I found that provosts and deans of color were under the most pressure to link excellence and diversity because their very right or qualification for being at the university was justified by this type of linkage. Many institutions tout the idea of "inclusive excellence," but what does this really mean, and can it have negative ramifications?

Is the idea that you have to say "diversity" next to "excellence" problematic? Is it a reinforcement of systemic racism? When I give talks, I often tell people that the only time we should link these two concepts is if we are pointing out that the only way we can truly be excellent is to be diverse. Convincing others of this idea can be difficult. A provost in the South admitted, "We have taken heat on this whole sacrifice quality for the sake of diversity [issue], and I've been very clear that we're not trying to sacrifice quality for the sake of diversity, that we actually believe it is possible to achieve both." She shared that her institution regularly distributes "literature on diverse organizations and how we're changing organizations for the better. We also bring in some best practices about how to diversify the pool."

Quality and merit are muddy and nebulous concepts that colleges and universities have been unable to get a grasp on aside from continuing to privilege those who already have privilege. Universities have a long-standing fear that if they are more inclusive they will become less—they will fall in the rankings, they won't be respected, they will lose prestige, they will lose access. These fears manifest in faculty members and administrators across institutions. Just as individuals must look inside and determine if they care more about only their own well-being or the greater good, institutions must do the same. And if faculties can center diversity and equity in discussions about diminishing quality, it seems wholly possible that they can center diversity and equity in discussion of improved quality.

4

What about the Pipeline?

We need to get more candidates [of color] to consider themselves in their own view qualified to apply for a faculty position at an Ivy League university. That's certainly the refrain that we hear when we speak to candidates—that they don't think they would even get an interview.

—AAU UNIVERSITY PROVOST

The most common excuse I hear from deans, faculty members, and search committees about the lack of diversity among faculty is "There aren't enough people of color applying for their faculty positions or in the faculty pipeline." It is accurate that there are few people of color in some disciplines. It is also accurate that there are very small numbers of Native Americans, Native Hawaiians, Alaska Natives, and Pacific Islanders across various disciplines, but even these individuals, once earning a PhD, have difficulty securing faculty positions (Shotton, Lowe, and Waterman, 2013). That said, there are ample numbers of PhDs of color overall in the humanities, education, and biology, yet, we still do not have great diversity on these faculties (Bastedo and Bowman, 2010; Smith, Turner, et al., 2004; Turner, Gonzalez, and Wood, 2008; Weinberg, 2008).

In the preceding chapter, I discussed the complicated nature of "quality" and the way that institutions define it—clinging to pedigree, sameness, Whiteness, and prestige. As part of this discussion, I explored the focus on the small and limited group of institutions that are deemed high quality by various AAU institutions. It seems to me that the scarcity of people of color in the faculty pipeline is linked to the overwhelming focus on hiring PhDs from this small group of institutions—a group that itself is not doing enough to recruit and retain PhDs of color. Those who earn PhDs from non-AAU institutions (and even some less prestigious AAU institutions)—despite attending research-focused PhD programs that are ranked the very highest quality by the Carnegie Classification system—are relegated to nonexistence (Clauset, Arbesman, and Larremore, 2015).

In this chapter, I will share data from the Survey of Earned Doctorates (2019), which depict the presence of people of color across the spectrum of the academy, with many disciplines considerably higher in terms of producing PhD holders of color than representation in the faculty. Table 6 displays the presence of people of color earning PhDs across the continuum of all institutions in the United States between 2011 and 2018. American Indians and Alaska Natives make up less than 1% of PhDs, Asian Americans account for 5%, Black people represent 6%, Hispanics account for 5%, and Native Hawaiians and Pacific Islanders represent less than 0.5%. Whites account for 48% of those who earn PhDs across the nation. Importantly, and indicative of Daryl Smith's comments on our success in internationalizing our future faculty, 29% of PhD earners across all disciplines are nonresidents of the United States (see table 6).

As mentioned above, whenever I give presentations on faculty diversity in hiring, one of the major pushbacks I receive is that the reason a particular institution does not have more diversity among their tenured and tenure-track faculty is that underrepresented racial and ethnic individuals are not in the pipeline. However, the pipeline is complicated and differs depending on the discipline and type of institution, as well as within various racial and ethnic categories.

If we are truly dedicated to hiring more African Americans to the faculty, it is important to look at their participation across disciplines

and institutional type. If we examine African American PhD production across all the biological and biomedical sciences, we see that
they account for 3% of all PhD holders in this field, and that of these
individuals, only 25% of them earn their degree from an AAU institution. In engineering, African Americans make up a mere 2% of PhD
earners, with 47% of these scholars obtaining their degrees from an
AAU institution. Four percent of PhD holders in English language
and literature are African Americans, with 45% of these individuals
securing their degrees from AAU institutions. Ethnic and cultural
studies boasts the largest production of African American PhDs,
with 21% of PhD holders in this area. Of note, 62% of these PhDs
earned their degrees from AAU institutions, which raises the question: are AAU institutions more likely to accept African Americans
into PhD programs focused on race, ethnicity, culture, or gender?
Or, perhaps African Americans are more likely to express interest
and apply to AAU PhD programs in these areas. African Americans
are barely represented among PhD holders in language and linguistics, making up only 1%. Sixty-seven percent of these individuals
earn their degrees at AAU institutions. In history, 5% of PhD holders
are African American and, of these, 62% earn these degrees at AAU
institutions. In the discipline of math, African Americans make up
only 1% of PhD recipients, with only 33% of these scholars earning
their degrees at AAU institutions. Four percent of PhD holders in
philosophy and religious studies are African Americans. Of these
individuals, 40% earn their degrees from AAU institutions. African
American PhD holders in the physical sciences are sparse at only
2%; of these, 40% come from AAU institutions. Psychology boasts
6% of its PhD holders being African American; however, only 21%
of these individuals earned degrees at AAU institutions. Imagine
what this means in regard to what we know about African American
mental health? Of course, one doesn't need to be African American
to conduct research related to African Americans and mental health,
but the research would be much richer if it had more African American contributions and voices. When we look at the social sciences,
some areas fare well while others are dire. Economics is particularly
troubling for African American PhD holders, as they represent 1%

Table 6

PhD Conferrals by Race/Ethnicity in Select Fields, 2011–2018 (All Institutions)

Field	American Indian	Asian American	Black/ African American	Hispanic
All Fields	1,748	26,721	29,006	24,769
Biological and Biomedical Sciences	180	5,317	2,164	3,223
Engineering	86	4,998	1,325	1,938
English Language and Literature/Letters	58	376	414	508
Ethnic, Cultural Minority, Gender, and Group Studies	39	55	186	115
Foreign Languages, Literatures, and Linguistics	26	349	122	924
History	37	207	372	519
Mathematics and Statistics	18	760	206	341
Philosophy and Religious Studies	22	213	238	209
Physical Sciences	94	2,193	868	1,446
Psychology	140	1,726	1,965	3,256
Social Sciences	111	1,316	1,157	1,310
Anthropology	47	188	159	298
Economics	5	434	117	191
Political Science and Government	19	274	287	256
Sociology	28	261	448	377

Source: National Science Foundation, Survey of Earned Doctorates, 2018, www.nsf.org.

NHPI	White	Two or More Races	Unknown	Nonresident Alien	Total
471	241,406	5,586	27,399	143,589	**500,695**
78	31,743	872	3,367	16,906	**63,850**
30	21,954	631	2,922	44,156	**78,040**
8	7,688	149	895	943	**11,039**
5	274	16	73	116	**879**
5	4,508	95	814	3,034	**9,877**
6	5,024	84	643	916	**7,808**
8	5,326	134	645	7,108	**14,546**
2	3,775	80	494	925	**5,958**
31	20,462	478	2,231	18,419	**46,222**
24	20,223	492	2,080	2,442	**32,348**
20	13,813	338	1,987	9,397	**29,449**
4	2,648	72	417	728	**4,561**
1	2,419	71	436	5,233	**8,907**
13	3,457	70	480	1,447	**6,303**
2	2,927	80	342	843	**5,308**

All Fields (%)	0%	5%	6%	5%
Biological and Biomedical Sciences	0%	8%	3%	5%
Engineering	0%	6%	2%	2%
English Language and Literature/Letters	1%	3%	4%	5%
Ethnic, Cultural Minority, Gender, and Group Studies	4%	6%	21%	13%
Foreign Languages, Literatures, and Linguistics	0%	4%	1%	9%
History	0%	3%	5%	7%
Mathematics and Statistics	0%	5%	1%	2%
Philosophy and Religious Studies	0%	4%	4%	4%
Physical Sciences	0%	5%	2%	3%
Psychology	0%	5%	6%	10%
Social Sciences	0%	4%	4%	4%
Anthropology	1%	4%	3%	7%
Economics	0%	5%	1%	2%
Political Science and Government	0%	4%	5%	4%
Sociology	1%	5%	8%	7%

0%	48%	1%	5%	29%	**100%**
0%	50%	1%	5%	26%	**100%**
0%	28%	1%	4%	57%	**100%**
0%	70%	1%	8%	9%	**100%**
1%	31%	2%	8%	13%	**100%**
0%	46%	1%	8%	31%	**100%**
0%	64%	1%	8%	12%	**100%**
0%	37%	1%	4%	49%	**100%**
0%	63%	1%	8%	16%	**100%**
0%	44%	1%	5%	40%	**100%**
0%	63%	2%	6%	8%	**100%**
0%	47%	1%	7%	32%	**100%**
0%	58%	2%	9%	16%	**100%**
0%	27%	1%	5%	59%	**100%**
0%	55%	1%	8%	23%	**100%**
0%	55%	2%	6%	16%	**100%**

of this group. Of this 1%, only 34% earned degrees at AAU institutions. Again I ask, what would we likely know about inequities in African American communities if universities, in particular AAU institutions, were more inclusive in their economics PhD programs? Likewise, in anthropology, African Americans make up only 3% of PhD degree holders; however, 59% of these individuals come from AAU institutions. African Americans fare slightly better in political science and sociology with 5% and 8% of PhD holders being Black, respectively. Of these, 43% and 52%, respectively, earned their degrees at AAU institutions (see tables 6 and 7). If we reflect on chapter 3 and the discussion of quality and pedigree, where an individual earns their PhD is important, given the insular nature of faculty hiring (Clauset, Arbesman, and Larremore, 2015).

As we move to an examination of Latino PhD production across disciplines and institutions, the results are slightly more positive in some areas. In the biological and biomedical sciences, Latinos account for 5% of all PhD holders, with 56% of these individuals earning degrees at AAU institutions. In engineering, Latinos hold a mere 2% of PhDs, with 61% of these degrees coming from AAU institutions. In English language and literature, 5% of PhD holders are Latino, and 52% of these scholars earned their degrees at AAU institutions. Much like African Americans, the greatest representation of Latinos in PhD programs overall is in the area of ethnic and cultural studies, with 13% of degree holders being Latino. Eighty-nine percent of these individuals earn their degrees at AAU institutions— begging the questions: Are AAU institutions more likely to enroll Latinos in ethnic and culture studies? Or are Latinos more likely to apply to these AAU programs? Unlike their African American counterparts, Latinos earn 9% of PhDs in foreign languages and linguistics. Of these individuals, 61% earn degrees at AAU institutions. In history, Latinos represent 7% of all PhD holders, with 55% of these scholars earning degrees at AAU institutions. Latino PhD holders don't do as well in math and the physical sciences, accounting for 2% and 3% of all degrees earned, respectively, 52% and 55%, respectively, of these individuals come from AAU institutions. In philosophy and religion, Latinos represent 4% of PhD recipients, with 49% earning degrees from AAU institutions. Latinos do fairly well in psychology, earning 10% of all PhDs. However, only 19% of these degrees are earned at AAU institutions, a situation that is highly problematic, given faculty members' negative dispositions toward non-AAU PhD degree holders and the privileging of AAU PhD degree holders (Clauset, Arbesman, and Larremore, 2015). As we look more closely at the social sciences, there is little representation in economics and political science, with Latinos holding 2% and 4% of all PhDs, respectively. Of these Latino PhD holders, 55% and 59%, respectively, earn their degrees at AAU institutions. Latinos do significantly better in anthropology and sociology accounting for 7% of PhDs in both disciplines. Interestingly 70% of Latino PhD holders in anthropology earn their degrees at AAU institutions, and 66% of those in sociology do as well (see tables 6 and 8).

Asian American PhD holders range from 4% to 6% across most disciplines, and a minimum of 56% of these individuals earn their degrees at AAU institutions. There are a few outliers in this group. Asian Americans only account for 3% of PhD degree holders in history and English. However, 84% of their history PhDs are from AAU institutions, and 66% of their English degrees are from this group as well. Asian Americans account for 8% of PhD holders in the biological and biomedical sciences, with 64% of these scholars earning degrees from AAU institutions. Of note, at 5%, Asian Americans earn fewer PhDs in psychology than both African Americans and Latinos; however, a greater percentage of their degrees are from AAU institutions (36%) than their Black and Latino counterparts. As I said when discussing Asian American faculty, I want to caution the reader about drawing too many conclusions and generalizations about the representation of Asian Americans, given that these data are not disaggregated (see tables 6 and 9).

American Indian and Alaska Native (AIAN) PhD production is almost nonexistent (0%–1%). With the numbers being so small in some disciplines (e.g., political science) that you can count PhD holders from 2011 to 2018 on one hand; and only one of these individuals earned a degree from an AAU institution. The greatest representation is in ethnic and cultural studies, with AIANs representing

Table 7	Black/African American PhD Conferrals by Select Fields and Institutional Type, 2011–2018			
Field	Total	AAU Institutions	Non-AAU R1/R2 (Carnegie 2018)	Other Institutions
All Fields	**29,006**	7,183	14,571	7,252
Biological and Biomedical Sciences	**2,164**	1,012	766	386
Engineering	**1,325**	634	671	20
English Language and Literature/Letters	**414**	188	202	24
Ethnic, Cultural Minority, Gender, and Group Studies	**186**	115	69	2
Foreign Languages, Literatures, and Linguistics	**122**	82	37	3
History	**372**	230	136	6
Mathematics and Statistics	**206**	68	137	1
Philosophy and Religious Studies	**238**	95	54	89
Physical Sciences	**868**	349	482	37
Psychology	**1,965**	408	1,103	454
Social Sciences	**1,157**	543	597	17
Anthropology	**159**	94	64	1
Economics	**117**	40	74	3
Political Science and Government	**287**	122	165	0
Sociology	**448**	235	202	11

Source: National Science Foundation, Survey of Earned Doctorates, 2018, www.nsf.org.

Total	AAU Institutions	Non-AAU R1/R2 (Carnegie 2018)	Other Institutions
100%	25%	50%	25%
100%	47%	35%	18%
100%	48%	51%	2%
100%	45%	49%	6%
100%	62%	37%	1%
100%	67%	30%	2%
100%	62%	37%	2%
100%	33%	67%	0%
100%	40%	23%	37%
100%	40%	56%	4%
100%	21%	56%	23%
100%	47%	52%	1%
100%	59%	40%	1%
100%	34%	63%	3%
100%	43%	57%	0%
100%	52%	45%	2%

Table 8	Hispanic PhD Conferrals by Select Fields and Institutional Type, 2011–2018			
Field	Total	AAU Institutions	Non-AAU R1/R2 (Carnegie 2018)	Other Institutions
All Fields	**24,769**	9,884	9,734	5,151
Biological and Biomedical Sciences	**3,223**	1,789	833	601
Engineering	**1,938**	1,190	700	48
English Language and Literature/Letters	**508**	263	231	14
Ethnic, Cultural Minority, Gender, and Group Studies	**115**	102	13	0
Foreign Languages, Literatures, and Linguistics	**924**	564	352	8
History	**519**	286	164	69
Mathematics and Statistics	**341**	179	162	0
Philosophy and Religious Studies	**209**	102	76	31
Physical Sciences	**1,446**	794	617	35
Psychology	**3,256**	608	1,136	1,512
Social Sciences	**1,310**	789	508	13
Anthropology	**298**	209	87	2
Economics	**191**	105	84	2
Political Science and Government	**256**	152	103	1
Sociology	**377**	248	122	7

Source: National Science Foundation, Survey of Earned Doctorates, 2018, www.nsf.org.

Total	AAU Institutions	Non-AAU R1/R2 (Carnegie 2018)	Other Institutions
100%	40%	39%	21%
100%	56%	26%	19%
100%	61%	36%	2%
100%	52%	45%	3%
100%	89%	11%	0%
100%	61%	38%	1%
100%	55%	32%	13%
100%	52%	48%	0%
100%	49%	36%	15%
100%	55%	43%	2%
100%	19%	35%	46%
100%	60%	39%	1%
100%	70%	29%	1%
100%	55%	44%	1%
100%	59%	40%	0%
100%	66%	32%	2%

Table 9   Asian American PhD Conferrals by Select Fields and Institutional Type, 2011–2018

Field	Total	AAU Institutions	Non-AAU R1/R2 (Carnegie 2018)	Other Institutions
All Fields	**26,721**	15,760	7,969	2,992
Biological and Biomedical Sciences	**5,317**	3,395	1,133	789
Engineering	**4,998**	3,642	1,287	69
English Language and Literature/Letters	**376**	248	118	10
Ethnic, Cultural Minority, Gender, and Group Studies	**55**	49	5	1
Foreign Languages, Literatures, and Linguistics	**349**	272	74	3
History	**207**	174	32	1
Mathematics and Statistics	**760**	495	257	8
Philosophy and Religious Studies	**213**	120	59	34
Physical Sciences	**2,193**	1,457	720	16
Psychology	**1,726**	629	764	333
Social Sciences	**1,316**	877	420	19
Anthropology	**188**	131	55	2
Economics	**434**	280	147	7
Political Science and Government	**274**	199	74	1
Sociology	**261**	175	78	8

Source: National Science Foundation, Survey of Earned Doctorates, 2018, www.nsf.org.

Total	AAU Institutions	Non-AAU R1/R2 (Carnegie 2018)	Other Institutions
100%	59%	30%	11%
100%	64%	21%	15%
100%	73%	26%	1%
100%	66%	31%	3%
100%	89%	9%	2%
100%	78%	21%	1%
100%	84%	15%	0%
100%	65%	34%	1%
100%	56%	28%	16%
100%	66%	33%	1%
100%	36%	44%	19%
100%	67%	32%	1%
100%	70%	29%	1%
100%	65%	34%	2%
100%	73%	27%	0%
100%	67%	30%	3%

4% of PhD recipients, and 74% of these individuals come from AAU institutions (see tables 6 and 10).

Native Hawaiian and Pacific Islander (NHPI) PhD holders account for 0% across every discipline, with the exception of ethnic and culture studies; 60% of these scholars earned their degrees at AAU institutions. There have been 471 NHPIs who have earned PhDs across various disciplines between 2011 and 2018; 188 of these individuals—less than half—earned their degrees at AAU institutions (see tables 6 and 11). As we saw in chapter 2, NHPIs are underrepresented in the AAU faculty as well.

White PhD production is a very different story from that of people of color. Whites make up 50% or more of PhD degree holders in biological and biomedical sciences, English language and literature, history, philosophy and religious studies, psychology, political science, anthropology, and sociology. In all of these areas, with the exception of psychology, at least 44% of these degree holders earned their PhDs at AAU institutions. Whites represented lower percentages among PhD degree holders (yet still relatively significant compared to their counterparts of color) in engineering (28%), ethnic and cultural studies (31%), math (37%), and economics (27%). In all of these areas, 50% or more of Whites earned their degrees at an AAU institution (see tables 6 and 12).

Given what Daryl Smith told us about the proliferation of nonresident PhDs in the faculty, I think it is important to point the reader to the disciplines where 40% or more of the PhD degree recipients are nonresidents. These include engineering (57%), math (49%), physical sciences (40%), and economics (49%) (see tables 6 and 13). Moreover, nonresidents make up at least 50% of AAU PhD degree holders across all disciplines, with the exception of English language and literature and psychology (see table 13). Nonresident PhDs have a significant advantage over US-born people of color, given their presence in PhD programs at AAU institutions.

If we spend some time looking at these data related to potential faculty pipelines from PhD programs alongside data pertaining to faculty diversity at AAU institutions (presented in chapter 2), we see an interesting and concerning landscape. The most current data (2017) on faculty diversity at AAU institutions available as I'm writing this book shows that 70.4% of tenure-track and tenured faculty are White, and 48% of the PhDs produced between 2011–2018 in the United States are White as well, with 44% of those individuals earning degrees at AAU institutions. Based on these two facts and the conversations I had with AAU administrators about pedigree and the privileging of a small group of institutions, Whites continue to have a strong advantage in faculty searches (see chapter 3). Likewise, 4.2% of tenure-track and tenured AAU faculty are nonresidents, and 29% of the PhDs produced between 2011–2018 in the United States are nonresidents, with 55% of those individuals earning their degrees at AAU institutions. These nonresident PhD holders have a significant advantage over US-born people of color, based on the privileging of graduates from AAU institutions in faculty hiring. Asian Americans also have a disproportionate advantage in terms of tenure-track and tenured faculty representation in AAU institutions; however, it is vital to understand that data pertaining to this population are not disaggregated and don't account for low-income and underrepresented Asian American populations, and that this advantage is in the sciences and engineering. Asian Americans account for 14.1% of tenured and tenure-track faculty in the AAU and 5% of all PhDs being produced between 2011 and 2018 nationwide. Importantly, 59% of Asian American PhDs are earned at AAU institutions.

The landscape of faculty diversity changes substantially when we examine African Americans, Latinos, American Indians and Alaska Natives, and Native Hawaiians and Pacific Islanders. African Americans make up a mere 3.4% of AAU tenured and tenure-track faculty overall and represent 6% of all PhD holders produced between 2011–2018, with only 25% of these individuals earning degrees from AAU institutions. Given the privileging of PhDs from AAU institutions and the emphasis on pedigree (see chapter 3), this systemic bias hurts African Americans, has done so over the long-term, and will continue to long into the future. As a group, they are the least likely to earn a PhD from an AAU institution versus a non-AAU

Table 10	American Indian/Alaska Native PhD Conferrals by Select Fields and Institutional Type, 2011–2018			
Field	Total	AAU Institutions	Non-AAU R1/R2 (Carnegie 2018)	Other Institutions
All Fields	**1,748**	663	791	294
Biological and Biomedical Sciences	**180**	99	54	27
Engineering	**86**	51	34	1
English Language and Literature/Letters	**58**	31	26	1
Ethnic, Cultural Minority, Gender, and Group Studies	**39**	29	10	0
Foreign Languages, Literatures, and Linguistics	**26**	22	4	0
History	**37**	20	17	0
Mathematics and Statistics	**18**	8	10	0
Philosophy and Religious Studies	**22**	11	7	4
Physical Sciences	**94**	56	38	0
Psychology	**140**	24	93	23
Social Sciences	**111**	63	48	0
Anthropology	**19**	14	5	0
Economics	**47**	29	18	0
Political Science and Government	**5**	1	4	0
Sociology	**28**	12	16	0

Source: National Science Foundation, Survey of Earned Doctorates, 2018, www.nsf.org.

Total	AAU Institutions	Non-AAU R1/R2 (Carnegie 2018)	Other Institutions
100%	38%	45%	17%
100%	55%	30%	15%
100%	59%	40%	1%
100%	53%	45%	2%
100%	74%	26%	0%
100%	85%	15%	0%
100%	54%	46%	0%
100%	44%	56%	0%
100%	50%	32%	18%
100%	60%	40%	0%
100%	17%	66%	16%
100%	57%	43%	0%
100%	74%	26%	0%
100%	62%	38%	0%
100%	20%	80%	0%
100%	43%	57%	0%

Table 11

Native Hawaiian or Other Pacific Islander PhD Conferrals by Select Fields and Institutional Type, 2011–2018

Field	Total	AAU Institutions	Non-AAU R1/R2 (Carnegie 2018)	Other Institutions
All Fields	471	188	201	82
Biological and Biomedical Sciences	78	44	16	18
Engineering	30	17	12	1
English Language and Literature/Letters	8	1	6	1
Ethnic, Cultural Minority, Gender, and Group Studies	5	3	2	0
Foreign Languages, Literatures, and Linguistics	5	1	1	3
History	6	2	4	0
Mathematics and Statistics	8	5	3	0
Philosophy and Religious Studies	2	0	1	1
Physical Sciences	31	18	13	0
Psychology	24	8	13	3
Social Sciences	20	4	15	1
Anthropology	4	1	2	1
Economics	1	1	0	0
Political Science and Government	13	2	11	0
Sociology	2	0	2	0

Source: National Science Foundation, Survey of Earned Doctorates, 2018, www.nsf.org.

Total	AAU Institutions	Non-AAU R1/R2 (Carnegie 2018)	Other Institutions
100%	40%	43%	17%
100%	56%	21%	23%
100%	57%	40%	3%
100%	13%	75%	13%
100%	60%	40%	0%
100%	20%	20%	60%
100%	33%	67%	0%
100%	63%	38%	0%
100%	0%	50%	50%
100%	58%	42%	0%
100%	33%	54%	13%
100%	20%	75%	5%
100%	25%	50%	25%
100%	100%	0%	0%
100%	15%	85%	0%
100%	0%	100%	0%

Field	Total	AAU Institutions	Non-AAU R1/R2 (Carnegie 2018)	Other Institutions
All Fields	**241,406**	106,721	100,866	33,819
Biological and Biomedical Sciences	**31,743**	17,746	10,559	3,438
Engineering	**21,954**	13,593	8,112	249
English Language and Literature/Letters	**7,688**	3,342	3,988	358
Ethnic, Cultural Minority, Gender, and Group Studies	**274**	209	57	8
Foreign Languages, Literatures, and Linguistics	**4,508**	3,606	854	48
History	**5,024**	2,918	2,058	48
Mathematics and Statistics	**5,326**	2,948	2,341	37
Philosophy and Religious Studies	**3,775**	1,912	1,460	403
Physical Sciences	**20,462**	13,125	7,238	99
Psychology	**20,223**	5,453	11,383	3,387
Social Sciences	**13,813**	8,062	5,614	137
Anthropology	**2,648**	1,691	947	10
Economics	**2,419**	1,516	878	25
Political Science and Government	**3,457**	2,105	1,340	12
Sociology	**2,927**	1,660	1,240	27

Table 12 White PhD Conferrals by Select Fields and Institutional Type, 2011–2018

Source: National Science Foundation, Survey of Earned Doctorates, 2018, www.nsf.org.

Total	AAU Institutions	Non-AAU R1/R2 (Carnegie 2018)	Other Institutions
100%	44%	42%	14%
100%	56%	33%	11%
100%	62%	37%	1%
100%	43%	52%	5%
100%	76%	21%	3%
100%	80%	19%	1%
100%	58%	41%	1%
100%	55%	44%	1%
100%	51%	39%	11%
100%	64%	35%	0%
100%	27%	56%	17%
100%	58%	41%	1%
100%	64%	36%	0%
100%	63%	36%	1%
100%	61%	39%	0%
100%	57%	42%	1%

Table 13 Nonresident PhD Conferrals by Select Fields and Institutional Type, 2011–2018

Field	Total	AAU Institutions	Non-AAU R1/R2 (Carnegie 2018)	Other Institutions
All Fields	**143,589**	78,710	58,946	5,933
Biological and Biomedical Sciences	**16,906**	8,622	6,007	2,277
Engineering	**44,156**	24,602	19,206	348
English Language and Literature/Letters	**943**	450	394	99
Ethnic, Cultural Minority, Gender, and Group Studies	**116**	88	27	1
Foreign Languages, Literatures, and Linguistics	**3,034**	2,379	645	10
History	**916**	721	189	6
Mathematics and Statistics	**7,108**	4,456	2,647	5
Philosophy and Religious Studies	**925**	514	281	130
Physical Sciences	**18,419**	9,615	8,715	89
Psychology	**2,442**	1,146	1,093	203
Social Sciences	**9,397**	6,151	3,200	46
Anthropology	**728**	572	154	2
Economics	**5,233**	3,535	1,675	23
Political Science and Government	**1,447**	912	531	4
Sociology	**843**	559	276	8

Source: National Science Foundation, Survey of Earned Doctorates, 2018, www.nsf.org.

Total	AAU Institutions	Non-AAU R1/R2 (Carnegie 2018)	Other Institutions
100%	55%	41%	4%
100%	51%	36%	13%
100%	56%	43%	1%
100%	48%	42%	10%
100%	76%	23%	1%
100%	78%	21%	0%
100%	79%	21%	1%
100%	63%	37%	0%
100%	56%	30%	14%
100%	52%	47%	0%
100%	47%	45%	8%
100%	65%	34%	0%
100%	79%	21%	0%
100%	68%	32%	0%
100%	63%	37%	0%
100%	66%	33%	1%

institution. If higher education leaders are serious about providing opportunities to African Americans on their faculties, they must address this issue now on three fronts: (1) expanding the definition of quality to be more inclusive and recognize the impact of pedigree on opportunity; (2) pushing back against the privileging of a narrow group of universities as areas for recruitment of faculty; and (3) recruiting and matriculating more African Americans into AAU PhD programs.

Although not nearly as dire relative to African Americans, we see a similar situation unfolding with Latinos. Latinos make up 4.3% of tenured and tenure-track faculty at AAU institutions and 5% of all PhD holders from 2011 to 2018, with 40% of those individuals earning PhDs at AAU institutions. Likewise, American Indians, Alaska Natives, Native Hawaiians, and other Pacific Islanders represent substantially less than 1% of all tenured and tenure-track AAU faculty. They account for less that 1% of PhD holders, and of those individuals roughly 38–40% earn their degrees at AAU institutions. It is imperative that colleges and universities, and especially AAU institutions, understand the implications of the low numbers of people of color earning PhDs within AAU institutions, given the pervasive biases toward pedigree in higher education and faculty hiring, in particular. AAU institutions either need to admit more people of color to their PhD programs or stop privileging graduates of AAU institutions in their job searches—preferably both.

Although a lack of people of color in the various disciplinary pipelines is used as an excuse and should not be, we must acknowledge that there is considerable bias and systemic racism in graduate school admissions, as demonstrated by Julie Posselt. In her book *Inside Graduate Admissions: Merit, Diversity, and Faculty Gatekeeping* (2016), she provides the reader with a window into graduate recruitment and admission, including issues of merit, bias, and diversity. One of the most salient findings in Posselt's work is that although faculty graduate admission committees talk a great deal about their commitment to diversity, they do not consider diversity to any significant extent in the admission process. They are more interested in reproducing themselves (i.e., sameness or Whiteness), and enrolling students that improve their standing as a program and as individual faculty members; an interest that mirrors the faculty hiring process (Clauset, Arbesman, and Larremore, 2015). Posselt found that faculties tend to only want to admit PhD students who are indisputable in terms of their assumed performance and feel like a good fit intellectually, although what faculties often mean is that a cultural fit is needed—they say intellectual, but mean cultural. She also sees AAU institutions as wanting to select

> faculty who seem like a safe bet to become the next rising star within their discipline, and if that's who they see themselves to be as a department, it gives them the grounds to privilege applicants who have a certain sort of record that requires a certain type of mentoring and investment and likely institutional pedigree and prior opportunities, which, at each of those levels, you're going to reduce the pool of people who cover all of those qualities and identify with an underrepresented racial or ethnic group.

In order to better grasp Posselt's work, I interviewed her for this book. I wanted to have a more thorough understanding of her thoughts on the connections between graduate school admission and faculty hiring as well as her perspective on using the pipeline as an excuse for not diversifying the professoriate. According to Posselt, who regularly interacts with faculty, department chairs, and graduate deans when conducting her research, "you hear all the time that the excuse is a pipeline issue" and that there is "an insufficient pool for faculty searches or for the graduate admissions process." Posselt notes that oftentimes search committees and institutions don't do their homework. For example, they often know what the application rate is for people of color in their specific search, but they don't know the degree attainment rates in their field, nor do they take the time to research them. If they knew the degree attainment rates, they could do two things: (1) Consider whether or not their application rate is congruent with degree attainment rates in their field and make changes if it is not. (2) If the degree attainment rates are low, work to make change in the field at their own institution, partner with a few other institutions, or work with nationally known

PhD preparation programs to identify students of color pursuing PhDs to create viable pipelines. In Posselt's words, "You can choose to blame the inequalities that were created before you [for the lack of diversity], or you can try to study the inequalities that you're presented with . . . [to make change]. I think the latter is a more empowering approach than to say 'Oh, woe is me; we get a pass. We're going to be unequal because the level before us was unequal.'" One of the most depressing and poignant pipeline examples offered by Posselt during our conversation was about a graduate dean's perspective on women and her institution's PhDs in philosophy. According to Posselt, "I definitely hear people say really awful things." A graduate dean told her, "'We know that there's inequality in the philosophy PhD program, but we also know that women tend to get hired less into PhD programs, into faculty positions in philosophy. So, if we have too many women in our PhD programs, we're going to end up with bad placement numbers because they're not going to be able to get jobs because of the problems in the job market.' She sits with that and sweeps it under the rug as opposed to saying, 'This is a challenge; what are we going to do to face it?'" As I listened to her recount the conversation with the graduate dean, I was reminded of Daryl Smith's comment about knowing that exercise is good for her but not doing it. We see systemic racism, we know it is wrong, yet far too few people act to change the system. If we reflect on Lauren Rivera's ideas about pedigree, our lack of action as Whites makes sense—why would we work to dismantle a system that benefits us? Higher education is not alone in its refusal to rethink a system that benefits Whites and holds tightly to narrow definitions of quality and the privileging of degrees from a small group of institutions. Lauren Rivera shows us that this is the case in the corporate world as well. However, as mentioned, colleges and universities pride themselves on embracing diversity, searching for truth and producing knowledge. How can these goals be achieved—how can academic excellence be real—without enlisting the perspectives of people of color in equitable ways?[8]

8. Of note, when my essay was published in the *Washington Post*, I received emails and letters from people across various industries—law, the military,

How AAU Institutions Use Pipeline Data

As I talked with the administrators at AAU institutions, many confirmed the prevailing myths about pipelines, using the same excuses, while others realized that such excuses are used regularly and worked to cut through them. Still others told me they don't hear the excuses anymore. A dean at a university in the Northeast expressed her frustration as "You've come to the heart of [it]. What you hear people say is that there are no candidates out there, there are no diverse candidates out there, we can't get them, and so then the question is what are you looking for, and how are you defining the candidates?" On the contrary, a vice provost in the Midwest told me that he rarely hears anyone say "they're just not out there" anymore as people feel that the expectation is to go and look for candidates of color rather than fall back on the excuse that there aren't any.

Most of the administrators at AAU institutions that I talked with did not use the Survey of Earned Doctorates or any pipeline-specific data in their faculty hiring processes. For example, a provost at a midwestern private university told me that his institution just began collecting data on hiring, admitting "I think it is a bit embarrassing, but that's where we are." He added that upon coming to the university, there weren't a lot of processes in place, stating, "A lot of my provostship is going to be that really sexy work of creating policies and bureaucracies. But I think they're vital when it comes to issues like this."

There were a few provosts who were beginning to use data and were encouraging deans and faculty search committees to use the resources available to them. One Ivy League provost mentioned, "What we started to do just recently is give [the search committees] access to data that we have put together from the doctoral clearinghouse, saying 'This is what the field looks like; if you look at the last three years of data on who is getting a PhD, what does it look like?'

---

libraries, corporations, nonprofits—sharing that the same issues that I brought up in my essay exist in their areas. Issues of systemic racism in hiring are not unique to higher education. However, the lack of racial and ethnic diversity among faculty has a vast ripple effect as colleges and universities create knowledge, disseminate knowledge, and share knowledge with students in classrooms.

and it's our expectation that the applicant pool should look like what the field looks like." He added, "For example, if we know we're doing some searches in engineering, we will then do some of our own data scraping to say this is what we know about who has recently earned a PhD in a particular subfield of engineering, in terms of demographic features, and why don't you go out and actively invite them to apply, as opposed to just waiting for them to apply." Taking the issue of diversity in faculty hiring to a new level, this provost added, "We ask people to do this work in late spring, and we want to see this whole plan before we give them an approval to start advertising. We collect data and we supply it to [the schools]." The way that this provost holds search committees accountable is a model for others, as he has achieved considerable results in diversifying the faculty over the past five years. His office provides search committees with three years of data on PhD production in particular fields and asks committee members to review the data and make sure that their candidate pools mirror this PhD production. Of importance, he doesn't approve advertising for the position until the search committee has spent time with the data and has prepared a plan to actively recruit people of color beyond their personal networks.

Some provosts step in to ensure that pipeline issues don't stand in the way of progress and movement in terms of faculty diversity. For example, a provost in the Northeast explained that once searches begin, he uses a web-based search tool to monitor the pools for faculty hires. He and the deans from the institution check to see if the demographics of the various faculty search pools match the pool of individuals that exists in higher education overall. In his words, "If we don't see diversity that reflects the larger pool of candidates, for example, if we see it seems to be heavily leaning towards men or heavily leaning towards Whites, even though there is diversity in the pool, we will then contact [the search committee] and say this is what we're observing. What's going on? We will use that to actually intervene at different times in searches, saying, 'We see that you have x number of people in the long list that are [from diverse backgrounds]. What's your plan for really looking at them carefully?'" Although this approach is labor intensive on the part of the provost's office, it has a significant impact on faculty hiring, with this Ivy League institution changing their faculty demographics at a faster pace than most other AAU institutions over the past five years. According to the provost, "Our hiring has gone very well since we launched this plan. . . . I have departments that are really actively trying to diversify their faculty."

In most cases, faculties don't look at pipeline data because they want to reproduce themselves. An Ivy League provost described the problem to me using an example from the sciences: "Earth and planetary science is a field that often is very White and very male. [Our department] wanted to hire another planetary scientist and so literally a table full, a group of them came to visit me, trying to lobby me to allow them to hire. It was [a list of] literally all White guys. I basically looked at them and maintained, 'I will not allow you to hire another person like you until you diversify your faculty,' and lo and behold, [the] next hire is a person of color, a postdoc from MIT. You know, all the right attributes, but they had to get out of their network to do that, and in fact the last two hires have been people of color in that department." Without a push from the provost, this department would have happily and comfortably reproduced itself without ever seeking out data on the growing diversity in their field.

Another Ivy League provost explained to me that his institution has begun sharing pipeline data with search committees. Using the Survey of Earned Doctorates, they have a tool that allows search committees to explore by discipline to determine which institutions are graduating candidates in the areas of interest to search committees. The use of this tool came out of the provost's experience as a department chair. All too often he would hear departments say that they wanted to diversify the pool, but they didn't know where to look. He wanted to eliminate that excuse by providing readily available data—the Survey of Earned Doctorates tells us exactly which institutions are producing PhDs of color. Despite these efforts, however, he reported that the pools of candidates are still not as diverse as he'd like to see. "I will say that the majority of our searches are majority—majority in terms of the candidates that are both applying

and come in—and so that's . . . a work in progress for us. We need
to get more candidates [of color] to consider themselves in their
own view qualified to apply for a faculty position at an Ivy League
university. That's certainly the refrain that we hear when we speak to
candidates—that they don't think they would even get an interview,
so they don't apply—and so we're trying to sort of change that."
When I pushed him on why a person of color might feel this way, he
replied, "I think it might be historical context. It might be looking at
our faculty and seeing what our faculty looks like. It might be sort of
what they view an Ivy League institution would be looking for [in
candidates]." Blaming the candidate and their lack of confidence is
quite common and surfaced often in my conversations with AAU
administrators. However, when I engaged with the many people of
color who wrote to me asking for help finding a faculty job after the
Washington Post article was published, they told me they applied
everywhere regardless of the type of institution. They wanted a faculty position, as they had spent years preparing for one. Likewise,
as I discussed in chapter 3, James Anderson and his research subject
Fred Wale found that institutions often blame the candidate for the
lack of diversity in the pools for faculty searches.

A dean at a midwestern university shared with me that the provost's office at her institution sends all of the deans AAU pipeline
data—"the percentages of how many PhDs are produced annually in
AAU institutions and the way that breaks down according to [the
various disciplines]." However, it is troubling that only AAU institutions are considered able to produce future faculty for AAU
institutions when there are many other universities that produce
PhD students across the disciplines. Of significance, this dean also
explained that her institution goes to great lengths to achieve diversity across disciplines: "We have to tailor-make our narratives for
each individual unit, rather than looking at a college-wide demographic. So this has been one of the changes we've made in the
last couple years, because it really doesn't mean, well, it means
something quite different to say you have *x* percentage of a particular category of faculty member across the college, versus what it
means at the department level."

Limiting "Qualified" Candidate Pools
to AAU PhDs Only?

Given my conversations with AAU administrators, I think it is important that readers understand what search committees and universities miss when they limit their searches to the few institutions in the AAU. It is important to consider that many of the non-AAU institutions are much more diverse than AAU institutions—at the undergraduate student level, at the PhD level, and even across the faculty ranks. Earlier in this chapter, I included a discussion on the production of PhDs by AAU institutions across various disciplines and considering race and ethnicity. I also included data on PhD production across disciplines by non-AAU but still "very high research" or "higher research" or other non-AAU institutions.[9] These non-AAU institutions (across Carnegie Classification) boast considerable diversity in the PhD ranks and include institutions such as Georgetown University, the University of Georgia, and Claremont Graduate University.

Within these non-AAU institutions (see tables 14 and 15) are many Hispanic Serving Institutions and some Historically Black Colleges and Universities, such as the University of Houston, the University of Texas at El Paso, Howard University, and North Carolina A&T University. Unfortunately, it is rare for AAU institutions to look to HSIs and HBCUs for candidates for faculty positions. These institutions are often seen as less than their majority counterparts, due to racism and a lack of knowledge of the contributions of HBCUs and HSIs to students, learning, and knowledge (Conrad and Gasman, 2015). Within this group of non-AAU institutions, we find universities such as Arizona State University, a "very high research" university that is considered one of the most innovative and inclusive universities in the nation under the leadership of President Michael Crow.[10] Why

9. These designations are included in the Carnegie Classifications of colleges and universities.

10. For more information, see https://www.usnews.com/best-colleges/rankings/national-universities/innovative. In addition, two of the ASU campuses are Hispanic Serving Institutions—ASU-Phoenix Downtown and ASU-West.

Table 14   Non-AAU Very High Research Institutions

Arizona State University-Tempe	Montana State University
Auburn University	New Jersey Institute of Technology
Binghamton University	North Carolina State University at Raleigh
Boston College	Northeastern University
Clemson University	Oklahoma State University-Main Campus
Colorado State University-Fort Collins	Oregon State University
CUNY Graduate School and University Center	Rensselaer Polytechnic Institute
Drexel University	SUNY at Albany
Florida International University	Syracuse University
Florida State University	Temple University
George Mason University	Texas Tech University
George Washington University	Tufts University
Georgetown University	University of Alabama at Tuscaloosa
Georgia State University	University of Alabama at Birmingham
Kansas State University	University of Arkansas
Louisiana State University and Agricultural & Mechanical College	University of California-Riverside
Mississippi State University	University of Central Florida

University of Cincinnati	University of New Mexico
University of Colorado Denver/Anschutz Medical Campus	University of North Texas
University of Connecticut	University of Notre Dame
University of Delaware	University of Oklahoma-Norman
University of Georgia	University of South Carolina-Columbia
University of Hawaii at Manoa	University of South Florida
University of Houston	University of Southern Mississippi
University of Illinois at Chicago	University of Tennessee-Knoxville
University of Kentucky	University of Texas at Arlington
University of Louisville	University of Texas at Dallas
University of Massachusetts-Amherst	University of Texas at El Paso
University of Miami	University of Wisconsin-Milwaukee
University of Mississippi	Virginia Commonwealth University
University of Nebraska-Lincoln	Virginia Polytechnic Institute and State University
University of Nevada-Las Vegas	Washington State University
University of Nevada-Reno	Wayne State University
University of New Hampshire	West Virginia University

Source: Carnegie Classifications of Institutions of Higher Education, 2020, https://carnegieclassifications.iu.edu.

Table 15 Non-AAU High Research Institutions

Air Force Institute of Technology-Graduate School of Engineering & Management	DePaul University
American University	Duquesne University
Arkansas State University	East Carolina University
Azusa Pacific University	East Tennessee State University
Ball State University	Eastern Michigan University
Baylor University	Florida Agricultural and Mechanical University
Boise State University	Florida Atlantic University
Bowling Green State University	Florida Institute of Technology
Brigham Young University-Provo	Fordham University
Catholic University of America	Gallaudet University
Central Michigan University	Hampton University
Chapman University	Howard University
Claremont Graduate University	Idaho State University
Clark Atlanta University	Illinois Institute of Technology
Clark University	Illinois State University
Clarkson University	Indiana University-Purdue University-Indianapolis
Cleveland State University	Jackson State University
College of William and Mary	Kennesaw State University
Colorado School of Mines	Kent State University at Kent
CUNY City College	Lehigh University
Delaware State University	Louisiana Tech University

Source: Carnegie Classifications of Institutions of Higher Education, 2020, https://carnegieclassifications.iu.edu.

Loyola University Chicago	Rockefeller University
Marquette University	Rowan University
Marshall University	Rutgers University-Camden
Mercer University	Rutgers University-Newark
Miami University-Oxford	Saint Louis University
Michigan Technological University	San Diego State University
Missouri University of Science and Technology	Seton Hall University
Montclair State University	South Dakota State University
Morgan State University	Southern Illinois University-Carbondale
New Mexico State University	Southern Methodist University
The New School	Stevens Institute of Technology
North Carolina A&T State University	SUNY College of Environmental Science and Forestry
North Dakota State University	Teachers College at Columbia University
Northern Arizona University	Tennessee State University
Northern Illinois University	Tennessee Technological University
Nova Southeastern University	Texas A&M University-Corpus Christi
Oakland University	Texas A&M University-Kingsville
Ohio University	Texas Christian University
Old Dominion University	Texas Southern University
Portland State University	Texas State University
Rochester Institute of Technology	Thomas Jefferson University

University of Akron Main Campus	University of North Carolina Charlotte
University of Alabama in Huntsville	University of North Carolina Greensboro
University of Alaska Fairbanks	University of North Carolina Wilmington
University of Arkansas at Little Rock	University of North Dakota
University of California-Merced	University of Puerto Rico-Rio Piedras
University of Colorado Colorado Springs	University of Rhode Island
University of Dayton	University of San Diego
University of Denver	University of South Alabama
University of Idaho	University of South Dakota
University of Louisiana at Lafayette	University of Texas at San Antonio
University of Maine	University of Toledo
University of Maryland Eastern Shore	University of Tulsa
University of Maryland-Baltimore County	University of Vermont
University of Massachusetts-Boston	University of Wyoming
University of Massachusetts-Dartmouth	Utah State University
University of Massachusetts-Lowell	Villanova University
University of Memphis	Wake Forest University
University of Missouri-Kansas City	Western Michigan University
University of Missouri-St. Louis	Wichita State University
University of Montana	Worcester Polytechnic Institute
University of Nebraska at Omaha	Wright State University
University of New Orleans	Yeshiva University

would AAU institutions not consider Arizona State University a well-qualified producer of PhD students? I also wondered the same thing about the CUNY Graduate School and University Center, as it is a significant producer of PhDs and a Hispanic Serving Institution. Of course, as some are reading this paragraph, they may be thinking, "but these institutions are not as good as AAU institutions"—I ask, how do we know? By what criteria are we judging these institutions that are considered research 1 and 2 institutions according to the Carnegie Classifications? What are AAU institutions missing out on when they limit their faculty recruiting to a narrow group of universities (Clauset, Arbesman, and Larremore, 2015)? Diversity, innovation, and creativity are three things that come to mind for me. And if that still isn't enough, what are recruiters at AAU institutions doing to diversify PhD pipelines? A commitment to racial and ethnic diversity is laudable, but unless the work is done to open up pathways that are privileged or to stop narrowing the group of institutions that are deemed qualified to produce PhD candidates, nothing will change and commitments are hollow.

When considering the full scope of PhDs being produced across disciplines and at various universities, the pipeline has considerable diversity and significant potential for adding to the intellectual, racial, and ethnic diversity of the professoriate. However, higher education must be open to recruiting from a more robust set of institutions than only the handful that so many universities deem appropriate. Assumptions about the quality of research-oriented PhD-producing institutions that are not AAU members must be challenged. Lastly, AAU institutions must study their data regarding race and ethnicity to ensure equity in the production of PhDs across disciplines.

5

Where Are the Leaders?

> There's no substitute for [search committees'] understanding
> that at the very top, people are really committed to this and
> that they're really going to push.
>
> —AAU UNIVERSITY PROVOST

I want to begin this chapter with two ideas: (1) university leaders
claim that race and racism are not issues on their campuses,[1] and
(2) university leaders have invested large amounts of money into the
hiring of a diverse faculty in response to calls for more diversity and
inequities across university constituents. When I think about these
two ideas, they seem to contradict. If there aren't issues around race
and racism on college campuses, why is there a need to invest so
much money to diversify the campus and alleviate inequities? Let
me provide more context on both of these ideas.

---

1. Of note, I wrote this book prior to the George Floyd protests of 2020. After
these large-scale protests, there was some temporary admission of racism on college campuses. However, prior to the 2020 protests, the majority of campus leaders were silent; many are still silent; and as I finish this book the admissions are
falling off.

In 2014, I wrote an essay for *Inside Higher Education* titled "Presidents in Denial" (Gasman, 2014). I wrote this essay after reading about the results of a survey that the publication had conducted with college presidents across a variety of topical areas.[2] I was struck as I read the outlet's results that "Most presidents (90%) say that, generally speaking, the state of race relations on their campuses is good." I was amazed because just two weeks earlier, the *New York Times* ran a story titled "Colorblind Notion Aside: Colleges Grapple with Racial Tension." Across the nation on college campuses, there were many racial incidents involving students, faculty, and administrators. I included the following incidents as samples in my article:

- A student at San Jose State University was tormented and ridiculed with racial slurs and the posting of the Confederate flag by three students for months (Kaplan, Murphy, and Early, 2013).
- The University of Alabama admitted that it tolerated racial segregation in its Greek system up until very recently, with Black students being targeted for discrimination across the system (Associated Press, 2013).
- Black students at Harvard University launched a Tumblr campaign called "I, Too, Am Harvard" to elevate the voices of Black students on campus because they are "unheard" (Butler, 2014).
- Black men at UCLA created a YouTube video titled "The Black Bruins" detailing the dismal statistics surrounding Black men on the Southern California campus. Likewise, law school students at UCLA have been bringing attention to the discrimination that they face on a daily basis through a social media campaign (Otani, 2013).
- The chancellor of the University of Illinois at Urbana-Champaign, an Asian American woman, experienced racist

2. See https://www.insidehighered.com/news/survey/federal-accountability -and-financial-pressure-survey-presidents.

slurs when she didn't cancel classes during inclement weather (Jaschik, 2014).

- Black students at the University of Michigan were protesting the racial climate on campus through both traditional means and social media (Vloet, n.d.).
- A fraternity at Arizona State University held a party at which White students dressed in "gangsta wear" and drank from hollowed-out watermelons (Farberov, 2014).

In the article, I discussed reasons why presidents might be ignorant to the racism on their campuses, including a desire to avoid negative attention, a possible belief in the myth of a post-racial world (given that President Barack Obama had been elected twice), a lack of awareness of what was happening on campus, an assumption that increased demographic diversity equals racial harmony, and lastly, an obliviousness to the lives of people of color. To me there was an enormous disconnect between reality and the views of college presidents.

Interestingly, in the years right after all of this racial unrest (and the survey results that denied it), we saw university after university—especially heavily endowed AAU institutions—with the support of their boards of trustees, pour money into faculty diversity in the area of hiring. Just a few examples include Yale University's commitment of $50 million, the University of Pennsylvania's allotment of $50 million, Cornell University's investment of $60 million, and Columbia University's massive commitment of $185 million. These investments and those of other universities are aimed at individual schools that lack diversity on their faculty, at provost-matching programs to incentivize hiring, implicit bias programs, faculty training around best practices in hiring, and building inclusive climates to foster retention of faculty and students. Given the newness of these initiatives, there are few results pertaining to the success of these efforts, but they are a testament to the lack of racial and ethnic diversity on college campuses among the faculty—an issue that presidents are well aware of even if they don't acknowledge it in surveys (Lamon, 2017; Schick, 2015; Xia and Percy, 2019).

Leadership at AAU Institutions

Scholars who have focused on diversity in faculty hiring for decades, such as Daryl Smith, tell us that success is rooted in the support of university leadership—beginning with presidents and including provosts and deans. And this support must be buttressed by university boards of trustees, which unfortunately mirror the makeup of faculty—they are overwhelmingly White and male. Without leadership and accountability, it's nearly impossible to gain momentum toward diversifying the faculty and to bring about a sense of equity on a campus. The first step is that leaders must value diversity, and the second is that they recognize that there is an inclusion problem and that systemic racism is at the root of this problem. In order to ensure that faculty-hiring search committees operate in the most productive and equitable ways possible, administrators use a variety of tactics. In my conversations with AAU administrators, they discussed strategies ranging from monetary incentives to sitting on hiring committees to using data to sway skeptical faculty members.

The way that leadership functions—or is allowed to—is fundamentally different across AAU institutions. Some universities have a decentralized system that operates using responsibility-centered management and budgeting, leaving every boat on its own bottom scrounging for funding. Other AAU institutions are more centralized with funding coming from the provost's office and deans submitting a yearly budget attempting to secure the funds. And still others are a bit of a hybrid, required to raise money for some costs but receiving centralized funds for others. These ways of budgeting and allocating funding have an impact on how leadership works. At some institutions, the deans have great autonomy to make faculty search decisions and assessments as to whether or not a school or department may launch a search. At others, the provosts make the final decisions about whether or not a search can move forward. Regardless of the approach, I talked to quite a few administrators at both the provost and dean level who use varying methods to influence faculty searches.

A Commitment from Leadership

Ensuring that diversity and equity issues are open for discussion is important for progress, and provosts are vital to the foundation of this open discussion across universities. However, these conversations can be difficult and controversial even when they are focused on improving campus systems and the overall climate. Of those AAU provosts and deans I spoke to, many had a firm commitment to diversifying the faculty, but some did not. Those that were most committed had personal experiences that changed their perspective or they were people of color; these individuals worked to establish policies aimed at diversifying both the faculty and students. I was particularly struck by one White man who shared his reasons for being ardently committed to diversity:

> I'm the first person in my family to go to college so I was pretty attuned to socioeconomic issues. Before coming to [my current institution], I had spent twenty-five years in the People's Republic of Cambridge. I felt that I was pretty progressive. In 2015, when a lot of mobilization on campus happened around issues of racism, diversity, and inclusion, I was already in a high academic leadership position, and I attended all those rallies. Sometimes it wasn't convenient for me, because with me there, they would sometimes turn the bullhorns on me, but I wanted to hear what was going on. I went to the staff meetings and the faculty meetings and I was really, really shocked with what I learned. First, shocked [about] how ignorant I was about the experiences of students, faculty, and staff of color in these universities and how [they faced], not just the microaggressions, but how often . . . and how in so many ways they were undercut. I basically listened to that, started reading a ton. I did any training workshop I could, and I thought this just has to change. If we're going to be a great university, then we have to make sure that we are genuinely inclusive to everyone, so we can attract the best and brightest and they can be their authentic selves. It's not only good for my university, your university, but it's what the country needs.

My conversation with this man led me to wonder how administrators and faculty who have not had experiences that allow them to relate to others—those who might not have the same privileges and access to resources—support equity. I also was left wondering how often they work to better their skills and to learn more about how racism and inequities manifest on campus, not only in the faculty hiring process but beyond. Having leaders who are open and who use their voices is essential, but not common. Having leaders who use these voices to enact equity-oriented campus policies is even more rare but needed in order to make systemic change.

A vice provost in the South explained how important it is to have the support of the provost on diversity and faculty hiring. Speaking of her own provost, she said, "This is really her vision. I think her success was, it wasn't dictatorial. She really recruited the deans to be on board with this . . . and the numbers show it. We dramatically, in every metric, improved on race and gender in our hiring." She added, "I think that often there's this assumption [that] the administration [is] imposing things, but the best policies are ones that are iterative and collaborative." She noted that her provost does have very specific ideas, but she is also collaborative and intentional in crafting equity-oriented policies that make a difference. She stressed that this approach not only leads to an improvement in diversity in hiring, but they are also seeing more satisfaction among those they hire, in terms of what they are accomplishing. She stressed that the deans are "all in" now because they can see that the provost's emphasis and strategy is working and they feel supported in their implementation of these strategies. Across my interviews, when results rolled in, faculty members were often convinced that faculty diversity plans were worth the time and effort.

Although the work of search committees is essential to attracting and recruiting a diverse professoriate, it is also imperative that deans and faculty overall are in a constant state of looking to diversify their faculties. A midwestern provost at a public university suggested bringing a diverse group of faculty to campus on a regular basis—"not in the context of a search, just in the context of, hey, let's get to know this person. Just build a relationship with this person.

Let's reach out to various networks across the United States to grow our relationships with underrepresented faculty." He also suggested "keeping eyes open" at conferences for new scholars and more established scholars that your institution may want to recruit. When I was a professor at Penn, my then dean Andy Porter used a similar approach to hiring a diverse faculty, an approach he learned at the University of Wisconsin. He launched a faculty of color series, where faculty of color throughout the country were invited to give talks on campus and our faculty could nominate people for visits. Unfortunately, we never hired anyone who visited through this program. However, these faculty visitors did have an impact on diversifying the faculty in other ways, bringing exposure to new, different, and varying ways of thinking, conducting research, and methodological approaches.

A dean at a midwestern university shared with me that when messages around diversity come from her, things change. When she came to her university, her school had almost no diversity in the faculty, and she immediately took on the issue and began talking about it to everyone in the school and those in upper-level administration. She made it a priority and pointed out the lack of diversity on a regular basis. As a result, the faculty members in her school are now becoming more diverse, and she will continue to push for more diversity among the faculty, requiring them to participate in implicit bias training (to be discussed in chapter 6) and including these issues in their annual strategic planning retreat. Unlike some administrators in the AAU who think that faculties can be resistant to diversity efforts, this dean feels that if you bring the issues to their attention, they will do the right thing: "A lot of us . . . just get focused on what we're doing and our research. I can speak from true experience about what it's like to be a minority in a field, but I would say that they're just focused on what they're doing. They just weren't aware, and then as you bring this to them and make them aware, they are engaged and interested. I think it's a matter of bringing it to the table and providing that knowledge." Although I appreciate the dean's optimism, I do wonder how any faculty members remain unaware of challenges around race in the twenty-first century—with all of the information available to them, including scholarship and more general resources, such as social media. A part of me continues to believe that these individuals are intellectually passive, even lazy, when it comes to race and its role in faculty hiring.[3]

Accountability across the Board

Shared governance—faculty participation in institutional governance including "personnel decisions, selection of administrators, preparation of the budget, and determination of educational policies"—is essential and works effectively to ensure thought-provoking curricula as well as intellectual integrity, but in other ways, shared governance allows faculties to perpetuate sameness in hiring and provides few outlets for those administrators who are equity-oriented to hold faculty members responsible for their actions (Association of University Professors, 1966, n.p.).[4] In an ideal system of shared governance, faculties would hold themselves accountable on issues of equity in hiring, but I have rarely seen that happen. The data don't indicate robust accountability in faculty hiring, and the literature shows no evidence either. As a result, there is a fine line between holding faculties accountable and violating the confines of shared governance and academic freedom.

Provosts and deans are walking an administrative tightrope at times with their faculties. It is typical for deans to take a back seat in faculty hiring once they let the faculty search committee know that it has the approval to move forward with a search. Deans will often wait until the end of the search to exercise direct influence on the

3. As I was working on the final edits for this book, the United States was in the midst of some of the largest protests that our nation has experienced. It seemed that White people were finally taking the time to educate themselves around issues of race. The *New York Times* best-seller list was filled with authors, mainly African Americans, writing about race, equity, equality, and being anti-racist. I hope that this type of self-education remains and that people don't continue to comment that they "just didn't know."

4. For the full statement on shared governance, crafted by the American Association of University Professors, see https://www.aaup.org/report/statement -government-colleges-and-universities.

process by being the one who makes the offer to the candidate. A dean of pharmacy at a southern university admitted that when she doesn't see a diverse pool when hiring faculty, she will push back, and she has even paid to bring in a fourth candidate if it helps to diversify the candidate pool. Likewise, according to a dean from a private research institution on the East Coast, "We're running two searches in one department right now, and when I saw the initial list of candidates, I was a little bit dismayed that they all seemed to be coming from really high profile institutions, but they were about half women, and in fact, our two finalists that we may or may not get—one is Mexican American and the other I think is Brazilian. . . . There were no African Americans in the finalist pool. This was a good outcome for this department, which doesn't have a lot of faculty of color."

Interestingly, a vice provost at a public university on the west coast told me that when he has surveyed the faculty across his institution, asking them roughly seventy-five questions about inclusive excellence and diversity, "Consistently, the question about diversity gets extremely positive responses." He noted that his institution uses these data to talk to faculty and deans, saying, "You reported in this anonymous survey that you want more diversity." From his perspective, there are three things that are important to fostering diversity in higher education: "One is that faculty in general are committed to the idea of diversity, but they struggle to hire [a] diverse faculty." As you may recall, this perspective is the same as Daryl Smith's view in chapter 1. "Two, we've invested in a wide range of hiring programs that complement the programs in the schools. These [central] programs are responsible for the lion's share of diverse faculty being hired. In other words . . . schools aren't hiring diverse faculty with their own budgets." He explained that when he asks his counterparts at other AAU institutions how diverse faculty hiring is funded, it's through targets of opportunity and central funds out of the provost's office. The third item he imparted was that schools that are majority men or majority women tend to reproduce sameness (i.e., Whiteness) in similar ways. Thus, a nursing school that is majority women will produce a racial and ethnic sameness just as an engineering school, which is mostly men, would. This vice provost maintained that it's important to be vigilant in one's support and to use data to make convincing arguments to the faculty.

According to a provost at a midwestern institution, "If you are setting diversifying the faculty as a priority . . . you have to have faith that the deans are on board. Nothing's going to happen except for the same old stuff [without them], and you might have to have a few uncomfortable conversations, and you have to decide if the dean is really an impediment, because he or she just isn't interested in [diversity]." He added, "You just have to decide, is that enough for me to change deans, as a provost?" He also noted that deans at his institution are judged on their success when it comes to hiring, recruitment, and retention of a diverse faculty.

Similarly, at a midwestern university that has experienced much controversy around racial issues, the provost holds deans accountable for faculty diversity in their performance appraisals. He admitted that this was not the case prior to the national controversies, but it must be the case now in order to ensure that the faculty is diverse. Both accountability and a commitment to diversity and inclusion are included in the university's new strategic plan. In addition to holding deans accountable in performance appraisals, the provost also provides funding matches for hiring faculty who can bring diversity to the curriculum, classroom, and faculty overall. This university has added a variety of diversity-related components to campus after experiencing national controversy around race—including spaces for students and faculty to come together and network as well as the addition of new positions completely focused on diversity and inclusion. A dean at this institution divulged that she often sees students and faculty using the space and notices that they tend to be African American.

Some AAU administrators are very heavily involved in faculty searches because they feel that they have to be in order to achieve faculty diversity and push back against the status quo. A dean at a midwestern university admitted that when he gets a list of final candidates that is all White men, he questions it and asks the committee for more information and a justification for the lack of racial and gender diversity. He can get a list like this approved by the provost's office, but it will take more work and committees have to answer the questions: "Have we done our best? Do we have the best candidates? Have we accidentally excluded someone or brushed over someone?" Similarly, a vice provost at a university in the Northeast told me that the provost's office will send a list of possible candidates back to the search committee if it is not diverse in terms of race and gender: "We'll say, maybe you should be keeping the search open longer and try to reach out to more people."

Taking things a step further, a provost at a southern university mentioned that she requires search committees to file a report, and they know that their work as a committee will be scrutinized and that they will be held accountable. In addition, she explained that deans are held accountable in their annual reviews for faculty diversity. The provost made it clear that the entire faculty knows that "diversity is important to the provost. They may not like that, but they all know it's important." Likewise, and a bit more systematically, a provost in the Midwest detailed how he holds search committees accountable. He stated, "We ask [search committees] to adhere to our policies and guidelines with respect to making sure that they do best practices for diversity, for building a pool of diverse candidates, and [are] using best practices in their searches and in their conversations about candidates and in their use of a standard set of criteria by which to judge every CV or every candidate." He added, "We ask [committees] when they finally get to where they're going to make an offer, we ask them to request permission to negotiate. I almost never would say no, but we ask them at the same time to fill out a checklist. Did you do all of these practices? We ask them to explain if they didn't, and then we might on the basis of that say, sorry, [the] pool wasn't big enough, but knowing that they're going to have to justify themselves at the end [means] they will at each stage keep track of it. Given the culture when I came, which was no interference whatsoever, I felt that was about as much as I could do this year."

A department chair at a southern university felt differently about accountability, stating, "I don't know any stories on accountability.

Not here." She then went on to compare her institution's hiring to NFL football and the Rooney rule. The Rooney rule is an NFL policy that requires teams to interview minorities for head coaching and senior-level operations jobs (Butler, Longaker, and Britt, 2010; Collins, 2007). She expanded, "They always know who they want, and they bring in, just for the purposes of window dressing or whatever it is they call it, they bring in a minority candidate with zero intentions of hiring him. You hear Black coaches talking about [how] it felt like a real interview. That's what they say." She added, "People get around what they want, and quite frankly, you just have to be intentional." She said bluntly, "Look, we don't have any Black faculty members and we want one, then you go hire one."

A vice provost in the Midwest told me that his institution doesn't hold deans accountable currently, but he noted, "My office is leading with some consultants, an institution-wide diversity, equity and inclusion, strategic planning process with the plan to be delivered [soon]. One of the things we asked the consultants to do was to give us some examples of what a scorecard might look like that we could use with deans and others to sort of assess progress made to date. So we don't currently reward those activities, but it is something that deans could be held accountable for and potentially awarded for in the future." Likewise, a dean in the Midwest let me know that he is not incentivized to bring in a diverse faculty but does it anyway. He added that search committees in his school have "complete autonomy" and that he doesn't "police the candidate pool at any levels." He added, "I know some of my colleagues do. I don't, and the reason I don't is that I haven't found the need to do that, because I actually interview, if I'm in town, I meet with every faculty candidate that comes through. I haven't seen the need to sort of come in and say let me be more in control of the hiring and not allowing you to hire if you don't have a diverse faculty pool. The faculty said they wanted to do this, and so I think it's much better that way than me policing it. They've just said they're going to do it, and they know if they don't [have a diverse pool], their chances of getting a faculty position in the next year drops significantly."

Incentivizing Diversity

Provosts can give incentive funds to schools and departments for diversifying their search or to reward success with faculty hires. These funds might include departmental resources and salary assistance for the hire. According to Ann Springer (2006), these types of funds should be "integrated into the department budget and not continue to be created as a separate source of funding in order to avoid creating a sense that the hire is a special hire and not part of the regular department" (n.p.). Perceptions of special treatment of a hire can lead to resentment on the part of some faculty members and this, in turn, will work against the retention of the candidate (Springer, 2006). One provost I spoke with, at a midwestern university, actively incentivizes faculty with money. He explained that "we have a little kicker that we give to the schools if they recruit someone who is underrepresented in their fields. It's [roughly] $30,000 a year for three years, but what that does is it gives the dean the ability to go to the faculty and say, if we recruit this person, I get this kicker from the provost's office, and I think that helps."

A provost at a public midwestern university disclosed that his institution uses incentives and rewards to motivate deans to hire a diverse faculty. He noted that his institution sets aside special funds that are "dedicated to help remedy the underrepresentation of various faculty." He explained that deans can tap into a fund that pays "75% of the new hire's base salary in perpetuity." This kind of support is helpful to deans who are operating with tight budgets. They are often able to hire two people rather than one, as the support from the provost's office allows for more flexibility. To complement this approach, the institution also prioritizes requests for strategic funds from deans by those who have put together a diversity plan. More specifically, he stated, "Suddenly I was getting emails and phone calls and meetings with the deans and associate deans [who wanted to access the funding]."

During my conversations with administrators at AAU institutions, some mentioned that they use financial incentives such as a dean's merit increase or school allotted funding to incentivize or reward diversity efforts. However, this was not the norm. According to the provost of a private research university in the Northeast, when I asked if her university uses financial incentives, "Well, you won't be dean anymore [if you don't embrace diversity in faculty hiring]. It's as fundamental as that. We don't use financial incentives, because I've been very clear that this is not a question of buying your participation in this [process]. If you're not on board with this, then you're not on the ship. I have been consistent in saying that a university that believes itself to be excellent cannot be excellent if it is not also diverse and representative of the community." This provost was the only one to define excellence as including diversity. Along the same vein, I asked a vice provost if her institution offers incentives to deans for bringing in a diverse faculty, and she responded with a quick "no." Expanding on her answer, she revealed, "I think we're wary of focusing on outcomes, because those issues are ethical, and I think also for legal reasons, we really focus on process, in the belief that the process will produce the numbers, which in our case it has."

Using Influence and Strategy

Provosts and deans who have the most success in hiring a diverse faculty have worked to make their searches as open as possible to ensure that the restrictions around the job are not excluding underrepresented groups. A vice provost on the West Coast told me that he encourages departments with subfields to make the search committees more heterogeneous to break up the groupthink; he also advises department chairs to ensure the entire department votes on searches in order to have more input. He added that he is trying to change things at his institution because search committees have a lot of autonomy and it's a "little bit of a Wild West at times." Of concern, he sighed, "Some of the problems with searching and with other things arise because people just kind of make it up and do it as they want." He doesn't want to get rid of autonomy, but he wants to have "more standardization"—his institution recently began using Interfolio as a way to "curtail the Wild West." Interfolio, a for-profit company, offers a variety of services for individuals and institutions. It currently works with nearly 275 colleges and universities, providing support for faculty hiring as well as faculty tenure and promotion. According to its website, it understands the difference between hiring corporate staffing and hiring faculty. More specifically, "Interfolio supports the academic requirements of faculty recruitment because it's a tool built for all of the nuances of shared governance (and the requirements of human resources). It provides powerful transparency into the talent, diversity, and accomplishments of your faculty population."[5]

A vice provost at a university in the South also mentioned Interfolio when discussing her institution's lack of records of its hiring data. She likes Interfolio because it allows the university to keep track of the demographics of a candidate pool and of those that the university overall hires. She added that Interfolio eliminates the need to have a department or school administrator writing down "what they know about the demographics of their applicants." She mentioned that her institution and others had pushed Interfolio to collect data in a way that could also be reported to the Integrated Postsecondary Education Data System (IPEDS)—a necessary task that all colleges and universities must complete. She's excited about this consistent collection of data, as being able to review a five- or ten-year period will help her to make the case for more diversity in faculty hiring if the institution isn't meeting its goals. As I was speaking with the vice provost, I was struck by her enthusiasm for solving problems and helping faculty to succeed. I asked her what makes her successful, and she responded, "I think it's intentionality."

Another strategy of note comes from a provost at a research institution in the Northeast. The provost suggested using the opportunity of having a new "crew of deans" to implement a large-scale push for faculty diversity. She requires the deans to submit a three-year plan and vision across their departments. These plans include requests for faculty hires and the identification of hiring gaps. Deans must also submit projections pertaining to enrollment of undergraduates (if applicable), masters students, and doctoral students. She also

5. Interfolio website, 2020, www.interfolio.com.

requires the schools and departments to provide an overview of how they will create a more inclusive climate for junior faculty joining the university. As a result, she and the deans have increased the hiring of faculty of color by 25% and have laid the groundwork for additional hires. She brought in a new mindset that embraces racial and ethnic equity as fundamental to excellence, and she has enacted policies that make success possible.

The Race of the Provost

As I was writing this book, there were twenty-four women and thirty-nine men among the provosts in the AAU institutions and eleven people of color (see table 16). I was able to speak with some of the provosts of color for this book, although I worked hard to disguise who they are due to the ramifications of what they shared with me. These individuals are in a peculiar situation—wanting to make systemic change, but being cognizant of their race and what it represents as they go about doing their job.

When talking with provosts of color for this book, I asked them if their race made a difference in doing their job. My assumption, based on my past research, reading of others' research, and my experiences, was that of course race makes a difference. However, I wanted to hear their perspectives firsthand. One provost told me that his race manifested in complicit ways, sharing, "I don't want to be the one in the meeting saying, we should be caring about diversity." He often feels "damned if you do, damned if you don't," given that he wants to speak up but doesn't want to be tokenized for speaking up for only the group he represents. He clarified, though: "I do think that I have a freedom to say 'Wait, what? You're doing what?' Like, 'No, no, no, you're not doing that,' and to be listened to, [compared with] someone else, from a majority background [chiming in]. So [my race] does alter the conversation, but in ways that are a little bit unpredictable, I think, or maybe at times counterintuitive."

Another provost in the middle of the country told me that although her university doesn't provide any written guidelines around issues of race and gender for search committees, including

Table 16	AAU Provosts Gender and Race
Women	24
Men	39
White	52
Black	4
Latino/a	3
Asian American	4
Women of color	4
Men of color	7
White men	32
White women	20

Source: Institutional websites, 2020.

training or guidelines for search committee composition, she speaks with committees about these issues. Much like most of the provosts of color and White women in the role of provost, she is the first person of color to hold the position. During our conversation, she joked about being in place for a few years and wondering how long that would last. As I submitted this book to my editor, she had already left her position.

Still others told me how lonely they were in their roles, given that there were very few people of color in administration at their institutions and few people in the provost role across the nation that they could confide in or relate to regarding the unique racial issues that they regularly face in their roles. Of note, while I was writing this book, several provosts of color at AAU institutions left their roles for other jobs—either lateral moves or for presidencies—after only a short time.

The voices and actions of leadership around the issue of enhancing faculty diversity in hiring is crucial to success. Without it, faculty and search committees, which we will discuss in chapter 6, are left to reproduce themselves and to hold tightly to the status quo—a status quo that reinforces and uplifts Whiteness. Provosts and deans who use their platforms to project a consistent message and enact equity-oriented policies are most successful in terms of changing the campus climate. Holding faculty and search committees accountable, while also allowing for the autonomy that is essential for a climate of shared governance, is a tricky road to walk.

6

Do Search Committees Know What They Are Doing?

We're trying to internalize in our processes what we know from the work of social scientists is most effective, which as you know, as a faculty member, we aren't so good always about bringing over what we know to what we do.

—AAU UNIVERSITY VICE PROVOST

Faculty search committees are part of the problem when it comes to the recruitment of faculty of color. They are not trained in recruitment, are rarely diverse in makeup, and, as we learned in chapter 4, are often more interested in hiring people just like themselves than in expanding the diversity of their department or school. They reach out to those they know for recommendations and rely on ads in national publications that are not aimed at diverse audiences. And even when they do recruit a diverse group of applicants, often those applicants are deemed "not the right fit" for the institution. Worthy of note, Julie Posselt found the same discussions of "fit" when researching her book, *Inside Graduate Admissions* (2016). Faculties hold tightly to maintaining the status quo and ensuring that they are comfortable in their environment. Given that 76% of tenure-track and tenured faculty are White and predominantly men at colleges and universities across the nation,[1] this results in an environment that is often not welcoming or friendly toward White women and people of color.

In this chapter, I will explore the faculty hiring processes at AAU institutions, how search committees are formed, their composition, the type of administrative guidance search committees receive, the work that they do and the role that training (specifically implicit bias training) plays in their work, and their level of autonomy in faculty hiring.

How Faculty Hiring Takes Place

As I discuss how faculty hiring takes place, I want to begin with a reminder from Lauren Rivera (2015). She argues in *Pedigree*, "[A]t each stage of the hiring process—from the decision about where to post job advertisements and hold recruitment events to the final selections made by hiring committees—employers use an array of sorting criteria ('screens') and ways of measuring candidates' potential ('evaluative metrics') that are highly correlated with parental income and education. Taken together, these seemingly economically neutral decisions result in a hiring process that filters . . . based on [parental] socioeconomic status"—or pedigree (p. 2).

At most AAU institutions (and colleges and universities in general), faculty hiring takes place in two to three main ways. The most prominent way involves deans asking the provost for permission to launch searchers in various departments. Another way involves targets of opportunity, which are focused searches that regularly involve financial support from a central pool of funding through the provost's office. A few institutions are using a third approach that is just beginning to become popular but is also controversial. This approach involves the provost's office launching searches in collaboration with schools and departments. These searches are focused on

1. Men constitute 62.4% of tenured and 51.6% of tenure-track faculty. For more information, see Finkelstein and Conley (2019).

increasing diversity across the entire institution and are typically not located in an individual school or college.

In the first approach to faculty hiring, deans put together information on their school's retirements, departures, and areas of new growth and also craft statements that detail the "pedagogical and intellectual needs" of the school. Many deans also try to make a connection between the hire and the institution's strategic plan, as this approach often enhances their chance for approval. At institutions that have a diversity plan for faculty, deans regularly make a link to this plan, hoping to secure central funding for their searches and increase their chances of approval. As discussed earlier, a review of the AAU institutions' strategic plans that are publicly available shows that verbiage around diversity and inclusion take center stage at most AAU institutions, but not all. According to a dean at a midwestern university, the strategic plan is focused on hiring in areas for which the institution wants to be nationally and globally renowned: "We have specific components of our strategic plan related to diversity and inclusive excellence."

Targets of opportunity, to be discussed in more detail in chapter 7, happen at most institutions but remain controversial among some, as they target specific individuals without conducting a national search. Targeted individuals are typically very prominent people and mainly people of color, but not always. Targets of opportunity are usually people who fill a specific need in a department or school, bring prestige, and are primed to leave their current institution (Bilimoria and Buch, 2010). In order to pursue a target of opportunity, approval is needed from the provost and faculty, within the specific school that is hiring.

The third approach, which is not standard, is a top-down strategy for diversifying the professoriate. Typically, the funding for this type of program comes from an allotment of monies for diversity efforts on campus. Rather than focus on specific disciplinary expertise, this approach is aimed at looking for candidates who have a commitment to diversity, equity, and inclusion among underrepresented groups. One of the best examples of this approach is at the University of California–Davis, which benefits financially from a system-wide commitment to diversifying the professoriate (Easley, 2018). I visited with the provost's office a few years ago while giving a talk on diversity in faculty hiring and asked one of the administrators in the central academic offices how he gets buy-in from deans and faculty. He noted that the special searches were taking place alongside traditional searches, and deans were given extra funds to matriculate faculty as well as funds toward salaries if one of these searches took place in their school. Still, these types of searches are quite controversial—often criticized for encroaching upon shared governance and academic freedom. If you have any doubt of the controversial nature of these searches, take a look at the comments section on national news stories that highlight these kinds of searches (see Flaherty, 2018b).

Some of the AAU administrators that I talked to use the faculty search process as an opportunity to push faculty "to have conversations about diversity in curriculum, the direction of the curriculum, and interdisciplinarity." And, along these lines, they are also asked to think about the types of faculty, in terms of expertise, that they need to carry out these changes. In these cases, AAU administrators described searches as being two years in length rather than one, with the first year being a silent phase—one in which the faculty invites people it would like to have as colleagues to campus through symposia and low-pressure events. Then, in year two, the faculty launches a national search and invites many of those individuals who came informally to enter the national search. I've seen this happen at several institutions, and it can be a powerful way to bring diversity to campus. It can also lead on less-experienced scholars, making them think that they are being courted when the department is really interested in multiple people. Clarity is essential when using this kind of approach.

A vice provost at a midwestern university pointed out that when "deans are required to submit their faculty hiring plans for all the positions that they have open, they are not only required to provide justification as to how these searches will help to enhance the scholarship and the research and teaching within their school, but also how it will help enhance diversity." He added that when the deans sit down face-to-face with the provost, they are "expected to talk about how these hires help enhance" intellectual, gender, racial, and ethnic diversity.

It is important to understand that the hiring of faculty in some areas requires or expects participation in hiring conferences. For example, law school hiring involves participation in the Association of American Law Schools (AALS) hiring conference. Most deans that I talked with noted that they interview roughly fifty to sixty candidates over a two-day period at the annual AALS conference. Some law schools also conduct Skype interviews to narrow the field before choosing a set of finalists. A law school dean in the West described his school's process of advertising to get a diverse pool as one in which it advertises very widely. The recruiters don't merely rely on the AALS process for hiring faculty but reach out across many outlets that they have crowdsourced over the years. However, more importantly, according to the dean, they use their personal networks, trying to reach out to as many people as possible with an eye toward getting some people that may not traditionally have [participated] in the search. Of course, if the law school lacks diversity, personal "known networks" might not yield a diverse pool, as I mentioned earlier in this book.

Of note, other disciplines, including the humanities, use hiring conferences (or did in the past) but not to the extent of law schools. Some disciplines, such as history, have eliminated their job centers at their annual conference and no longer provide interview suites. Instead, they encourage institutions to use video conferencing. For example, the American Historical Association (AHA) website states, "As of 2019, the AHA urges hiring departments to schedule teleconference interviews or on-campus visits for first round interviews. The AHA will not maintain the AHA Job Center or provide interview suites. First round interviews may be conducted through phone, videoconferencing platforms, or in-person if arranged by the department."[2]

2. For the organization's full guidelines and standards for hiring, see: https://www.historians.org/jobs-and-professional-development/statements-standards

The Composition and Work of Search Committees

I found it difficult to ascertain from my conversations with AAU administrators what search committees do in terms of work, as most of their work is "in the weeds" and doesn't rise to the level of involvement from provosts and deans. As expected, I was able to gather more knowledge from the search committee chairs and department chairs with whom I talked. Research tells us that search committees should be thinking about both the small work and the larger visionary work for their departments (Gillies, 2016). One of the larger tasks of search committees is thinking about where the department wants to be in ten or twenty years and how the hire will shape this vision. They should also be thinking about which new fields in their discipline are emerging (Gillies, 2016). Of considerable importance is a discussion pertaining to what perspectives and experiences are missing based on race, ethnicity, gender, sexuality, et cetera, and how the search process can contribute to closing these gaps. Search committees need to grapple with how the position adds to goals of diversity, inclusion, and justice if they are focused on these goals (Griffin, 2020).

Search committee composition is very different, depending on institution, school, and department. Within the AAU institutions, according to my interviews, most—not all–committees have a graduate student (typically with no influence and who does some of the grunt work of the committee), several faculty experts in the field, sometimes a diversity representative (either faculty or staff), and sometimes someone who is outside of the department or school to offer balance of perspective. Based on my extensive conversations with AAU administrators, their institutions envision committee members as being objective, neutral, and well intentioned. However, the truth is much different from what is expected for these entities. The majority of AAU deans are focused on inclusivity, reflecting

---

-and-guidelines-of-the-discipline/guidelines-for-first-round-interviews. The Modern Language Association (MLA) has also issued guidelines in recent years—https://www.mla.org/Resources/Career/Career-Resources/Guidelines -for-Search-Committees-and-Job-Seekers-on-Entry-Level-Faculty-Recruitment -and-Hiring. For more information see Flaherty (2018c).

the overall academic community, and disciplinary expertise. When thinking about search committees, a law school dean in the West told me that "When we're hiring, this is a committee where we're going to want our good players on there, because it's a big decision. We think about trying to get a good balance and diversity on the committee too. That's not just with respect to gender or minority status. Those are considerations for sure, . . . [b]ut also thinking about diversity in subject matter, thinking about people who can engage well with the candidates. You have to have a good sense of judgment. I guess the last thing is because it's a faculty decision and we want to engage the whole cross section of the faculty, thinking about putting together a group that can engage with all the different segments of the faculty, so that they are a conduit for all the various opinions to make their way to the committee process."

A vice provost at a university in the South relayed, "We're very concerned about inclusivity and ensuring that we have a faculty that reflects in all respects the community that we serve, the community of scholars, the community of students." She added, "We found that that kind of intentionality has really led to much better evaluation of candidates as they come forward and helps to minimize implicit bias." However, search committee composition doesn't always come easily. A provost at a public Midwestern institution revealed that sometimes his office has to be more forceful with some schools and departments in the composition of search committees. He acknowledged that some departments don't "appreciate the heavy hand of the administration." Explaining that his institution "prides itself on faculty governance," he added, "And part of that is that we encourage the development of protocols at the department level. The guidelines for hiring—just all the basic policies and procedures in hiring, tenure, and promotion—all of those—we tried to articulate down across the campus in all the schools." He shared that there is pushback if the "administration intervenes or plays a heavy hand in the selection [process]. [This dissatisfaction] is often conveyed by the chair of the department on behalf of the department to the dean."

A provost of an Ivy League institution described his approach to forming search committees: "We suggest faculty from a diverse background that might have a range of ideas and expertise, including subdisciplines, gender, race, and ethnicity. We also advise [people] forming the search committees that in many cases, women and underrepresented minorities get asked to serve on committees [too frequently]." He noted that although some committees have a diversity representative who is responsible for "checking that the pool is diverse," some schools have charged the entire committee with this task.

Offering a different perspective, a vice provost in the South told me that her institution used to require diversity on search committees and that the guidance for this diversity came from the Equal Opportunity and Civil Rights office on campus. Her institution operated with this in mind for years. However, "At one point the people in charge of our ADVANCE grant [discussed earlier] pushed back, saying we're overtaxing our [White] women and minority faculty in the fields. They asked us, where those individuals are such a small minority, do we absolutely have to have gender and racial diversity on every search committee? Can we move away from that? And we did move away from that." Research tells us that White women and people of color are often saddled with more service responsibilities within the academy and are rarely rewarded for this service in promotion and tenured processes or financially, in terms of salary (De Welde and Stepnick, 2015). Unfortunately, search committees that lack diversity are more likely to reproduce uniformity and, in the case of the academy, Whiteness (Morgan et al., 2021; Nietzel, 2021).

The vice provost added, "We want to have diversity on the committee in terms of gender, racial, and ethnic diversity. But that's tough because we don't have enough people to go around sometimes. And so we also want to make sure that the same person from an underrepresented group isn't put on multiple searches in the same year or multiple searches year after year because that's really draining. We want to make sure that people who have appropriate rank are on the search. We consider it fine to have a mix of seniority on the search. So, a very junior person could be a member of a search committee, but it shouldn't be chaired by a junior faculty member. And we do try to protect people who are close to going up for tenure."

Populating a search committee is a dicey task for a dean, as reaching the right mix of people is hard and avoiding tokenism of people of color is tricky as well. In the words of Sensoy and DiAngelo (2017), due to the lack of diversity in departments, the same people are asked to serve over and over and are taxed in terms of their service commitment. In addition, the dynamics can be difficult to navigate. They warn that members of search committees are "presumed to be objective and neutral" with the exception of those perceived to be token members (p. 565). They also note that these token members of search committees are often assumed to have expertise and knowledge related to "race and racial issues, but *only* on these issues" despite having disciplinary expertise. Lastly, if token members of search committees call out racism, they "are often met with resistance" and their contributions are disregarded (p. 565). Unfortunately, it is frequently the case that Whites think that if the process feels comfortable to them, it must be comfortable to everyone.

AAU universities run the gamut in terms of how their administrators populate search committees and what is valued. By and large, however, most institutions consider racial and ethnic diversity, gender diversity, and intellectual diversity. They also want to include people who best represent the institution, department, or school and who will get the work of the committee done in a timely manner. Ensuring that search committees have diverse representation across a variety of factors, and that all members are empowered to speak freely and without intimidation, is essential to hiring a diverse faculty. Confidential evaluations of the search committee process are an effective way for deans to better understand issues that might arise and to curtail them in the future.

The Search Committee Diversity Representative

Most AAU institutions have a diversity representative on their search committees; in fact, most institutions require them. These individuals are often faculty, sometimes staff, and occasionally the chief diversity officer of the institution. The politics involved in serving in this role can be difficult. Faculty members in these positions are often looked upon as spies for the dean or as policing the committee. Some of the deans I talked with noted that for searches for junior faculty, sometimes the diversity representative is an untenured faculty member. This situation can be dangerous for junior faculty. Imagine questioning senior faculty members, who are determining your tenure at the institution, about their lack of support for faculty diversity. Likewise, staff in these diversity representative roles have little power, as they don't have tenure and are often afraid to speak up, given the disproportionate role that the faculty plays on search committees. According to a chief diversity officer at a university in the Northeast, "The diversity representative often was not prepared to have conversations about diversity, equity, and inclusion. And [the] person served [more] as a de facto, powerless member of this committee who the committee members viewed as just someone who was supposed to make sure that the search was equitable in whatever way that meant." Frustrated by the ambiguity and lack of any influence or power on the part of the diversity representative, the chief diversity officer decided to meet with all of the search committee chairs to educate them around "multi-systemic privilege and oppression and the ways it could impact the search." She also implemented sessions on implicit bias (discussed later in this chapter) and hosted informal meetings with members of search committees to answer questions such as "If someone who has lost hearing is coming to campus, how do I ask them what they need?" or "What do I do if somebody who is nonbinary is coming to campus and my department really doesn't know what to do around that or around gender pronouns?" In this case, the chief diversity officer found that committees had a lot of questions and were quite ill-equipped to handle them. She also found that many members of the search committees eventually asked for help with writing interview questions and locating resources for candidates on campus during their visits.

At some AAU institutions, whether or not a university has a diversity representative on the committee is haphazard. One dean told me: "If we can represent diversity, [we do]—which sometimes we can and sometimes we can't." These same institutions try to ensure there is a woman on the committee as well, but it's not always possible from their perspective. According to a vice provost on the West Coast, "We have a set of milestones. We're looking at the pool characteristics, and so an equity advisor will look at, when the search committee is submitting their proposed short lists, the equity advisor can see the pool characteristics, as well as the characteristics that are available on the proposed short list. They can sort of see to what extent there is a significant disparity or divergence, and probe questions until they are satisfied." At this point the search is paused and it comes to him for approval. Once the list is approved, the committee can reach out to candidates for campus interviews. During this discussion, I was curious about the equity advisors—how many are there and do they feel empowered to do their job, as it can be a tricky one. He noted that he has roughly fifteen equity advisors (faculty members) that are spread across the various schools on campus. These individuals apply for the position and are also nominated by deans. Once appointed, they are thoroughly onboarded as part of a campus-wide team, which meets on a monthly basis. They are a resource to the various deans. One of the most difficult parts of their role is reminding faculty search committees of campus expectations. The vice provost added that the equity advisors have the "authority not to approve something." He also reminds them that if there are ever issues with a search committee process, they need to go directly to the dean, as the searches are under the purview of the dean and he "doesn't want any friction."

As I probed a bit more about the pressure these equity advisors must be under, based on my own experiences as someone who has been outspoken about systemic racism, the vice provost explained, "I think [it's] a very valid concern that you pointed out, that in some cases folks are uncomfortable, but it's a three-year term and generally by the second year or third year, they have a better sense of how the process works. The bottom line is in holding colleagues accountable; it is uncomfortable inherently because it's not about the research; it's not about evaluating their teaching or their service. It's basically about ensuring that what they say they're [going to] do, they are actually engaged in doing. So yes, it's hard." He added, the equity advisors "have authority to actually pause the search, and they really serve as a confidential resource." Of interest, this process grew out of a National Science Foundation ADVANCE grant (discussed earlier in this book). In the vice provost's words, "As you may know, ADVANCE, in the original award, focused exclusively on gender, not race and ethnicity. When I came [to the university], I revised the mission to be broader. Then we started formalizing the program with nominations, onboarding, and greater authority. What I'm suggesting is that over time, the image of our ADVANCE program has changed, but essentially it's still grounded in peer-to-peer engagement." With the implementation of equity advisors, this institution, by far, had the most developed, well thought out, and advanced process for ensuring equity-based checks and balances on search committees. Imagine if this type of process were implemented across all the AAU institutions.

When describing what it is like to sit in a room in which a faculty search committee is making hiring decisions, a diversity representative avowed, "It's incredibly uncomfortable. It also depends on the relationship that I have with the people in the room. I might have a good relationship with the chair of the search [committee], and there might be somebody who is part of the search committee who has a lot of power on the faculty at the university who's saying all kinds of problematic stuff. [Sometimes] I can rely on the chair to manage that but not always. [Sometimes] I have a separate conversation with the chair to anticipate that some of this might come up and [think about] how we manage it. Sometimes I manage it and ask some questions about what's really going down. What are we talking about here, and now that we've talked about implicit bias can we connect with some of the concepts? And they say nothing." Part of the issue is the lack of movement once the problematic language surfaces. Diversity representatives often have their hands tied or have little power, and tenured faculty members serving on search committees either don't want to speak up or are afraid to confront their colleagues out of fear of retaliation (Hollis, 2015).

An associate provost for diversity in the Northeast asserted that her influence is stronger because she also holds the position of full professor. Because she has gone through the tenure ranks and sat on search committees as a faculty member, she is fully aware of the strategies that are used to avoid bringing in a diverse pool of candidates. She differentiated herself from those chief diversity officers who have only worked in administration, noting that she has a lot more influence, having worked in and fully understanding the system. In her words, "I'm a full professor. I know the okey doke. I know the games people play. I've been on search committees and when they say something [strange around diversity issues], I say, 'Come on. You know that's not the case.'"

Chief diversity officers, who are rarely ever tenured faculty, are becoming more involved in the faculty hiring process at many AAU institutions, but their role is undefined and many faculty members don't understand their position, their work, or their role in the hiring process. Moreover, some of the faculty don't want their involvement as they think faculty hiring is a faculty decision and should not have input from outsiders. They see administrative diversity efforts as an impingement on their academic freedom and the foundation of shared governance. In the words of one chief diversity officer in the Northeast, "Some folks have said 'I don't get why you're even here' or 'I don't know what to do with you.'" Most diversity officers are in understaffed offices of one or two and have small budgets that allow them to do very little. In 2018, researchers conducting a peer-reviewed study found that the hiring of diversity officers has had little significant impact on faculty diversity in colleges and universities (Bradley et al., 2018). However, shortly after the publication of the article, diversity officers pushed back—using Twitter—against these findings, sharing their extensive work on college campuses to influence faculty hiring. In reality, the role of diversity officers is not the same from campus to campus. At some colleges and universities, these individuals are more focused on student life issues, while at others, they are invited to offer perspective on faculty hiring. Without faculty rank and standing, however, they can have very little influence in the actual hiring process (Bradley et al., 2018).

Crafting the Job Description

The way a faculty job description is written is directly tied to the success of the search. According to Denise Lach, the director of Oregon State University's School of Public Policy, in a special report by the *Chronicle of Higher Education*, recruiting begins with the job description. She advises search committees to "start with the job description and try to take out hot-button words or words that look like code" (p. 9). She elaborates with an example, noting that search committees often want candidates that have secured specific kinds of grants. Lach asks what kinds of candidates typically receive these types of grants? And she notes that one must have a "good mentor who is connected to the funding agency and is also a good grant writer" (p. 9). After a conversation, the committee members that Lach worked with realized that they were "privileging people who had already been privileged in their graduate program" (*Chronicle of Higher Education*, 2018, p. 9).

Daryl Smith and her colleagues (2004) found that if a job description includes a link to diversity in the form of practice or scholarship, the search is more likely to result in the hiring of a person of color. Likewise, Sensoy and DiAngelo (2017) recommend operationalizing diversity in the job description: "If the job announcement states that yours is a campus that 'promotes diversity,' the committee needs to set clear targets by operationalizing the term. For example, decide what explicit evidence you will use to determine that the candidate has promoted (rather than simply values) diversity" (p. 563). They also warn that if the search committee cannot operationalize diversity, they should not include a reference to it in the job description, as this is disingenuous.

A vice provost for diversity at a private research university in the Northeast, frustrated by the system, told me, "In the academy, the search process is the most passive process I've ever seen. You write an ad, and then you put it out into the world, and then you just sit back and wait, and then you review, and you don't do any pre-work. You don't prep the ground; you don't do anything. You just sit back and wait. You don't even change the language to be more inviting to people from underrepresented groups. You just use the same language, the same elitist language. And then you complain that people of color aren't swarming to you." She added that people often tell her they don't have the time to invest, and she replies, "Well, then, you are going to get the same results." When I was talking with Daryl Smith, she recounted that when she is doing her research with universities on increasing diversity in faculty hiring, she often finds that the job descriptions are organized in the same way they were in the 1950s: "People took [the job description] out of the file. They took the old job description, they changed the date, posted [it] and prayed. Praying, meaning I pray that they'll have some diversity." Failing to put the time and effort into crafting a strong job description is detrimental to the diversity of the pool.

According to Gillies (2016), job announcements need to include information related to how candidates can succeed in the faculty position. In addition, job announcements must reflect a diverse range of experiences and interests in order to attract a diverse group of candidates. Gillies also suggests that the position announcement describe the "role, its impact, and how it contributes to diversity, inclusion, and justice." Of course, this last suggestion is controversial, as some faculty members do not see a need to connect their work or themselves to diversity.

A dean at a university in the South mentioned that with her school's search committees, she is "intentional and purposeful." The committees represent diversity broadly in terms of race, gender, ethnicity, but also diversity across the curriculum. She added, we write "our hopes and dreams into the position announcement." In contrast, a chief diversity officer at a northeastern university shared with frustration, "Surprise, we were posting the ads in all the same places every year and expecting that our pool was going to be more diverse, which is silly. I did just a little bit of research because it doesn't take much, actually, and [identified] some other possibilities for posting. I don't know how much that helped with this last search, but I do know that some of the folks that we hired this last time around are people of color or nonbinary." She also helped the search committees rewrite their job descriptions: "Every job ad that was sent out came across my desk first. [It's a big deal.] I was also in conversation with the chairs and the deans about [using] a standard template for what we want to say about ourselves as to who we are and who we're looking for."

A dean, also at an institution in the Northeast, let me know that it's rare that universities really study where they are advertising for faculty positions, as hiring faculty is greatly decentralized. He noted that his institution did an analysis and found that the places they advertised and the resulting pools were inadequate and overly narrow. After realizing where his team was failing in faculty searches, he began having a central staff member evaluate the advertising strategy for each search. In his words, "We've instituted policies about tapping networks, but also documenting the networks that we're tapping so that they don't [merely] replicate bias in terms of the recruitment committee. I've hired someone to certify the searches." This dean has a staff member that lets him know if searches will garner a diverse pool of candidates based on the committee's strategy, and if it's not feasible, the staff member leaves the search open. In order to be convincing to his colleagues and the institution overall, this dean brings the diversity of the search back to being an institution with "a core mission around the social policy of social justice."

A law school associate dean and past department chair in the West communicated that "[crafting] position descriptions in a way that's broad enough that we're going to capture the greatest potential of getting more diverse applicants under our initial construction of the pool so that we can get eyes on them [is vital]. Because if we don't, we're never going to be able to look a little closer." Likewise, an Ivy League provost relayed, "We want to word the job description as broadly as possible so that it can be inclusive of many different types of people. We want to lay out what's your plan for how you are going to advertise for this position. What are you going to be doing to enhance the diversity of your pool?"

A law school dean on the West Coast shared with me, "We had discussions about whether or not we could write a posting that would be more welcoming and at the same time not overwhelming, because sometimes people think if I don't have all of these things then I shouldn't apply. We worked on the language of the postings in an effort to get a more diverse pool." However, Sensoy and DiAngelo (2017) caution search committees to avoid "coded language" such as "urban, inner city, and disadvantaged." They consider these terms uncritical and alienating to candidates of color (p. 563).

Some AAU institutions have standardized the entire search process, evaluating how committees work, how job descriptions send messages, and how general correspondence about faculty hiring with candidates is linked to hiring a diverse faculty and maintaining these hires. A vice provost on the West Coast at a public university shared that once a search is approved, search committees have to prepare a plan that includes data about the potential pipeline for the position. He requires committee members to understand the pipeline before advertising the position. The deans are also provided with various standardized tools, including sample announcements, letters that they can customize, and information on inclusive excellence to be incorporated in all outreach.

As I was interviewing an associate provost of diversity, she revealed deep frustrations with faculty biases. She told me there is a "sort of passive racism that undergirds the practices in the academy. . . . It's allowed to go unchecked; it's a bunch of this sort of mythology and spewing and petulance and upsettedness." She offered an example, "We have this senior faculty member who was really an ally, and we were talking about embedding diversity indicator language into the search ads, and he [would] not listen. He was not happy about it at all. It was really striking to me because he's such an ally. I asked him, 'What is your objection to the [diversity indicator language]?' And his objection was, 'If I was on the market today, I would not be able to get a job because I would not know how to answer that question.' And I said, 'Did you see all the junior people—White, Black, whatever—standing around the edges of the faculty meeting nodding?' He said, 'Yeah, I saw them.' And I said, 'But they all know how to answer the question because they are coming into the academy to get competencies that include pedagogy and mentoring of underrepresented people.' You should have seen the look on his face. He said, 'Really?' I said, 'Yeah.' He replied, 'Oh, well, I'm fine with it.' I would suspect that [some faculty members] are not interested in fairness. They [also] don't want to find themselves making less than people of color [or losing a job to them]." Of importance, she added, "I think the question about what people fear is real, and I don't think enough folks pay attention to it and listen deeply enough to it. I think that's to our detriment. If I had not gone and talked to my senior colleague who was like 'No' [to including diversity language in the job description], I would not have known that the reason he was so against the [diversity language] was because he was fearful of his former self, and therefore fearful for people like him. And once we worked past that with him, he was able to get on board again. I think the educators in us should also be trying to think about how do we educate folks who have very long held beliefs and [whose beliefs] the system has helped support."

Search Committee Training

There are several kinds of training that search committees should require, but training is not systematic and is not guaranteed across all AAU institutions. Part of the issue is that members of faculty do not like to be trained, and they also approach being on a search committee as something they already know how to do—mainly because they were hired through a search process. Most of the administrators from AAU institutions whom I interviewed have their faculty search committees undergo training for legal issues involved in faculty hiring—for example, questions that can and cannot be asked, and the confidentiality of search materials.

The type of training that is more controversial and less frequent is implicit bias training or any kind of training related to diversity. This type of training, if provided, happens in one of several ways. Some institutions offer implicit bias training for the entire faculty at the school level—usually through regular or special faculty meetings; others make implicit bias training an option for search committee members, and still others require implicit bias training in order to serve on a search committee—with some requiring it every three years.

According to Jennifer Eberhardt, author of *Biased: Uncovering the Hidden Prejudice that Shapes What We See, Think, and Do,* our unconscious or implicit biases can be at work and present when we don't even realize it. As she explains, even when we seek to treat people fairly, we have stereotypes ingrained in our heads that can have an impact on the way we see or visualize others and our behaviors. She warns us that our unconscious biases can shape equity in education, hiring, the criminal justice system, housing, and many other areas. Biases have an impact on all aspects of life (Eberhardt, 2019).

The national training organization ELI, which does extensive work within the areas of government, nonprofits, and higher education, offers a few good research-based examples that help people to understand what implicit bias is and its ramifications in the workplace and everyday life. The first example pertains to technology (remember Daryl Smith's wise words in chapter 1 regarding technology). When YouTube unveiled a new video upload feature, it noticed that roughly 10% of the videos were uploaded upside-down. The application developers at Google were confused, as they didn't understand how a significant percentage of their users were shooting videos incorrectly (Bock and Welle, 2014). After considerable study of the problem, the engineers discovered that they had designed the application for uploading videos for right-handed users. They had not considered that left-handed users rotate their phones 180 degrees when using them, causing videos to be uploaded upside-down (ELI, n.d.).

Another example cited by ELI involves managers reviewing resumes and relies on the work of Marianne Bertrand and Sendhil Mullainathan (2003). In Bertrand and Mullainathan's study, managers were given a group of resumes. Some of these resumes were exact duplicates with only the name changed and nothing else. The resumes with "Anglo-" or White-sounding names were flagged for a callback substantially more often that those with "diverse" names. In addition to names, activities or hobbies triggered other assumptions among the managers. Those activities that sounded more important or prestigious privileged candidates. Those who had played polo, rowed crew, or rode horses were more likely to be flagged for further consideration than those who played basketball or softball. Assumptions regarding financial stability and success resulted from the types of activities listed on the resumes.

Requiring implicit bias training can cause some backlash, as faculty members don't like to be forced into anything mandatory, including training (Schneckenberg, 2009; Watty, McKay, and Ngo, 2016). They often consider it a violation of their academic freedom. However, the provosts and deans among the AAU institutions that do require diversity or implicit bias training consider it part of the faculty duties. When I asked one Ivy League provost how the faculty responds to mandatory implicit bias training, he emphasized, "They know that I'm such a champion of this, that at least in front of me, they're polite. I don't know what they are saying behind my back." He added, "I'm very involved in the development of our diversity and inclusion plan. I was very actively involved during the [writing] process and since that process."

A dean in the social sciences at a Big Ten institution told me that his university doesn't allow search committees to post a faculty job description until everyone on the committee participates in diversity training: "Every single committee gets this diversity training sponsored by the college." He added that search committees have to repeat the training every year, sharing that he himself had just gone through the training again, as a member of the search committee for an administrative position. The dean articulated that the trainings often differ by school and department—some are more intense and rigorous while other trainings are more surface-level trainings. I asked him if faculty members resent attending the trainings and he offered that he rarely hears complaints as most of them understand the intensity of hours involved in serving on a search committee, and diversity or implicit bias training only adds one extra hour.

A business school dean at a public university in the South shared that he requires implicit bias training for all search committee members. I asked him how the faculty responds to the requirement, knowing that most faculty members are not keen on mandatory anything. He responded with "That's actually a really good question, because we have found in my experience in general, when you mandate something, there's a lot of resistance. But, I think recruiting is important, and people like to be involved in recruiting because they're hiring people that are going to be their colleagues. I feel like if you want to do this job, you better do some training." He added that at his university, there is a universal message that diversity and implicit bias training is important and "something that you need to be thinking about." Likewise, a provost in the Northeast shared excitedly that she sees a link between newly required implicit bias training and her success in hiring a more diverse faculty. She explained that she used to have the diversity representative participate in the implicit bias training, but that individual was later disregarded in committee meetings and not seen as an expert in the field. She now targets the search committee chairs and thinks it "really helps." She noted that the training has put the onus of diversifying the pool and reaching out to a wider audience on the shoulders of the search committee, with no excuses. This past year, she hired twelve new tenure-track faculty members in the College of Arts and Sciences and over half were faculty of color.

A dean at a university that has faced many controversies around racism stated that she is "very proactive" and that her institution "trains every search committee"; she also makes sure "every ad includes inclusive language." Seeing substantial increases in faculty diversity in recent years, she noted that national controversies resulted in the formalization of a lot of approaches and policies that were handled haphazardly in the past. As I talked with this dean, who wasn't at the institution when the controversies surfaced but had been hired afterward, I wondered if significant change can only happen as a result of protest and national controversy? As a historian, I know that throughout the history of higher education, protest on the part of students and others has led to systemic change. For example, one of the reasons why we have Black studies, Latino studies, women's studies, and LGBTQ studies is due to protests, sit-ins, and demands for change by students (Rojas, 2007; Williamson, 1999).

Some AAU institutions take implicit bias training to a higher level, using external or on-campus theater groups to act out scenarios with which faculty grapple. The scenarios might include "how to discuss candidates that come from institutions you're not aware of" or "what to do when letters of recommendation have gender-biased language in them." According to one Ivy League provost who uses this approach, initially these types of trainings were optional, but recently, the institution has made them mandatory for anyone on a search committee. Sometimes when search committees are participating in the theater-based training, the entire department will join in, exposing the whole department to their biases and opening their minds. Likewise, an institution in the South is capitalizing on the talent in their theater department. In the past, they would hire acting troupes from other universities—which several AAU institutions do—but they have recently worked to develop their own troupe. The provost's hope is that the university can "offer to go into departmental faculty meetings or different groups, so that if they can't come, if they won't come to us, we'll just go to them. By seeing it acted out, even individuals who are closed-minded about the notion [of bias], the hope is they'll start getting the sense that well, yeah, there's a better way of doing it than the way that we did it back in the eighties."

A provost at a public midwestern university shared that at his institution, what began as recommended diversity training is now required. He explained that he began with a modest start to the requirement: "The requirement [works] like this; at least one member of each search committee that has been formed must attend a hiring workshop. Each year, committees must send one person and it cannot be the same person that attended last year. And the purpose for that is really to get more and more people trained in thinking about diversity and thinking about identifying bias." He stressed that the trainings present "strategies for blocking bias, or at least identifying it to become conscious about bias. And then [we help them] to work against [bias] and to articulate specific criteria for evaluation rather than implicit criteria." He added that he had to hold two workshops in the past year as an increased number of faculty wanted to attend. Most diversity trainings for faculty hiring at AAU universities are focused on eradicating implicit biases, but they do not focus on expanding the definition of excellence so that diversity is integral to excellence. Diversity trainings miss an opportunity by neglecting to work with faculty to expand their ideas of excellence to include a commitment to and foundation of racial and ethnic diversity.

A vice provost for diversity in the Northeast explained, "I provide three distinct trainings—one for search committee chairs, one for search committee members, and then an open training which is focused on developing a deeper pool of applicants. This year we are going to start requiring [search committee members] to attend the trainings. The trainings include some implicit bias education but not a lot. They are more focused on good search practices. I think the implicit bias trainings are a little overwrought. Implicit bias training is not the end-all, be-all. I think you can train people against bias maybe, or you can put people in front of them that knock the bias out of them, or at least knock it far enough to the side. The negative narratives in the academy around intelligence are so deeply rooted that the only thing that almost ever gets past that is proof in the [presence of a real] person." Being pragmatic, a dean in the Midwest at a public university asserted that his institution requires bias training, and they think about it much like training for Institutional Review Board (IRB) approval. Just as a professor needs to apply for IRB approval and complete various modules and training in order to conduct research with human subjects, those on search committees must undergo training when working with candidates.

When interviewing administrators across the AAU institutions, one institution in the Midwest stood out in terms of their explanation for why they don't require implicit bias training. A dean told me, "We decided explicitly to make [implicit bias training] voluntary, not required. This [idea] came from some of our social scientists, who warned us that if we make it required, it may have negative consequences. Behavioral psychologists were making the point, and I don't know if it's true or not, I'm trusting them—to be careful before you require someone to do something like this sort of training, because unconsciously, [the training] itself can bias people in unexpected ways." As a compromise, her university strongly recommends the trainings but doesn't require them. Although there has been some support for implicit bias training by behavioral psychologists, there have also been critics among this group who don't think this type of training makes a difference or should be required. It seems behavioral psychologists have strong feelings about the subject on all sides (Azar, 2008).[3]

A dean from a midwestern university told me that at her institution, she "strongly encourages but doesn't require [the faculty] to watch a series of videos on implicit bias." And in order to prevent implicit bias from seeping into the interview process, she mentioned that her university has a standard set of questions for every candidate. However, she divulged, "We also recognize [that] the departments feel very strongly sometimes that each individual candidate's content of their work will require different conversations. So that's something I'd say we're still working on, to try to produce the right level of generality of the questions, so that we can hand it to each committee and say this is what you agree to ask the candidates. We also don't want to micromanage them. We really want to say each committee should come up with sets of questions, and we may step in, but I don't think we have the bandwidth to review every single set of questions."

According to a vice provost at a southern university, the faculty hiring system is fraught with long-standing challenges. She shared, "I think the challenges are the same everywhere. The faculty mob is one that has such longevity, we have people here [that] were hired in the seventies and eighties and feel that they can conduct searches the same way as they used to back then, so not open to change, not open to new ideas of what excellence does mean, and how we can move the faculty forward. These individuals don't want to be trained, and they refuse to abide by best practices, and so we're kind of stuck. The problem is . . . when these individuals are the ones that are bringing in the multimillion-dollar [grants], and they're the person in the department that is seen as being somehow most valuable, and so

3. For additional information on the Implicit Association Test, see Greenwald, Banaji, and Nosek (2015) and Oswald et al. (2013).

they end up chairing the search committees. That's a big challenge." She added that the messages are very strong around pedigree, but her institution tries to counter them by offering both online trainings and in-person workshops—although these are not required, they are highly recommended by the provost. Her institution avoids requiring the trainings, as they worry that requirement will backfire. She elaborated, "You know faculty—there are those that really care deeply about hiring diverse faculty, and those who will still today tell you, we want to 'just find the best person,' as if this is somehow separate from diversity. Those who believe will take the training seriously, and those who don't believe will just click and get done with it. I think that that's going to always be true. This is a hard job."

Some AAU administrators boasted high attendance at implicit bias trainings. A provost at a private midwestern university mentioned that the implicit bias trainings that the university offers are well attended and very popular. "We don't have to hassle people to show up for them." He thinks that offering these trainings is important, but stressed that he is not in the business of "telling schools whom to put on a search committee." He added, "I don't get down in the weeds." A vice provost in the South explained that her institution offers implicit bias training at the beginning of the year, but also throughout the year "in recognition that you have to be fluid and respond to people's availability." She added that her institution offers basic training in how to do searches as well as support from the Office of Inclusive Excellence. They have very high attendance, with 100% of committee chairs attending and most search committee members in attendance. Interestingly, she mentioned that her institution takes attendance at implicit bias seminars into account when reviewing offers to candidates: "they have a real incentive to go." Basically, if a search committee presents a slate of candidates or makes a final offer without appearing to have fully vetted the pool, the committee is trusted more if the members attended an implicit bias seminar: "we require [a list of] who has attended in the offer and requests memo from the dean." According to the vice provost, "Implicit bias is not just based on race, gender, sexual orientation, etc. It can be based on all kinds of things that are an illegitimate basis, or just not the basis on which we want to make decisions. If you have criteria, if you ensure that you return and constantly use those criteria to visit and evaluate candidates, it goes a long way." It's important to note that of all the interviews I conducted for this book, this vice provost is the only person to refer to using literature or reading literature to make decisions. She added that she has seen candidates where it's clear that the faculty really liked them, but the committee struggled with how to justify pursuing them, given that on the criteria, other than likability, they just don't rise to the same level."

A vice provost for faculty on the West Coast remarked that he put together a handbook for faculty hiring. The book takes deans through each stage of the hiring process, including "long-range planning, scouting for potential candidates, hiring approval, setting up search committees, and how to give a hiring charge to a hiring committee." He also does trainings for search committees on how to write job ads, how to use assessment rubrics, how to think about implicit bias, how to mitigate against implicit bias, and how to think about your campus allies. In addition, he spends time training search committees on the interviewing process—on campus and during the narrowing phase. And lastly, he includes a section on retention, which is just as important in the hiring process. Although his institution offers a handbook and various trainings, none of the trainings are required. When I asked him about the reaction he received when conducting trainings, he commented "I think people are becoming more and more receptive. My experience has often been [that] the first time I go someplace, [there] are lots of people in the room with their arms crossed. The body language is very clear that they don't want to be there. I think they're often surprised. My approach is not a kind of scolding approach, which I think some people take [as saying], 'You're all terrible people. You don't have any diversity.'" He added, "I think that sometimes, especially in [a] unit that's very homogeneous, some of the STEM fields, but even something like classics, they're kind of braced to be scolded and I don't take that approach. I come in very much that what we're going to talk about is how to run an effective search, an efficient search. If one of your goals is to diversify your faculty, here are things that will help you do that, but the overall big goal is effective and efficient searches, try to be humorous and be funny and [have a] light touch, and not come in with the kind of wagging the finger." When he first started doing trainings, he would come in with a lot of data because people fetishize data—but it puts people on edge when the first thing they see in a training is how terrible they are doing in terms of faculty diversity and hiring. "You haven't hired a person of color in ten years and you haven't promoted anyone. It just puts people on edge, and so I come in with a different approach and it seems to be working."

Seemingly surprised, the vice provost told me, "I have to say, I've had some real converts that have been shocking. I got the math department last year to completely revise the process. [For a math department], it was really the rank of the institution that the candidate was coming from, who was the advisor and what the advisor's letter [says]. That was their way of thinking about candidates. They kept hiring the same people over and over and not having very diverse finalist pools. In working with their dean and their chair . . . it really took a village." He expanded, noting, "We convinced them to rethink their process and to include a diversity statement for a math hire, and they were a little freaked out because they'd never seen one. They don't know what one is." One of the strategies that the vice [provost] used is having the math department chair and the dean support these efforts in separate settings. In his words, "we staged it really purposefully." He added that the math department faculty members were shocked by what they learned. He exclaimed, "They found it really revealing, oh my God, all of these candidates, we've never asked them before, what are your experiences with diversity? Suddenly, people were telling them all about these amazing tutoring programs and summer programs and bridge programs that they had worked on."

Another way that the vice [provost] asked the math department to make changes was to have them do preliminary interviews—in the past they had reviewed four hundred applications and tried to narrow to five people. They would do this by looking at people from Princeton, Johns Hopkins, and other institutions with which they were familiar. The vice provost had to convince the math department to conduct preliminary Skype interviews—and this strategy put a more diverse group of candidates in front of them, but also allowed them to keep their "slam dunk" candidates that made them feel more comfortable. As a result, the math department "brought in the most diverse set of finalists they ever brought in, and then they hired a mathematician of color, which is fairly unusual." He continued, "It wasn't easy, but they're pretty convinced, and now I have them telling other people." When I asked the vice provost if he had a substantial budget to do all of this training, the handbook, and outreach, he emphasized, "I'm a pretty lean operation." He has roughly $50,000 a year to help departments in the area of diversity—a small amount, but if used creatively by a determined leader, it can make a difference. Using strategies like these is a powerful way to make change, but it takes a brave and persistent leader who is willing to push back against those who seek to protect the status quo.

Overall, AAU institutions are inclined to offer some sort of implicit bias or diversity-related training. Provosts and deans are divided on whether or not these trainings should be required for various reasons, mostly related to the stubbornness of old-guard members of faculty who don't like to be told what to do or to be "trained." However, there is a push toward "interrupting" the stubbornness. Perhaps an African American department chair in the South captures it best: "I love implicit bias [training] because as you know, we all have implicit biases, and sometimes people—you need to interrupt the cycle for them to understand what they are doing." She added, as if speaking to Whites, "You keep hiring your kind, your type, and it's not so much they're anti–other people; they just want to be comfortable and to be used to their own kind." Implicit bias training makes the faculty aware of its consistent and pervasive need for sameness—in a majority White academy, that means Whiteness—and comfort at the expense of diversity and opportunity for others (Morgan et al., 2021). Although implicit bias training is essential, it is also vital that we realize that once people are aware of their biases, but continue to act on them, these biases become explicit. Perhaps the bias that upholds sameness in the academy is already explicit, given the way that many faculties fetishize pedigree despite knowing the impact of these actions (Morgan et al., 2021).

Faculty Hiring Handbooks

As mentioned above, some chief diversity officers at AAU institutions have manuals that offer guidance on how to put together a search committee using a diversity and inclusion lens. A law school dean at a midwestern university explained that she tasked a committee with putting together a hiring manual that could be passed on from committee to committee and updated when needed. She felt compelled to create the guide because search committees are made up of different people every year and there is rarely consistency, given the large amount of work that goes into the hiring process: "The document lays out the barriers, landmines, silence, and untruths [that faculty of color face]." This law school dean wants to ensure that committee members are fully aware of the experiences of people of color when navigating the hiring process. From her perspective, to be successful, the individual must be "like a unicorn." Once again, I am reminded of Lauren Rivera's words in *Pedigree* (2015), "Since elites usually set the rules of the game, it is not surprising that in whatever manner merit is defined and measured in society's gatekeeping institutions, elites seem to have more of it" (p. 9). As such, none of the endurance and pain that people of color experience in the PhD program or along the tenure track are acknowledged as skill, talent, or for that matter "grit" as Angela Duckworth (2018) has pointed out in students. In the words of a chief diversity officer from the Northeast who thinks it is vital for search committees to be informed with regard to the experiences of people of color prior to engaging in searches, "How dare you talk about quality . . . for a person to have survived the experience, they are often the most incredible people on the planet."

Given the biases and the hoops that people of color must jump through in the faculty hiring process, having a handbook can be a first step in mitigating challenges. University-written faculty hiring handbooks have statements pertaining to diversity in them. Often these statements are rich in terms of embracing diversity, even though they also maintain a firm distance from asking faculty to challenge systemic racism in hiring. Columbia University offers an extensive handbook—*Guide to Best Practices in Faculty Search and Hiring*, which details all aspects of faculty searches—it reads like a "how to" for search committees. Not only does the document provide guidelines, but it also points the committee members in the direction of resources and data that they can use to bolster the candidate pool and take a more informed and data-based approach to the search. The guidebook calls for a diversity advocate to be appointed to the search committee and stresses the importance of having a search committee chair who is dedicated to diversity and its value. Search committee members are also prompted to ask candidates how they contribute to diversity in the institution, curriculum, and in their research, if applicable (Columbia University Office of the Provost, n.d.)

Michigan State University parlayed resources from its ADVANCE grant into creating a faculty search handbook—*Faculty Search Toolkit: A Resource for Search Committees and Administrators*. Funded by the National Science Foundation, it's no surprise that the underlying message of the handbook is to take a scientific and evidence-based approach to faculty searches and hiring. With that said, the handbook does include sample candidate evaluation forms, specifically focused on the candidates' diversity competency, as well as sample diversity-related interview questions. It also contains an extensive section pertaining to the hiring of White women and people of color (Roehling and Granberry Russell, 2012).

Likewise, Harvard University's *Recruiting for Diversity* (Harvard University, 2013), a guide that is readily available on the institution's website, beautifully speaks to the values of diversity in the introduction, noting, "Not only is diversity recruitment the right thing to do, it is the smart thing to do. . . . Having diverse staff enables us to understand and meet the needs of people from diverse perspectives, and creates an atmosphere that supports positive relationships and communications" (p. 12). Moreover, the guide pushes the reader to understand the deeper ways that diversity enhances environments, claiming, "Different backgrounds and perspectives lead to a variety of ideas, knowledge, and ways of doing things. The converse is often true as well: team members from the same background may take actions based on a narrow range of experiences. By ensuring that your team includes staff from various social and cultural backgrounds, you will widen the range of perspectives, knowledge, and approaches from which decisions are made" (Harvard University, 2013, p. 12). There is no explicit mention of "quality" in this discussion although it seems to be implied. Would it be more powerful if Harvard's guide challenged faculties in terms of their beliefs in what constitutes "quality"? Yes.

Harvard's guide is delicate, and although it asks readers to reflect on their implicit biases, it does so in a way that avoids pushing readers or making them uncomfortable: "We all have certain leanings or preferences—often called biases—and often we are not even aware of them. Focus on uncovering your own biases, so that they won't get in the way of your making the best hiring decisions" (Harvard University, 2013, p. 13). Although soft in tone, Harvard's guide does address some common biases in faculty hiring, asking, "Do you tend to 'tune out' those with foreign or regional accents? Feel uncomfortable around people with disabilities? Make assumptions about graduates of religious schools, Historically Black Colleges, or women's colleges, or scholarship in women's or minority studies?" (Harvard University, 2013, p. 13). The guide even recommends that readers consider taking an Implicit Bias Assessment, which is available to the general public through the Implicit Bias Project on Harvard's website.

Some institutions use the Implicit Bias Assessment prior to engaging in formal implicit bias training.[4] It flashes a series of photos and words at viewers to help them to understand the associations that they have with the words and photos and their implicit biases. The beauty of these assessments is that they can be taken alone in a

---

4. The Implicit Bias Assessment is located at https://implicit.harvard.edu /implicit/takeatest.html. Anyone can take the tests, but participation indicates a willingness to be a part of a larger study on implicit bias.

private setting, and users do not have to undergo the embarrassment that they might feel in a larger training session if biases are revealed.

In addition to various university-specific faculty hiring handbooks that are readily available online, there are two major books pertaining to faculty hiring—Daryl Smith's *Diversity's Promise for Higher Education* (2020) and Caroline Sotello Turner's *Diversifying the Faculty: A Guidebook for Search Committees* (2002); none of the institutions I interviewed assigned these books to search committees. When I was a faculty member at the University of Pennsylvania, I asked one of my deans to purchase Turner's book for all of the faculty search committee members, as it offers very concrete information about diversity in faculty hiring. Although as faculty, we are continually reading to enhance our knowledge in our discipline, we often are unwilling to do the same to enhance our skills in our day-to-day profession. I have found that faculties are intellectually passive, even lazy, when it comes to understanding systemic racism in faculty hiring and how to be more inclusive; they won't seek out materials the way they would in their own research area. As such, I have included a supplementary bibliography of books and articles, focused on the various aspects of faculty hiring and diversity, at the conclusion of this book. Given the vast amount of research in this area, there really aren't any excuses for failing to understand the impact of systemic racism in faculty hiring, our role in it, or our role in dismantling it.

Overall Patterns of Search Committees

Even with extensive training and guidance from provosts and deans, faculty search committees can fall into old patterns without someone overseeing their work. It is essential that these patterns are acknowledged and avoided in order to ensure that equity can be achieved in faculty hiring. A law school dean with whom I talked related, "I asked fellow law school deans who had had some success at their law schools in increasing diversity in a meaningful way on their faculty, I asked them for advice. The advice I was given was that I needed to be heavily involved in the search process throughout, because despite our greatest intentions or in spite of our greatest intentions, the committee is going to default into old patterns, old habits." She added, "I think that this is really key, to keep talking about [diversity] throughout the process so we don't ditch the rails. We might start out really doing well and having a great, diverse pool in the beginning, but then as we get closer, we start going back into our traditional sense of what makes an excellent candidate." Most of those I talked with for this book told me that the larger faculty hiring pools were diverse and that the issues around bias come into play in the final cut of candidates. This result is consistent with what I have seen in the academy for the past twenty years and what I have pushed back against, only to receive anger and defensiveness in return.

Another issue that AAU administrators grapple with are the legal ramifications of faculty hiring—these differ depending upon the public/private nature of the institution and upon the state in which the institution is located. A dean at a private research university in the Northeast explained: "In theory, the way that we were told to think about [faculty diversity] by our lawyer is that essentially it should be color-blind, because what you're doing is you're trying to diversify the pool, but any decisions beyond that, you're not taking race into account, and I think that search committees that are trying to support the idea of diversification have a hard time with that, and I kind of don't think that's where we're at now, but I haven't had any recent conversation with the lawyer about what we can or cannot do." The dean added, "We were told that we can't release self-identifying information about candidates to search committees. That sort of leaves the search committee doing what they had for years, sort of searching for clues in the applications themselves. Oh this person had a diversity grant at some point, things like that, which just seems dumb." This dean feels trapped by the perceived legalities of faculty hiring in her attempts to make change in the regular patterns of search committees, which tend to reproduce sameness in the faculty.

Another story relayed to me points to the stagnant and unchanging nature of faculty search committees. A provost at a southern university told me, humorously, "I know that Moses handed down a couple of tablets that you shall bring three candidates in to interview [for faculty searches]. It's written in some divinely delivered process. So we say, well, what if we brought in five? When you hire someone, even if they don't get tenure, you're talking about a minimum million-dollar investment. Spend an extra couple thousand dollars interviewing five instead of three, and then what we find is that they're much more open to looking at different kinds of candidates." She added, "the first three people they select are the people who they would select, according to the criteria that they've always used that has led to the faculty that looks like what it has always looked like, but then they have a couple more, so it's like well, we could try something a little different, experiment, take a risk. So [the committee] ends up inviting a couple of other people, and then through this process, the diverse candidates kind of rise to the top. They've got a chance to get into the pool, and then they've got a chance to get interviewed, and once they get interviewed, there's not a lot of pressure. They rise to the top in a really wonderful [way]." However, she cautioned, "It doesn't always work. It's not like every faculty member we've hired has been a [White] woman or a person of color."

Unless provosts, chief diversity officers, deans, search committee chairs, and committee members themselves disrupt the patterns of search committees, which often reinforce sameness (i.e., Whiteness), the results of searches will remain the same. At nearly every AAU institution in this study, search committees have profound autonomy and power. They are made up of strong faculty members, and the structures of shared governance—stronger at some institutions than others—provide immense support for search committee decisions and the maintenance of the status quo (i.e., sameness and Whiteness). For example, a dean at a Big Ten institution shared with me that the search committees at his university have considerable autonomy. As dean, he doesn't interfere with the makeup of the search committees, nor does the provost's office. Instead each committee has a faculty excellence advocate to assess the makeup of the committee as being representative of diversity. This advocate is typically a faculty member with equal power on the search committee to the other members. The person is normally tenured, however, not always—which, as mentioned, can be problematic. He noted that as dean, he is quite "passive" in the process and lets the search committee decide on the various roles everyone on the committee will play. Search committees have to weigh the input of the overall faculty and that of the dean. They are under constraints to please various constituents within a school or department. Faculties are the arbiters of who gets through the process, of who gains entry into the academy (Fraser and Hunt, 2011). AAU institutions, and others, can have statements about "inclusive excellence" or their commitment to diversity, but until faculties see diversity—in particular, racial and ethnic diversity—as integral and essential to academic excellence, we will not see major changes in faculty diversity.

7

Should We Require a Diversity Statement?

> People will gravitate toward the scholarly work, their teaching, and their leadership or service. But a diversity statement can convey whether or not [an] individual is going to actually contribute to the diversity that [the] university values and whether they've thought it through.
>
> —AAU UNIVERSITY DEAN

One recent trend aimed at attracting a diverse faculty pool is asking faculty candidates, regardless of their discipline, to write statements on diversity, equity, and inclusion and how they personally contribute to these ideas as part of their application packet. Diversity statements take many forms. There is not a standard approach to crafting a diversity statement, and most institutions requiring them do not give specific guidance to candidates in the faculty job description. According to Karen Kelsky (2014), former associate professor at the University of Illinois and founder of The Professor Is In,[1] a diversity

---

1. The Professor Is In is an academic coaching service. See http://theprofessorsin.com for more information.

statement "can address how you deal with a diverse range of students in the classroom. It can address how you incorporate diversity into your teaching materials and methods. It can also address how your personal background has equipped you to deal with diversity among your students. Beyond teaching, the statement can also discuss how you administratively support diversity among staff and faculty. And it can consider how you address diversity in your own research and writing." Kelsky acknowledges that the process of writing a statement, which is often quite personal, is jarring for some candidates and that they worry about offending people given how subjective the hiring process can be and how sensitive people from all perspectives are about diversity discussions. Any admission of a stumble or discussion of growth and discovery can be misinterpreted in a nation that is anything less than forgiving on all sides of the political and cultural spectrum. And for those search committee members who are vehemently against the use of diversity statements, a candidate's full embrace of diversity could be a detriment to their success.

Tanya Golash-Boza (2016), a professor of sociology at UC-Merced, has offered advice on how to write a diversity statement and provides context for how these statements are often read (or not read) and used by search committees. From the outset, she explains that some "faculty members overtly reject campus efforts to enhance diversity and equity. . . . Just like search committee members who do not care about teaching gloss over teaching statements, those who do not care about diversity gloss over diversity statements." She suggests that faculty job candidates write statements for those people on the committee who do value diversity. Golash-Boza also notes that most universities are just beginning to use diversity statements, are still developing ways to assess the statements, and do not have clear guidelines for submitting statements, making them tricky and ambiguous. Lastly, she cautions faculty candidates who are writing statements to avoid false comparisons, urging them to write about personal experiences and to not make assumptions about the experiences of other groups. This last bit of advice is essential, as diversity statements can be misread and misinterpreted, and diversity as an issue is contentious among various groups and for different reasons. Many faculty members have expertise in other areas—outside of the social sciences—and are not used to writing about themselves and their perspectives on diversity; writing a diversity statement can feel like walking through a landmine.

According to a study conducted by the National Center for Institutional Diversity at the University of Michigan, diversity statements tend to be most effective when the instructions are very specific (Langefeld, 2018). The authors also found that those institutions requiring diversity statements generated hiring pools that were much more diverse, as the requirement of a diversity statement sent a signal that people of color and diversity and inclusion were valued.

Several studies that rely on the same data set, conducted by Schmaling and colleagues (2015; 2019) and Baker and colleagues (2016), found that search committees did not pay as much attention to diversity statements as they did to where candidates received their PhD. Thus, even when institutions went the extra step to require diversity statements, search committees still remained laser focused on pedigree. The authors of these studies recommend that more attention be paid to diversity issues and questions throughout the application and hiring process. They also suggest that administrators make known the importance and value of contributing to diversity efforts and the ability to conceptualize these contributions in a written statement. Unfortunately, efforts to recommend or require the use of diversity statements are not implemented hand-in-hand with efforts to ensure that the faculty understands that academic excellence must include racial and ethnic diversity or it is rendered less than excellent.

Mixed Responses to Diversity Statements

Having candidates submit diversity statements has become quite controversial in recent years. In November of 2018, the former dean of Harvard University's medical school—Jeffrey Flier—tweeted, "As a dean of a major academic institution, I could not have said this. But

I will now. Requiring such [diversity] statements in applications for appointments and promotions is an affront to academic freedom, and diminishes the true value of diversity, equity of inclusion by trivializing it." Flier was responding to an article posted by Robert Shibley, the executive director of the Foundation for Individual Rights in Education (FIRE). Shibley was incensed about many of the University of California schools requiring a diversity statement of faculty candidates, noting that from his perspective, statements like these infringe upon academic freedom and allow campus administrators to "rely on broad, subjective and ideologically-loaded terms to influence hiring decisions" (Flaherty, 2018a). When I saw the tweet, I began paying attention to those who were supporting Flier's comment and those who opposed it. I also downloaded all the tweets—109 pages' worth—to analyze later for this book.

The Twitter response to Flier's tweet was mixed, with many academics supporting Flier and others calling his ideas into question. Paul Bieniasz, a virologist at Rockefeller University offered full support, tweeting, "I completely agree with this. Some of these statements, particularly those required by UC [University of California] schools, appear to be political litmus tests. I will never make such a statement myself and will aggressively oppose their introduction elsewhere." Critics of diversity statements warned of the way they could be used by those on the far left to ask faculty to align to a "very specific leftwing ideology," noting that equity statements "sound good on the outside but are trojan horses for bad policy." These same warnings were also put forth by those advising faculty candidates on how to write diversity statements for their application packets. They wanted to make sure that candidates knew when they were raising red flags and that their words could be misinterpreted (Golash-Boza, 2016; Kelsky, 2014).

Benjamin de Bivort, associate professor of evolutionary biology at Harvard University and a critic of Flier, tweeted "As part of coming to your view that diversity statements trivialize diversity, did you listen to STEM [people of color], [White] women, LGBTQ voices? Because they don't seem to agree with you." And Jim Johnson, a psychologist at the University of British Columbia responded with,

"Well congrats you've got the tiki torch boys[2] all revved up. But I'll bite, how does a statement describing one's efforts towards diversity affect academic freedom? I also had to make statements about my teaching philosophy and research approach for tenure and my freedom survived." He later added that if he were to write a diversity statement, he would "say I'm committed to understanding my own biases and systemic underrepresentation and correcting it. I'd also just simply point to my hiring and mentoring track record, both in academia and industry, and let it speak for itself. Not that hard. I don't see what the fuss is about. I'm happy to be asked tough questions [as] should anyone in leadership." Another psychologist at New York University, Lexi Suppes, tweeted, "I read these statements as asking all faculty to make a commitment to educating every student that walks into your classroom, regardless of background. A university has not only a right but an obligation to expect faculty to adhere to this." Siobhan Cooker, a professor in the medical school at Johns Hopkins University commented, "If an applicant has never thought about what it would be like to teach or work with people who are unlike them, the diversity statement is a great time to start to do that. It will make them a better researcher and quite frankly a better more compassionate person." Many faculty members in the Twitter exchange couldn't understand how a one-page statement impedes upon their academic freedom, noting that these statements aren't any more or less political than teaching and research statements. Confused as to how writing a diversity statement could jeopardize academic freedom, Arya Boudaie, a former graduate student at Brandeis University, tweeted: "It's an affront to academic freedom to ask professors to talk about how they want to promote diversity in their labs and making their labs inclusive, supporting minorities who historically have an awful time in academia?"

2. Tiki torch boys refers to a group of White supremacists who marched through Charlottesville, Virginia, during a Unite the Right rally. They chanted anti-Semitic and racist sentiments meant to threaten people. For more information about the march and the Unite the Right activities, see https://www.splcenter.org/unite-the-right.

In my conversation with Daryl Smith, she added an interesting perspective to the debate around diversity statements. She shared, "The challenge for the diversity statement is [it] could be pro forma, when the point is to bring in people who have capacity to see how diversity is embedded in scholarly work." Smith offered this example: "If you're going to bring an environmental scientist [in], you want to have somebody perhaps who [has] done work in urban toxic lead in the soil or the water crisis in Flint, Michigan, right?" From Smith's perspective, the diversity statement should not be linked to political correctness, and she believes "we've allowed that" to happen. As a result, she has "no doubt that somebody will write a politically correct letter and it [will] be superficial." Based on her research, Smith believes that a diversity statement can be used to express how a faculty member has mentored students in research and in their careers. For example, if you have an NIH grant, what has been your success in mentoring a diverse group of new scholars as part of the grant?

Daryl Smith believes that you have to argue for diversity among the faculty using intellectual approaches rather than *only* talking about community, equity, and justice. These issues are important, but having intellectual rationales for diversity, according to Smith, is essential. She believes that we have to move away from ideological arguments (i.e., diversity is a moral imperative) and toward intellectual ones, especially when discussing faculty hiring, which is "fundamentally about academic excellence." My sense of justice leads me to want institutions to connect these diversity commitments to equity and fostering justice while simultaneously linking to excellence. It is imperative that the definitions and understandings of excellence within AAU institutions (and beyond) are fundamentally linked to racial and ethnic equity or they are rendered anything but excellent.

Diversity Statements at AAU Institutions

Those AAU institutions that have decided to ask that candidates submit diversity statements are doing so because they think these statements will be a good signal to candidates that the institutions care about these things. Many institutions also feel that these statements allow candidates to "speak to some of their background experiences or their research interests," and this opportunity "could make them stand out in a way that they might not" if not given the opportunity. Those I spoke with at AAU institutions were mainly positive with regard to the use of or requirement of diversity statements in hiring packets. A law school dean explained that she just started requiring candidates for faculty positions to include a statement as to how they contribute to diversity, equity, and inclusion, explaining that she had learned about it in a training class on campus. She sees diversity statements becoming more of a standard practice and "a good signal to candidates that we care about these things." The associate dean at the same law school added that the diversity statements give candidates an opportunity to speak to experiences and skills about which they might not otherwise be asked. She also divulged that after securing the initial statements from candidates, the search committees asked candidates to expand or elaborate on their statements during their interviews: "I thought it was a really effective tool. I think it was a good signal to those candidates that we were serious about [diversity], but for us, I think we got some great answers from candidates that we otherwise wouldn't get, [these answers were] able to show some depth of thinking and from candidates that from their scholarship it wasn't obvious that they would have." She added, "I remember we had a candidate who was a law and philosophy contract scholar but had one of the very best answers to that question when it came up in the screening interview, and so I thought that was a really, really effective tool." This law school also asks for input from students in regard to the diversity statement and the depth of the candidates' answers in this area.

Some AAU administrators are still conflicted over the usefulness of diversity statements, and their adoption is recent. A vice provost on the West Coast mentioned that the diversity of the pools on his campus increased when they began requiring candidates to submit a diversity statement with their applications. However, he added, "Now, whether they actually believe [their statement] in their heart of hearts, we can never know." Knowing if candidates are genuine is something that can't be determined until they are hired and have time to demonstrate their commitment through actions. That said, the same is true of what is written in teaching or research statements, which are regularly required of candidates applying for faculty positions. A dean in the Midwest told me that her university is hesitant about implementing a diversity statement, but not because of pushback from White members of faculty. Instead, she noted pushback from some faculty of color. The latter think that diversity statements may "add an extra burden to applicants." She added that we often forget that there is much diversity of thought among people of color—between and among various underrepresented racial and ethnic groups.

I found the words of another provost in the Midwest to be particularly poignant on the topic of diversity statements. He revealed, "We suggest to hiring committees that they [have a] diversity statement. [However], they're scared, and forgive me but they're scared to death, scared as hell for sort of stirring the pot by saying or making a move they're not familiar with, which is how would you evaluate a diversity statement?" He added, "I always suggest the broader, the better. Just give the person a chance to unpack ways that through their research, their teaching, or their community engagement, they advance diversity. I let them talk about it in the span of a page or two, and they may or may not have a direct linkage to diverse communities, but in some way everybody [is] whether you live in an interconnected world [or not], so everybody's doing some kind of work in diverse communities." During our interview, this dean continued to reflect on the requirement of a diversity statement, explaining, "What it does is gives [candidates] a chance to talk about their commitments, and it gives us a chance to project that those commitments matter." He also added that diversity statements don't have to be a deciding factor in hiring; they can be weighed differently from other criteria—they are one factor. "People will gravitate toward the scholarly work, their teaching, and their leadership or service. But a diversity statement can convey whether or not [an] individual is going to actually contribute to the diversity that [the] university values and whether they've thought it through."

What I found interesting about the search committees' fear of evaluating diversity statements is that they evaluate teaching statements on a regular basis with no training as to how to do this properly either, but they don't see it as an issue. The vast majority of faculty members receive no training related to classroom teaching and know very little about how to evaluate the teaching of others. Even those in education schools don't have this kind of training, as there is rarely ever a class on higher education teaching, and it is vastly different from teaching at the K–12 level (Richmond, Boysen, and Gurung, 2016).

As diversity statements become more common, AAU administrators and faculty will need to grapple with how to evaluate them and other aspects of the hiring packet. To date, there are few research studies related to diversity statements and we know little beyond institutional experiences about their impact. A true commitment to diversifying the professoriate necessitates doing the hard work around gathering as much information and data about candidates as possible to make the best decisions with regard to faculty hiring.

8

Exceptions? No! Excuses? Yes!

Whereas if it's somebody that everybody is on board with, there's all these "Oh, they've been doing administrative roles, and that's why they haven't published in the last ten years."

—AAU UNIVERSITY ASSOCIATE PROVOST

I have focused this chapter on exceptions and excuses and how they are used and accepted in the academy across various levels. However, I want to begin with a story that highlights issues of systemic racism in faculty hiring.[1] The story is about exceptions and how easily they are repeatedly—without objection (and thus systemic)—made for White candidates for faculty positions by those who hold positions on the faculty, as deans, and in upper-level administration.[2]

Let me set the stage. An AAU institution advertised a search in the social sciences. The pool that they attracted, being a prestigious institution in a major city, was highly diverse—roughly 40% people of color. When the search committee presented the final slate of

---

1. The story told above is based on actual events.

2. For an interesting quantitative perspective on the law school reproduction of hierarchy, see the study by Katz et al. (2011), "Reproduction of hierarchy? A social network analysis of the American law professoriate."

three candidates to the larger faculty meeting, all three candidates were White, despite having a diverse pool—two White women and one White man. Of interest, the department that was hiring was made up of all White women, so the White man's inclusion in the pool wasn't an issue. However, it is concerning that the committee wanted to bring in two White women candidates to a department that was composed entirely of White women. Upholding White-ness is one of the main manifestations of systemic racism. Noticing this issue, a faculty member asked the search committee about the qualified candidates in the pool and the diversity of those candidates. The committee shared that 25% of the qualified pool was people of color. The concerned faculty member then asked why none of the final candidates were people of color. The search committee chair provided answers, explaining that these were the best can-didates, but also mentioned that there was a fourth candidate—an African American man—who was well qualified, but the school's budget didn't allow the committee to bring in a fourth candidate. The concerned faculty member asked to see the fourth candidate's CV and found that he was on par with the other candidates and, in fact, stronger than some of them by all of the objective measures noted by the committee.

At this point, frustrated, the concerned faculty member said, "This is what systemic racism looks like." When you have a department that is all White women and you aim to hire more White women (without objection from the larger faculty) even though you have highly qualified people of color in the pool—that is the perpetuation of systemic racism. The faculty became uneasy, no one supported the concerned faculty member's viewpoint, and some colleagues wanted the conversation to end. The lack of support and clinging to sameness is, yet again, the manifestation of systemic racism. After the meeting ended, several other faculty members approached the concerned faculty member, offering support. They had been too afraid to speak up during the meeting despite having tenure or in some cases being full professors. Perhaps they were focused on keep-ing their jobs, although tenure provides ample protections in all but a few cases (Whitaker and Grollman, 2018).

Over the course of the next few weeks, the faculty candidates in the search came to visit the campus. Neither the search committee nor the faculty overall was happy with the candidates in terms of their job talk performances and interactions in individual meetings with the faculty. In need of a new faculty member and worried about a failed search, the search committee had a plan. They called their friends at other universities—their known networks—looking for great candidates. Rather than going back to the pool of candidates that had applied, including the African American man, who was fourth on their list of highly qualified candidates, they found another White woman who was the advisee of a famous person at an "elite" university. She wasn't in the pool of faculty candidates nor did she apply for the position, yet they wanted to bring her in for a campus visit. When this idea was brought to the faculty as a whole, the concerned faculty member spoke up again, noting that just a few weeks ago, the school didn't have the budget to bring in the highly qualified African American man (who also did research related to queer and African American men, adding to the intellectual diversity of the department and school). Yet, all of a sudden the budget to bring in another White woman was available. The only answer the search committee provided was that the candidate came highly recommended by her advisor. At that point, the concerned faculty member made it clear that the process was an obvious example of how systemic racism works and urged people to look closely so that they could recognize it in the future. As in the past, no one supported the concerned faculty member during the meeting. Unfortunately, the faculty was willing to uphold a process that had privileged Whiteness in the past and was doing it again now; the department of all White women, once again, failed to engage the highly qualified people of color in the applicant pool and were not held accountable for their actions. The failure of administrative leadership and faculty to hold search committees accountable for engendering processes that reinforce racism is at the core of systemic racism.

In the following weeks, the new faculty candidate visited the campus. When her candidacy was brought before the faculty meeting for discussion, nearly everyone expressed interest in her. She had the right advisor and the right pedigree; she didn't have any publications as she was just finishing her PhD and hadn't completed her dissertation yet. However, people were willing to take a gamble on her because of the national stature of her advisor. Recall Lauren Rivera's description of how pedigree privileges certain candidates and cements systems of discrimination. The faculty voted to make the candidate an offer. Still, there was one issue. According to the bylaws of the university, all faculty candidates had to be discussed twice—at two different faculty meetings, held a month apart. The search committee members were worried that this candidate would be offered another position before the next faculty meeting and that they would lose her. In an interesting twist, the faculty voted to adjourn the meeting and began a new meeting in the same room—a second meeting—so that they could meet the requirements of the university policies. The faculty disregarded the policy of having a month between meetings to give its members time to think about the candidate, further review materials, and ask questions; they moved forward. Once again, the concerned faculty member spoke out in the meeting, noting that this was an example of systemic racism in all of its forms. The issue was not with the particular White woman candidate—these actions on the part of the faculty members were not her fault. The issue was that the faculty was doing anything it could to hire another White woman—including breaking university policy—and overlooking the African American candidate in the original pool completely. Would they have fought for a candidate of color in this same way?

Over the course of twenty years as a faculty member, I have learned that faculties will bend rules, knock down walls, and build bridges to hire those they want to, but when it comes to hiring people of color, they insist on "playing by the rules" and get angry when exceptions are made to accommodate people of color. They sometimes claim reverse racism and discrimination to avoid making exceptions. However, the biggest "secret" in the academy is that exceptions are made regularly for White people; exceptions are the rule in academe. During my time as a professor across several universities, I have seen faculties fight for average candidates, nearly all of whom "deserved" their positions because they were friends with those doing the fighting—the system works for White faculty.

In the balance of this chapter, I will draw upon interviews with those involved in faculty search processes—from deans, provosts, and search committee chairs—to understand the various perspectives on special forms of faculty hiring and to uncover the excuses that uphold systemic racism.

Formal Exceptions

As mentioned, in my experience, exceptions are made for White candidates, but I rarely see them made for candidates of color (DiAngelo, 2018). However, there are those who would argue that I'm wrong, and the evidence that they use is typically to point to target-of-opportunity hires. As mentioned in chapter 6, target-of-opportunity hires are outside of the traditional faculty search process. They are special hires focused on individuals who bring significant value and acclaim to the institution. Although they are often used to recruit faculty of color, they are not used in this way exclusively. Among the AAU administrators I talked with, the most common interpretation is that using a target of opportunity gives the university a chance to hire someone who can bring "unusual preeminence" to the institution. They are also used to "diversify the faculty or curriculum in significant ways." And sometimes this practice is employed "to hire someone who can strengthen or maintain a discipline or field that is key to the institution."

Because target-of-opportunity hires are not nationally advertised, some faculty members object to them. And, because they are often focused on diversifying the faculty, some members disagree with using them as a hiring process. One of the AAU provosts disclosed that she is philosophically opposed to having faculty lines dedicated to hiring diverse candidates. When I asked why, as most provosts I interviewed were supportive of targets of opportunity focused on faculty of color, she responded: "I don't want people thinking about diversity on Tuesdays at 4 p.m.—I want them thinking about diversity all of the time. I don't want them thinking about diversity when they happen to run across someone who's Black or Hispanic or Native American and maybe I can get an extra line out of it. I want them thinking about diversity on every single faculty hire, and I want every single faculty hire that we make to feel that they have earned their place at the institution." She added, "I'm sure there are some people who might be in favor of the fast and special diversity lines, but I feel that if we have these special diversity lines, it devalues their presence at the university. So, did you hire me because, would you have hired me if I wasn't Black? That has the capacity to really undermine the case for diversity." Adding nuance and justification for her views, she told me about conversations she has had with faculty: "I just had a conversation with someone who said to me, 'I don't understand why the provost's office won't do these diversity lines [target-of-opportunity hires]. That used to be the policy before you arrived here, and I feel like my department would be more on board if we didn't have to give up one of our other lines.'" The provost responded, "I know that was the policy prior to my arrival, and let me point out to you that in the ten years prior to my arrival, the net increase of Black faculty on our campus was zero. In the years that I have been here, we've had a 60% increase in Black faculty. So, if you're thinking that the previous approach worked, the data says it didn't." She also expressed, "I have Black faculty who will not allow their students to apply for jobs at universities that have these special lines for diversity hires because their view is, 'We've worked too hard on the quality of our research and to build our reputation for you to go anywhere where you got in [via] a diversity hire as opposed to you got in because you were excellent.'" Given that other AAU administrators told me that they were able to achieve more diversity in hiring by letting committees bring in an "extra diversity candidate," this provost might be onto something—that faculty may consider hiring a person of color as something that they will do as an extra but not as the norm. In effect, traditional search lines are reserved for White candidates. In addition, as I reflect on my conversation with this provost, I'm cognizant that "diversity hires" are often demeaned as not being as good or excellent and as being hired just because of the diversity they bring and not their intellectual assets. These ideas are even internalized by people of color at times.

Cluster Hires

Some institutions use cluster hires to diversify the faculty, which are an aggressive approach to hiring that brings groups of faculty to a department or across a school. This approach to hiring is often quite successful but can also be controversial among those who feel that these hires are circumventing the traditional hiring process. According to those who have had great success with cluster hires, their accomplishments have not happened without "some instances of miscommunication, mistrust, and skepticism" (Freeman, 2019). The logistics of the hiring process for hosting many searches at the same time is difficult and often leads to miscommunication. In addition, the search committees are all happening simultaneously and take considerable effort in terms of faculty time. Sometimes there are objections to cluster hires because it appears that the administration is trying to set "diversity as an explicit goal" when the faculty wants to hire "the best" candidate (Freeman, 2019).

According to Needi Bhalla (2019), a scientist at the University of California–Santa Cruz, cluster hires not only help to diversify an area, but they support retention efforts because faculty of color are not isolated—they are part of a larger community. She also acknowledges the invisible labor often done by faculty of color and states, "Hiring several faculty from underrepresented groups ensures that some of this necessary, invisible labor will be more evenly distributed" (p. 2748). Researchers who have examined cluster hiring warn that it is only effective if there is support from deans and upper-level administration, both in terms of financial support and administrative support, as the processes can be laborious and complicated (Sgoutas-Emch et al., 2016).

One of the AAU institutions that I visited had considerable success by hiring to fill an African Diaspora cluster. From the perspective of the dean, "The big advantage I saw there was that these people were not all going into African and African American studies at our institution." They were being hired in history, sociology, and other areas, adding to the diversity across the institution. Likewise, a provost at a southern university explained that he is a "strong proponent of cluster hires," with another provost in the Midwest agreeing: "I'm a big believer in cluster hires as a strategic way to diversify the faculty." He added that in fields that are inexpensive—such as the humanities—cluster hires are cost effective. However, he mentioned that "if chemistry were to come up to me and say, 'We need to do a cluster hire,' I'd say 'No, we can't afford it.'" From this provost's perspective, funding for labs in the sciences makes it too costly to hire a cluster of individuals at the same time.

A vice provost in the South highly recommends cluster hiring, sharing: "We've been able to bring in faculty with levels of diversity that are unprecedented at [our university] through [cluster hires]." She added that when you have a very diverse search committee— across disciplines, which is a necessity in cluster hires—you have more clarity around what quality is and what excellence is. In her words, "When you allow people to say and to discuss what is the excellence of someone who's in a field [that is] very different from [your field], you really have to define what excellence means. You have fewer preset biases and prejudices of thought, and if you allow diversity, any kind of diversity, if you create search committees that are very broad and have many different perspectives, then that opens [up] everyone to a vision as to who would fit. As we know, it's that notion of who would fit that keeps us from reaching out to diverse candidates." In addition to the outcome of hiring a diverse group of faculty, the cross-department or cross-institutional search committees that are needed in cluster hires can lead to important and long-lasting cross-pollination and learning among faculty.

In states that are under legal decisions that prevent them from using affirmative action, cluster hires have been a successful way of adding diversity to the faculty. As I was talking to a department chair at a university in the South, she revealed that she was hired as a result of affirmative action over twenty-five years ago, noting that her university can't use affirmative action anymore. However, they can talk about diversity broadly—and that kind of talk "salves the wounds of the sensitive." Although the cluster hire is around a topical area, provosts ask for diversity of all kinds in the cluster hire, and this approach has led to additional diversity.

Targets of opportunity and cluster hires are becoming widely recognized and, for the most part, accepted by faculties, with a few outliers. However, other exceptions to policies are more objectionable when it comes to candidates of color, but often seem fine when the candidate is White.

Giving White Candidates a Pass

In this section, I discuss how White candidates are often given a pass when everything doesn't line up on their CV, in their career, or during their on-campus interview, and how excuses are used to justify the failure to hire candidates of color. I want to begin with an experiment put forth by Özlem Sensoy and Robin DiAngelo in a 2017 article in the *Harvard Educational Review*. They suggest engaging in this thought experiment:

> A predominantly White hiring committee with a White person as chair hires a White person. The next hire is a White person. The next hire is a White person. The next hire is a White person. I could go on for years this way, and the people who might raise a red flag are most likely only faculty of color or others working from a critical social justice framework. In fact, one of us taught in a department that went seventeen years without hiring a single person of color. Now imagine that a Black person is chair of the committee, and two or more members are Black. The committee hires a Black person. Most (White) people would raise the red flag right there, but certainly they would do so if the second hire and the third and fourth hires were also Black. But when a red flag is raised on the continual pattern of White hires, justifications often surface, including:

- There just aren't many qualified people of color in this field. People of color who excel usually don't choose to go into education because the pay and status are low.
- We did everything we could to recruit candidates of color, but they just aren't applying. We can't create people who aren't there.
- We needed someone who could hit the ground running.
- Are you saying we shouldn't have our jobs? (p. 573)

As one does this experiment and begins to replace Black with White in these final justifications, it becomes clear to nearly anyone that these justifications are ridiculous and nonsensical excuses for not hiring people of color and that we would not accept them if they were used to justify not hiring Whites.

According to an associate provost and former department chair in the Midwest, "I think there is a stated definition [of quality in hiring] around where you've published, how much you published, how much of an impact [your] work has made. Do we see you cited? Do we see you doing a lot of talks? Do we see you out on the scene, getting a lot of attention for your work? Are the letters of recommendation good? What's the quality of the outlets where you're publishing? What is the quality of the fellowships that you're getting? Those are the benchmarks, but I would say there's an unspoken piece of [hiring] around fit. At the junior level that doesn't come up as much, because we usually don't know who the candidates are, right? But for senior candidates, things like collegiality, things like 'Is this person nice to work with, or going to be a disruptive force?' I have seen that come into play, whether implicitly or explicitly." The associate provost continued to elaborate, noting, "Sometimes when it's implicit, it gets defined as qualifications, and people start attacking qualifications, and that's where it gets dicey. You'll see somebody who has a really solid CV, but then there's this very nitpicky conversation of 'Well they published one of the most influential [articles] in the field, but that was ten years ago. If it was someone who folks really liked, and didn't have any concerns about in terms of 'Is this person going to rock the boat, or hold our feet to the fire a little too much, or just not be the most fun person to be around,' then all of a sudden their qualifications are called into question. Whereas if it's somebody that everybody is on board with, there's all these 'Oh, they've been doing administrative roles, and that's why they haven't published in the last ten years.'" She added, "There are ways that we tell stories where our biases come into play. That's the unspoken messiness that I think comes into play." We tend to give those we know, trust, and like a pass, and given that the academy is overwhelmingly White, White people and Whiteness have an advantage in this system (Morgan et al., 2021; Nietzel, 2021).

A provost in the Midwest shared that with regard to people of color, "It's more about they [the faculty] don't like that individual person, but the way it gets talked about can sometimes be a little problematic, racially. All of a sudden, this person's credentials are not that good, where for the faculty of color in the room, that feels like well, you all are moving the goal posts. These are the credentials that matter in our field and this is what we've all been striving for and this person has that, and all of a sudden you're degrading [their qualifications] again, discounting [them], and it feels problematic to hear that as another faculty member of color, when in fact, it's just that you don't like the person. We wish you would just say that or 'I think she's a jerk' and here's why. That's where it gets kind of weird and dicey." As this provost was talking with me, using analogies about "moving the goal posts," I couldn't help but reflect on Lauren Rivera's caution that those in power (mainly Whites within the academy) make the rules and change them as they see fit to maintain power and control.

In the wise words of Sensoy and DiAngelo (2017), search committees are focused on two ideas—fit and merit (or quality). Drawing on Lopez's (2015) research, they explain that "fit" is the dog whistle of search committees and that faculty use discussions of fit to discuss race without being explicit. They believe that "candidate fit" "means [the committee's] ability to keep White people racially comfortable and their likelihood of leaving Whiteness (or the status quo) undisturbed." They urge everyone involved in hiring to push against discussions of fit, and narrow constructions of merit, and to interrogate them.

Geographical Excuses

Another excuse for not having a diverse faculty that I hear quite often is that because the area surrounding a university is not diverse, it is not possible to recruit a diverse pool of candidates. It is accurate that a university is more likely to attract Latinos, for example, if there is a middle-class Latino population nearby (Ponjuan, 2011). However, as we saw in chapter 2, there are institutions without significant Latino populations nearby that have been successful at attracting Latino candidates (e.g., Johns Hopkins University), and there are institutions that have been less than successful despite a significant population of Latinos in the area (e.g., Rice University). Geography can be a factor, but it's not the only factor, and it should not be used as an excuse. A vice provost at a northeastern university told me when I asked her why her faculty pools were not diverse in terms of race: "Part of the problem is that the region around [us] is not a very diverse region. It's an expensive area and we don't provide housing benefits or anything like that. So we need to make sure that when we bring faculty from [Black and Latino] backgrounds that we try to connect them with the university and try to make sure that they understand that there is a community around. That is a struggle, and the fact that we're not in an urban area is also an issue." She admitted that there have been times when they have lost "amazing candidates" because the institution wouldn't provide funding for housing. What's most telling is the fact that White faculty candidates don't seem to need funds for housing as the faculty candidates of color do. This situation points to the inequities in society—in the funding that various students have when in PhD programs, and the student loan debt that people of color take on to complete their education (Goldrick-Rab, Kelchen, and Houle, 2014; Scott-Clayton and Li, 2016; Steinbaum and Vaghul, 2016). In addition, given the large investment that universities make in tenure-track faculty, it seems shortsighted and disingenuous not to provide supplementary funding to a candidate that brings rich diversity and meets institutional goals. Part of the issue is that the current faculty often sees this kind of support as unequal even though, based on past discrimination, it is equitable and is making up for societal and institutional disparities.

A provost in the Midwest discussed the same geographical issue with me. He stated, "It's not a very diverse city, and although we have a pretty sizable African American population, we don't have a very sizable African American middle class. I've heard many African Americans who are professionals say, well, I chose to leave [this city] because there's no middle class [here] for me. I think that's an interesting and kind of sad challenge, a difficult challenge we have, to recruit people despite that, especially African Americans." As he spoke, I wondered what I wonder every single time someone gives me this reason for low representation of African Americans—what is the university doing about this problem now that you've identified it?

He then moved on to discussing Latinos: "When it comes to Latinx people, we have virtually no community there at all. Our industry fell apart in the late seventies, early eighties, and that was maybe just before the big Latinx influx. There were no jobs. The city was emptying out just when that population was growing. [Our city] has been a little left behind. I was reading the numbers today, some incredibly low number of people who were not born in the United States; only 4% of the population [in our city] is born out of the United States. We have these long-standing ethnic communities, but they're all European—Polish, Irish, Italian, German—and so it's challenging to attract minorities. They don't see themselves so much in this city." I wondered how he knew that Latinos don't see themselves in the city. Had the university conducted a research study, focus group interviews, or a landscape analysis? I also wondered why Latinos were being viewed as "not born in the United States."

Excuses and resistance to revising or rethinking policies are common in the academy. I want to end this chapter with a short story that highlights how resistance to making changes to achieve equity reinforces the status quo. A couple years ago, I visited a university to talk about faculty diversity in hiring. Over the course of two days, I gave three talks and I met with various campus administrators—in one-on-one meetings and over meals. I could tell that most of the people I met with were truly interested in revising the institution's process and making change on campus. They thought they would become a stronger institution as a result.

On the final day of my visit, I gave a talk that was focused on myths surrounding faculty hiring for the center for teaching and learning. My host had told me that the university had a particularly hard time attracting Black women—which seemed very odd to me given that the university was located in a predominantly Black city with a robust Black middle class and was near other universities with substantial Black student bodies and relatively diverse faculties. Over the years, I had heard countless Black academics and professionals talk about longing to live in this particular location. During my talk, I showed some pipeline data in an effort to break down myths around various disciplinary pathways to the professoriate. As I was speaking, I saw three White men in the back of the room whispering. During the question period of my talk, one of the men raised his hand and said, "The reason why we can't attract Black women is that we can't afford them. They are made offers by other institutions that are much higher than we can afford." Given what I know about faculty salaries and the mythical bidding wars for people of color, I knew that there was more to this story (Smith, Wolf, et al., 1996). As a solution, I suggested that the team of White men, who were all from the same science-focused department, offer the Black women higher salaries in order to matriculate them. They immediately pushed back at me, saying, "That's not fair. If we did that, these Black women would be making more than many other people in the department." I then said, "We aren't aiming for fairness, we are aiming for equity, and equity means that you need to make up for past inequities by offering a higher salary. If you truly want to attract more Black women and you think the problem is salaries, you have to offer them more money to achieve your goal."

When I talk at various universities across the country, the administration and faculty often tell me that everyone is fighting over one or two people of color, and this makes it impossible for them to matriculate candidates. I wonder what would happen if search committees expanded their interests to a greater number of candidates. Many institutions and even prestigious institutions promote the notion that there are bidding wars—a notion that endorses the idea that people of color are chosen over White men. These "ordinary institutions" believe that they don't have the resources to attract the small number of candidates who are in high demand by the prestigious institutions (Smith, Turner, et al., 2004). Faculty will often give the excuse that all of the top candidates of color for positions secure jobs and are fought over for positions at the top institutions. However, according to Smith, Wolf, Wolf-Wendel, and Busenberg (1996), in a study that followed the careers of nearly four hundred men and women, including people of color who had received prestigious fellowships from the Ford, Mellon, and Spencer Foundations, even those PhD candidates at the most prestigious institutions were rarely recruited. Only 11% of the PhDs of color were recruited. The study showed that White women and people of color with PhDs did not experience any advantage in the job search and in securing a job.

I have found that you can often discover how much someone or an institution cares about an issue by following the money. I have also noticed that we are good at identifying the problem but not as good at solving it. When I finished my response about paying Black women more to attract them to campus, the three men scoffed at me and proceeded to talk over me until the session was finished. To the contrary, the few Black women in the room just smiled and nodded their heads. We invest in what we value. As I recall this incident, I am again reminded of Daryl Smith's comment about exercise. She knows she needs to do it and it's good for her, but she often can't compel herself to get up off the couch in the later afternoon to do exercise. Again, we say we want to diversify the faculty, but actually doing the work to make diversification happen is where colleges and universities get stuck. Only with leaders who put words into action will we change the status quo in higher education. Moreover, although I appreciate Smith's analogy pertaining to exercise, given what I have learned about pedigree from Lauren Rivera and from the interviews I conducted, I wonder if not doing anything to make change (or doing very little) in the area of faculty diversity (not exercising) is really Whites maintaining the power and reinforcing Whiteness. I want to be optimistic, but what I know is that if I really want something, I work hard to get it.

9

Dismantling and Reforming the System

A CALL TO ACTION

> You know, the old system, it got me a job, so I'm not going to complain about it a lot, but you know, the right advisor calling the right people and recommending you for a position, . . . today, that's just not sustainable.
> —AAU UNIVERSITY VICE PROVOST

If we truly want a diverse faculty, we have to approach the faculty hiring process in a much more thoughtful and informed way than we currently do. We can't continue to reproduce the status quo, and we have to be brave enough to push back against our colleagues who are dead set on maintaining the academy as it is—that is maintaining a commitment to sameness and Whiteness being the norm. It is essential that current faculty members think more deeply about their role in recruiting and hiring faculty and their role in maintaining the status quo. In this final chapter, I will offer a call to action with tangible recommendations, based on examples from across the spectrum of colleges and universities and on my research within the AAU context.

At the crux of making systemic change in higher education is a need for a belief among faculties that having a diverse faculty strengthens the curriculum, bolsters the academic environment in their department and school, enriches the overall institution, and is the foundation of academic excellence. Getting to this belief is a challenge. A law school dean in the Midwest acknowledged to me that conversations around diversity are very difficult. In her words, "I think a challenge that we face is that on my faculty, not only is there no consensus that diversity is an appropriate goal, but there are a number of people who think that any discussion of race is actually in violation of the law, so that any sort of conscious effort to say we want to have a more diverse pool or we want to hire this person is in part because we want to diversify our faculty, so just the prioritization of diversity as a goal is quite contentious." Even greater systemic change can take place if the faculty embraces equity. However, embracing equity means that sometimes seismic shifts need to take place, and these often make people uncomfortable as they feel that they will lose something if others gain. Yes, you may lose some advantages, but perhaps you had more than your share.

As Lauren Rivera tells us, those who design hiring systems are the same people who benefit from them. Being more egalitarian and including more and diverse voices in faculty hiring means that those who benefit may change, and policies, conversations, and values may change within an institution (Griffin, 2020). Not everyone is comfortable with this type of change, and faculties often hide behind shared governance and academic freedom to uphold the status quo that benefits them. Although embracing diversity and pursuing equity are essential goals for systemic change in higher education, they are slow coming in reality. As such, I present detailed strategies that help to reform the current system even in the midst of human obstacles—those holding tightly to the status quo and attempting to maintain a system that privileges Whiteness.

Action: Leaders Must Lead

A strong and consistent message from leadership at all levels is essential to dismantling systemic racism and hiring a diverse faculty. It is important that presidents, provosts, deans, department chairs, and search committee chairs all communicate the same messages about the institution's commitment to hiring and retaining a diverse faculty and how this diversity is central to academic excellence. Institutions have mastered the art of issuing statements on their websites, including a commitment to diversity in their strategic plans, and talking about this commitment in sound bites. However, a message in every setting that permeates the campus environment, policies that hold the faculty accountable for its faculty hiring practices, and equity-oriented action is what is needed. Moreover, leaders must express a firm acknowledgment of systemic racism, the impact of racial micro-aggressions, and the presence of both implicit and explicit bias on campus, and they must act to address all of these issues.

Often when people enter a leadership role, they have both concrete and visionary ideas for how to make changes. Yet, they quickly digress, often saying very little in an effort to avoid upsetting various constituencies. I understand the desire to stay above the fray, especially in the current climate in which leaders are attacked from all directions, even those that generated excitement upon their selection for the leadership role. However, being a leader and taking on a leadership role means that you have to make hard decisions and be open to criticism around those decisions. If leaders stand firm in their well-thought-out decisions and beliefs, most critics move on after a short time. The most ineffective and disappointing academic leaders are those that spew out policy-speak and say nothing due to their fear of not being liked or not being rewarded personally.

As I talked with provosts and deans, they would often make excuses for faculty members—"they just don't know, as diversity is not something they have disciplinary expertise on." Having interacted with faculties across the nation in all types of colleges and universities, I know two things: (1) When they want to know about something that is of value to them, they will investigate it, read about it, and hone their skills. (2) They know very little about hiring a diverse faculty and the experiences of faculty of color because they choose not to. I think leaders have allowed faculties to be intellectually passive—even lazy—around issues of racism, equity, and diversity. Yes, faculty roles focus on research, service, and teaching, but issues of diversity, equity, and race permeate all of these areas. Even when faculty members don't conduct research with any connection to race, equity, or diversity, these issues still play a role as to whom they work with, whom they offer opportunities to, and who has the chance to become their colleague. As our nation's classrooms become more diverse, it is important that faculties know how to engage an ever-changing classroom and a more diverse set of colleagues (Conrad and Gasman, 2015).

Action: Work to Dismantle and Reconstruct Search Processes

As Lauren Rivera reminds us, hiring processes benefit those who designed them and those for whom they were designed. In colleges and universities, by and large, these processes were designed more than fifty years ago for White men. If an institution continues to have mediocre results in terms of hiring faculty of color, it is time to redesign the faculty search process. One of the best ways to tackle an out-of-date and inherently biased faculty hiring process is to use an outside consultant from a similar institution that has a substantial track record for recruiting faculty of color. A provost in the Midwest told me: "The only way you can succeed is if you add things to the process that enhance the chance that you won't get the people that the process was basically designed fifty years ago to get, and also send a message to the people who are being recruited that yes, these processes have been unfair to people who look like you for fifty years, but we're changing it. The extra effort that we're putting into this is showing you that this is a fair process that you can trust. And it makes sense that people of color wouldn't trust these processes because these processes have been producing White male faculty members for fifty years or more, depending on how long we've been doing this kind of thing. We try to add a whole bunch of stuff, so that people who are of different identities trust us and trust the process and feel like they have a fair chance to compete, and that they're not going to be just taken all the way to the end so that we can say, we had a finalist who was an African American or Latino." I was struck by the candidness of this provost, as he was much more open and transparent than many with whom I spoke. I asked him when he realized that these hiring systems weren't designed for people of color or White women and that they put these groups at a disadvantage. His reply was just as candid as the rest of our conversation: "The chancellor told me he wanted me to work on this [issue]. You know, that's when it dawns on you kind of how this whole thing works. It's tough, I guess, for some people to acknowledge it, because they don't want to think about the fact that they had an advantage when they went through [the process]. I'm completely comfortable with that. I definitely had an advantage when I went through [the hiring process]. They probably also don't want to face up to the fact that they've been part of a system that hasn't been fair to everyone. But these are the transitions that we need White allies to go through, if we're going to do anything about all this, so we've contributed to it. Not everybody is comfortable saying that. I keep telling my friends it's liberating to get there on this, but it's hard for some people." In order to change the hiring process, it needs to be designed by a broad spectrum of individuals across various aspects of diversity; shared governance and faculty input must be central to the change process. However, all those involved in the process must be open to change and to the possibility that the system has a different impact on different people, depending on a variety of identities, including race, ethnicity, gender, sexuality, and religion.

As I discussed overhauling hiring processes with provosts and deans, those who were engaging in these processes were doing so at many levels and were also including the curriculum and co-curriculum as areas for change. They are often making these large-scale changes as a result of uprisings, sit-ins, and protests on their campuses during which students demanded change. According to one dean of a northeastern university, "There was a great deal of concern by the students with the slow movement in terms of making our faculty look representative. I think our student body [is diverse], both with our domestic students and overall, but we did not look so good in terms of our . . . faculty." Likewise, a provost from a private research university in the Northeast communicated that when protests erupted on her campus, the faculty members were very supportive of students. However, she wanted them to go further than merely offering support, asking them to make "their own commitment of activities that they were going to undertake and to post them publicly. That generated department and program discussions about, and self-examination about, what they were doing and how they were doing it and how they were thinking [in terms of faculty hiring]." She added, "I think [it] also helped contribute to a reexamination of whether or not our rhetoric on how open and inclusive we were [across various areas] was actually matched by the reality on the ground. That triggered a lot of soul searching, which I then think some of these other things that we've been doing on hiring and training, it's been easier to do [then] because of that earlier work."

Another strategy for changing status quo search processes is to identify similar institutions that have had more success and seek out their advice, learning from them and perhaps building networks that better inform faculty hiring. Once strategies that work are identified, these can be applied and implemented with faculty input. Far too often, administrators know there is a problem or work to identify a problem but once it's known, the problem is not acted upon. As Daryl Smith reminds us, it's one thing to understand that your body needs exercise, but it is completely different to actually exercise. I would go as far as saying that it's negligent to know that a problem exists—in this case, systemic racism in faculty hiring—and fail to work to solve it in serious and meaningful ways.

A strategy that can help in terms of rethinking the faculty hiring process is to examine the placement of people of color across various faculty roles both in the school and at the department level. Ask the following questions: Where are faculty of color located? At the assistant, associate, or full professor level? Where do they cluster? Do faculty of color tend to be in lecturer positions? Are they hired mainly as adjuncts? Depending on the answers, what is the institution going to do to rectify the inequities? If these types of questions are asked regularly and the answers are required before searches move forward, it is less likely that the effects of systemic racism will persist.

At the same time as requiring that deans and department chairs look closely at the positioning of faculty, it is also advantageous for faculty overall, search committee chairs, and search committees to meet with the chief diversity officer of the university. There will be pushback, as some search committee chairs and members will think they already know how to do the work of faculty hiring, and others might feel that they are prepared due to "their own experiences of marginalization" in other areas. However, anything that can add to the faculty learning process around faculty hiring is advantageous and important, and it is imperative to a system of faculty governance that centers equity and justice for all. Moreover, it is essential that faculty members know that they are being held accountable for hiring a diverse faculty.

Action: Question Definitions of Quality

One of the most important things that we can do is to have the courage to challenge colleagues when they bring up the word "quality" during discussions related to diversifying the faculty. An immediate assumption that quality will suffer with an increase in diversity is racist at its core, and we must be steadfast in making sure colleagues know that these types of conversations are unwelcome. Diversity increases quality rather than decreases it. In particular, search committees need to keep in mind how candidates rise to the top of a search pool. Is their ascension a result of their research and teaching qualifications or a result of whom they know? Of note, search committees need to recognize that CVs are not neutral data sources. They are a product of whom candidates know—of their social capital. Likewise, search committees should consider the time involved in doing research depending on the type of research, not merely the outputs. Moreover, it is important to remember that just because candidates of color (or anyone, for that matter) might do diversity work, it doesn't mean they can't be generalists in a field as well. We should consider that being able to educate and serve a diverse nation is vital to any faculty member in the twenty-first century. Part of being a high-quality candidate for a faculty position includes not only having content expertise, but also being able to communicate that expertise to a myriad of students from different backgrounds. It means situating one's content expertise in the larger history and context of one's field.

When discussing quality, it is also important that search committees acknowledge that we have consistently moved the bar in regard to issues of quality—making it more difficult for people of color to succeed. And as Lauren Rivera reminds us, since elites and those with power usually determine the rules of the game, it is not shocking that in whatever manner merit is defined, discussed, and measured in institutions, elites have more of it and more access to it. Moreover, when they notice that others are gaining more access to opportunity, they will often change the rules of the game. People of color will have more opportunity if we work to expand the definition of quality to be more inclusive and base this expansion on empirical data and not on intuition and connections.

One of the most effective ways to expand the definition of quality is to push back against faculty members' efforts to limit recruitment to a predetermined list of institutions from which candidates can hail. It's important to discuss the results of this practice and the limits it puts on faculty diversity, given the access that most people of color have to these types of universities. Remember how few African Americans are admitted to AAU PhD programs, for example. Across research universities, we should be asking, "What happens if we step away from this practice of only hiring from a small group of institutions? Of only hiring from AAU institutions? What do we gain? Do we lose anything? What new ideas will surface? How does the institutional environment change? What will be the impact of upsetting the status quo in this way? Will we achieve more equity by being more inclusive of various types of institutions? Having this conversation will lead to more inclusivity and a broader, not less rigorous, definition of quality. And, yes, there will be profound resistance to the idea of broadening the definition of quality, but if colleges and universities truly care about the diversity and equity that they discuss in statements, it is essential that proclamations and definitions of excellence have racial and ethnic diversity at their core. Lastly, when our definitions of quality are narrow and based on whom one knows, we limit our possibilities by keeping people out who could possess some of the most novel and innovative ideas.

Action: Require Training for Search Committees

Unfortunately, a faculty member can be a premier biologist or anthropologist yet at the same time may have no experience serving on a search committee and no understanding of diversity and equity issues as they pertain to faculty hiring (and beyond). In order to achieve racial equity in higher education, faculties need to understand racism, bias, institutional policies, and the importance of expanding the definition of quality to pursue diversity and equity and placing this pursuit at the core of their institution's understanding of excellence. This type of work requires training. Although implicit bias training is controversial and not a panacea for racist behavior and racial biases, it does have an impact on faculty and gives them an opportunity to reflect on their personal biases even if they are not willing to discuss these publicly. Given how sensitive and private people are about prejudices and biases, we may never know the impact of implicit bias work. Thus, one of the most effective strategies is to use Implicit Association Tests, as they are private (beyond anonymous participation in a research study) and personal, and cover a range of topics. These assessments also give participants immediate personal feedback on their implicit biases and time to reflect.

In my experience, implicit bias training can be volatile and deeply controversial in many ways. Yes, there are those faculty members that don't want to participate and will be resistant. However, there are also faculty members who typically support hiring faculty of color but might not like the way the implicit bias training is presented. It is best to have an outside group conduct the trainings, or someone from the chief diversity officer's staff instead of faculty colleagues. And using empirical data as a foundation for the training helps to convince skeptical faculty of the need for the training. Based on twenty years of being a faculty member, the one thing I know about presenting in front of the faculty or facilitating a workshop with faculty members is that if they don't think the information applies to them or is valuable, they will work to disrupt or dismantle the entire session. In order to counter this disruption, it is important to have enough supporters in the room who will speak out about the importance of the material being presented. When implementing implicit bias training, it is vital to do the preliminary work to gain support on the ground for it in advance of the training.

Action: Rethink Search Committees

As we have learned, search committees are different, depending on the institution. Some universities are quite purposeful in choosing who participates and how committees operate. Others merely let the search committees form and leave them on their own to conduct their work. In order to make long-lasting change and move closer to hiring a more diverse faculty, oversight and intervention need to take place. Best practices include ensuring that search committee chairs or the entire search committee meets with the chief diversity officer to better understand expectations for the search and the institution's commitment to hiring a diverse faculty.

In order to avoid overburdening faculty members of color, it is important to identify and recruit White allies who are willing to serve on search committees and advocate for equity in the faculty hiring process. Of the utmost importance is having a search committee chair who is committed to racial equity and diversity. This chair must have power and influence in order to be able to negotiate with members of the committee who are not supportive of faculty diversity. The chair must also be willing to stand firm against the power structures that protect the status quo.

So as to be more equitable, it is important that search committees begin their work with an ethos of being more inclusive rather than more exclusive. Colleges and universities pride themselves on who they keep out—bragging about their selectivity—while diversity and equity is tied to whom we let in and how we welcome new voices to the academy. When engaging candidates, questions from the search committee should be tied to inclusivity rather than exclusivity.

Some of the most effective and successful search committees are those that have a diversity representative on them who is a tenured, associate, or full professor. These representatives, if they are willing to speak up, have the power and authority to ensure that search committees stay true to their stated mission of hiring a diverse faculty and promoting equity. Oftentimes, the disconnect between a diverse final list of candidates and the replication of the status quo is the voice of a strong advocate for equity.

Action: Promote Learning in the Hiring Process

If colleges and universities are truly serious about increasing faculty diversity, why don't they visit institutions that have achieved success and ask them how they recruit a diverse faculty? Consider the diversity on the faculty of Historically Black Colleges and Universities, which boast some of the most diverse faculties in the nation: 56.3% Black, 2.4% Hispanic, 0.5% Native American, 9.5% Asian American, 0.2% Pacific Islander, 22% White (the remaining percentage includes people of two or more races). Or perhaps colleges and universities should consider talking with those at Hispanic Serving Institutions, which have faculties that on average are 5.3% Black, 18.4% Hispanic, 0.6% Native American, 9.7% Asian American, 0.2% Pacific Islander, 60% White (the rest claim two or more races) (Esmieu, 2018). In this country, we have many colleges and universities with significant diversity among the faculty, but all too often, we fail to seek advice from institutions that have the most success and the most experience.

Making data available on institutional faculty diversity is also important and leads to better transparency across the university. A provost at a private mid-Atlantic university shared with me that public visibility of data on diversity is vital. At his institution, "everyone sees the report"—the board of trustees, deans, and faculty. He noted that "the deans take the report seriously. They go back to their departments. Talk about the reports with them. I think that serves as the internal kind of mirror, holding up the mirror to ourselves." He added, and I think this is key in the quest for faculty diversity, "I think about [our transparency and process] in terms of outcomes and sustained outcomes. It's very easy to hide behind process or inputs. But the bigger question is, did it move the needle?"

Action: Confront Excuses

One of the most effective methods of ensuring equity is to confront and push back against the typical excuses that derail candidates of color. Some AAU deans have a running list of common excuses and point them out when they are used. The most common excuses focus on search committees assuming how candidates will behave in terms of whether they will take a job based on location and whether the institution can meet the salary requirements, given their belief that the candidates are being pursued by many institutions in a bidding war.

JoAnn Moody, the author of *Faculty Diversity: Removing the Barriers* (2012), calls assuming how candidates will behave an extraneous assumption. Faculty members assume that candidates of color won't come to their institutions without ever contacting them. An administrator at a private research institution in the Northeast explained, "faculty will say [even though] we are in a large city, 'Brown people aren't going to come here. Our data show that.'" But in reality, "the data tell us that when we make an offer to Brown people, [they] will come." "One of the things that I think we're beginning to understand, a lot of it, or at least some piece of it is, can [members] of an underrepresented group see themselves at your institution? And having an invitation to apply to [an] institution is going to help them to be able to see themselves at your institution." There is a myth that the slow progress in terms of diversity in faculty hiring is due to factors in the candidates themselves (Fraser and Hunt, 2011; Smith, Wolf, et al., 1996). We must reject this myth.

When I talked with Daryl Smith, she relayed to me that deans, department chairs, and provosts have told her many times that one of the reasons that they can't attract a more diverse faculty is that they can't afford to pay them the high salaries that they command. Many senior administrators often say, "They won't come here, we can't afford them, and they won't stay." As a result, there is an unwillingness to invest in faculty diversity in serious ways across colleges and universities. Based on her research, Smith found that these "statements [are] deeply held beliefs and myths." She also noted that having worked in diverse communities of color and with a rich diversity of scholars, "I didn't observe the phone ringing off the hook for most of them. So if you're Cornell West, the phone will ring off the hook. But by and large, really good people that I know had to work hard to find a job, and in the fields with the least diversity (e.g. science), there are more people taking positions outside [the academy] because they couldn't find faculty positions."

Interestingly, one of the Big Ten deans with whom I spoke told me exactly what Smith expressed. He emphasized, "I think the competition is so much fiercer now. That's the biggest thing. That's frankly the most difficult thing that we're dealing with, it's not even so much the hiring, it's the retention of underrepresented [faculty], because the salaries, the salary differentials are becoming problematic. I handle the retentions so when we're trying to hire, we're trying to poach, for example, somebody from another institution, another Big Ten school. The salary differentials for underrepresented minorities, particularly African Americans, [the situation is] moving beyond the level that we can justify without causing all kinds of other problems within the departments." He also worries that the salary differentials in his departments will soon become tied to something other than productivity [inferring someone's race] and that's the big [issue]. He is likewise concerned that his institution will not be able to continue to fight off poaching institutions that have larger endowments, while at the same time, he doesn't have the funds to poach faculty from the middle-tier institutions.

Smith's research revealed that, in many leaders' minds, everybody is "getting a million job offers that [their institution] could never compete with." As a result of listening to leaders across the country, she decided to construct a research study around individuals who had received prestigious national fellowships. She identified three hundred people of color and interviewed all of them, eventually finding that these people "were not getting ten job offers" as many administrators had thought. They were getting far fewer than ten, and if they were in math and science, they had even less opportunity. Among many of the AAU institutions, there was a sense that the reason that they were unsuccessful in recruiting a diverse faculty is because these candidates had so many options and thus chose their competitors over them. However, this presumption is rarely the case. Sometimes institutions claimed that they couldn't meet salary requirements; in the sciences, institutions claimed that they couldn't meet the start-up package requirements. Oddly, White faculty recruited to these same universities seemed to be willing to "settle" for the lower salaries and the lower start-up packages. Some AAU administrators with whom I talked tackled concerns from deans and search committee chairs about not being able to meet salary requirements by presenting data on faculty salaries across the campus and from peer institutions. These data show that high salaries among people of color are aberrations and not the norm; for example, within public universities, we see tiny increases that are statistically insignificant for Black and Latino faculty at the most selective, highest-ranked institutions and with the greatest productivity (Li and Koedel, 2017; Eagan and Garvey, 2016; O'Meara et al., 2017; Ordway, 2017). In fact, according to a 2017 national study, spanning six disciplines and focused on selective public universities, White men continue to have the highest salaries among faculty, and Black and Latino faculty have the lowest salaries, earning between $10,000 and 15,000 less depending on the discipline. Of note, "the unconditional gender gap is larger at just over $23,000" (Li and Koedel, 2017, p. 348).

Action: Rethink Recruitment Processes

One of the impediments to hiring a diverse faculty is that search committees don't spend time thinking through searches before posting them or bringing in candidates. All too often, departments are very eager to hire new faculty to fill workload needs, and thus they want to move forward without time for reflection on what they are looking for in a faculty colleague to complement their strengths and patch their weaknesses. In order to make a serious effort to hire a diverse faculty, deans and search committees need to ask themselves some important questions. These include (Harvard University, 2013): What are the department or school's current strengths with regard to diversity across the faculty and curriculum? How can new faculty hires build upon current strengths and complement them? What kind of diversity related challenges does the department or school face?

In addition to questions pertaining to the overall tenor of the school and departments, there are questions that should be asked pertaining to creating a diverse applicant pool. For example, when thinking about recruiting, think about the following questions (Harvard University, 2013): Which racial and ethnic groups do we tend to fail to attract to the faculty applicant pool? How and where might we find them? Whom can we contact to recommend strong faculty candidates who will advance diversity in research and teaching? What strategies can we use to reach out to colleagues and candidates from demographically diverse institutions?

Before reviewing candidates in the applicant pool, it is essential that the search committee ask some questions. These questions are focused on being more inclusive rather than exclusive, and this focus makes a fundamental difference (Harvard University, 2013). Does the pool of applicants mirror the nationally available pool of recent PhD graduates from underrepresented racial and ethnic groups? If not, how can we reach those applicants that we have missed? What criteria will be used to screen candidates? Are these criteria equitable? Have we allotted enough time to discuss each applicant in full? How will we determine which candidates are qualified for the position? Should the search deadline be extended to accommodate a more diverse pool? What criteria will lead to a rejection?

Once candidates have been reviewed, there are more questions that search committees can ask. These questions include (Harvard University, 2013): How did we determine which candidates to include and exclude? Are we making assumptions or speculating about candidates in ways that are exclusionary? Were decisions fact-based? Does the list of final candidates have people of color on it? If the overall candidate pool was diverse, why isn't the final list of candidates diverse? How do the gender, racial, and ethnic demographics of the search committee's shortlist of candidates compare with the overall pool of qualified candidates, and with the national pool of recent PhD graduates? What criteria did we use to eliminate candidates of color? Should we review the candidates a second time to be more inclusive?

Areas that are ripe for enhancing the diversity of the applicant pool and providing more opportunity to candidates are the adjunct and part-time faculty ranks (Springer, 2006). These faculty members are typically overlooked when search committees are conducting searches; yet, the adjunct ranks are often filled with people of color who have not been able to secure tenure-track faculty positions. According to a study conducted by TIAA, 58.2% of people of color holding faculty positions are part-time adjuncts, and 17.1% are full-time non-tenure-track faculty (Finkelstein and Conley, 2019). We must ask ourselves why so many people of color with high-quality degrees are relegated to part-time and non-tenure-track jobs.

Another area that is rich with potential faculty candidates is the postdoctoral ranks across disciplines at research universities. During my discussions with the AAU administrators, a provost shared that her institution has several pre-faculty programs that are focused on bringing in a diverse group of postdocs and that these programs make an attempt to bring in scholars from institutions outside of the top echelon of research universities. However, she also made it clear that these programs are not an "automatic pathway into an Assistant Professorship." Likewise, according to a dean of a Big Ten university, "We've created a postdoc program to allow faculty with diverse backgrounds and maybe academic credentials that might not otherwise meet the standard for what we would expect at Big Ten institutions, for whatever reason, but also people we think had a lot of promise. So we created this postdoc program, which gives them two years of time off the tenure clock, with the expectation that if their productivity and progress along that path are good, they'll be transitioned to the tenure system at the end of the two years." He added that they hired four of these postdocs last year. In essence, these postdocs have an eight-year "clock" to tenure instead of six, and the university is making a substantial investment in them. The dean speaking with me about his program noted that over 150 applicants applied for four spots. In his words, "We're optimistic. . . . I was shocked." Although this program has led to more inclusion, I remain concerned that some AAU administrators see those faculty candidates from underrepresented backgrounds as less than prepared.

Because research tells us that many postdocs, especially those outside the sciences and those focused on diversity, are not hired for tenure-track positions at the institution where they are postdocs, I asked the dean what makes the difference at his university. He thinks the difference is that the postdocs are linked to a dean's office rather than a particular department. The postdocs are centralized and highly interdisciplinary, allowing people to get to know them outside of one department. Unfortunately, postdocs are often overlooked and not taken seriously as candidates. It is vital that these valuable members of the academic community be treated with respect. I have witnessed, on several occasions, the abuse of postdocs inside and outside of the science-related fields. Postdocs live in the midst of other academics and are privy to ongoing faculty searches. If a search is happening and there are postdocs within the department or school that apply for the position, it is important to take care with them and to be honest if they are not going to be seriously considered for open positions. I have seen abuse of postdocs of color in the form of leading them on with regard to their consideration for faculty positions, only to have them endure the entire search in real time knowing that they were led on and not taken seriously as candidates.

In order to change recruiting success and engage a more diverse candidate pool, search committees must be intentional about job descriptions, working to make them broad, inclusive, and targeted for the specific skill set that candidates need. Moreover, it is helpful to be clear about how candidates can be successful in their application process.

Despite objections, requiring diversity statements can help to diversify the field and send a sign to candidates that the institution values them and possibly their work. Institutions benefit from working with faculty to learn to evaluate diversity statements and understand their value. When people object to requiring diversity statements as part of the application packet, perhaps we should ask, "Don't we want people across all disciplines to add to the diversity of the institution and respect all people regardless of their racial and ethnic backgrounds (or other identities)?"

Action: Create and Tap Pipelines and Pathways

The faculties at AAU institutions often complain that the pipeline is not filled with candidates of color, and in some disciplines it is not. However, it is not an insurmountable task (nor too costly) to create pipeline programs that lead toward the diversification of the professoriate. There are myriad examples of programs that create pathways to the faculty that institutions can work more closely with and/or create programs that emulate their strategies. These programs include the Mellon Mays Undergraduate Fellowship, the Liberal Arts Diversity Council, the Big Ten Alliance, the McNair Scholars Program, the Leadership Alliance, the Institute for the Recruitment of Teachers, and the Hispanic Serving Institutions: Pathways to the Professoriate program. All of these programs are rich sources of future faculty of color, and their participants benefit from extensive training, professional development, and mentorship. Moreover, they span various disciplines and draw from a diverse group of institutions, including AAU institutions as well as Historically Black College and Universities and Hispanic Serving Institutions. There has been considerable research related to most of these programs that details their success rates and the strategies that they use in order to create pathways to the professoriate that contain fewer roadblocks to success.

Action: Climate Issues and Retention

Administrators must have an even commitment to recruiting and retaining faculty of color, as these issues work hand-in-hand and can't work without each other. If faculty of color are regularly leaving an institution, it becomes difficult to convince other people of color to join the faculty. Many people complain about the lack of candidates of color in the pipeline to the professoriate, but when these candidates are in the pipeline they are often not hired, or if they are hired they are not retained with intention. According to a provost at a midwestern university, "there's a turnstile effect of people leaving [the professoriate] after three years; we've wasted a lot of time, energy, and momentum in bringing them in." Oftentimes faculty members who are not supportive of hiring a diverse faculty make it difficult for new faculty of color to feel welcome, build roadblocks, and disrupt their pathways to success. The turnstile or revolving-door effect of losing faculty has a negative impact on future recruitment because word gets out that various departments, schools, and institutions are not good places for people of color and thus should be avoided.

Retaining faculty of color begins during the recruitment process. In the words of a provost at a public university in the Midwest, it is essential to "get folks to imagine themselves living" in the community and to "give them an idea of what the community might look like and ways that they can engage with communities—plural—whatever their understanding of community is, whether it's religious, or whether it's cultural or linguistic or racial. Whatever it means to them, meaningful connections to other people, getting them to see themselves, making those connections [at your institution]." He also added that "the first step in retention is the job ad. What are we projecting about ourselves and our values?" Another provost cautioned deans and department chairs to spend ample time on retention and to check in on faculty of color regularly, noting that "if we allow our best faculty, our diverse faculty, our senior [White] women to imagine themselves in another university, they're already half[way] out the door. We know that preemptive [retention] is cheaper than reactive retention."

In the words of a provost in the Northeast, "I'm looking for significant changes in how we approach hiring and, beyond that, a commitment. It's not enough to just hire somebody . . . and say, well, let's see how you do. How are the schools supporting our faculty when they get here and mentoring and developing faculty? The deans are required to report to me on what programs they have in place [to support new faculty]." She reiterated, "And that's not just something [they do] at the end of the year. That's an ongoing dialogue that I have with the deans about what they are doing to support the junior faculty . . . and to make sure that everybody, when they come here, actually feels a sense of belonging."

Action: Acknowledge and Confront Anti-Blackness

As shown in earlier chapters, African Americans account for 3.4% of AAU tenured and tenure-track faculty and represent 6% of all PhD holders produced between 2011 and 2018, with only 25% of these individuals earning degrees from AAU institutions. African Americans are the least likely racial or ethnic group to earn a PhD from an AAU institution versus a non-AAU institution. Given that AAU institutions privilege PhDs from AAU institutions and place an emphasis on pedigree, the small numbers of African Americans being admitted to AAU PhD programs prop up systemic racism now and will continue to in the future. If college and university leaders are serious about creating opportunities for African Americans on their faculties, they must address this issue now on three fronts: (1) expanding the definition of quality to be more inclusive and recognizing the pervasive impact of pedigree on opportunity and diversity; (2) challenging the privileging of a narrow group of universities as acceptable areas for recruitment of faculty; and (3) recruiting, admitting, and matriculating more African Americans into AAU PhD programs.

Concluding Statement

If we as the academy are honest in our commitment to hiring a diverse faculty, we have to get off the couch and get on the treadmill—as Daryl Smith reminds us—to do the hard work of dismantling a system that was built to support White men and exclude White women and people of color. We've made progress with White women, demonstrating that we know how to make change that leads to more inclusivity. Instead of congratulating ourselves on the mediocre success we have achieved with regard to diversifying the professoriate, we must be honest about the lack of substantial progress we have made, the pervasiveness of systemic racism, the role that the negative aspects of shared governance plays in the maintenance of the status quo, the privileging of pedigree and narrow definitions of quality, and our roles in stymieing opportunity for people of color who want to pursue faculty careers. Only then can higher education begin to live up to the lofty ideals expressed around academic excellence in every college and university mission statement.

Approach to the Study

In order to write this book, I used a variety of data sources. First, I drew upon the National Center for Educational Statistics and Integrated Postsecondary Education Data System (IPEDS) data to fully understand the state of faculty diversity for tenured and tenure-track faculty in the AAU institutions. Second, I used data from the National Science Foundation's Survey of Earned Doctorates to better understand the pipeline for future faculty across various disciplines. Third, I examined the websites of the AAU institutions to review their faculty diversity statements, faculty hiring materials, institutional missions, and strategic plans, and the ways they represent their faculty diversity to the public. Lastly, I conducted interviews with provosts, vice provosts for faculty, vice provosts for diversity, deans, department chairs, and search committee chairs across the AAU institutions.

I contacted each of the sixty AAU institutions, requesting an interview with the provost as well as a cadre of deans, department chairs, and anyone the provost deemed would be important to interview. As a result of my including "anyone the provost deemed would be important," I interviewed several chief diversity officers, general counsels, and chiefs of staff in addition to the positions named above. Out of the sixty AAU institutions, forty-two responded to my inquiry. I provided each of the AAU institutions with a copy of the IRB approval letter, the questions I'd like to ask, and a consent form. Of the group that responded, several asked for additional information before participating, while three declined immediately. Other provosts told me that they personally didn't have time to participate in this research project (which I noted would take no more than forty-five minutes), stating, "Please feel free to contact deans and department chairs to see if they would like to participate. However, this is not a project I feel I can devote my time to." Others told me that participating in this research project was "a major time commitment for their team" and "respectfully declined." Still others told me when I reached out in January 2019 that they were "just beginning the budget planning process that will last through July, so this is an especially busy time of the year." There were also institutions that asked me for a copy of my book proposal (I declined), book contract (I declined), and did interviews with me about my career and qualifications to write the book before deciding to participate (I agreed to the interviews).

Overall, thirty-six of the sixty US AAU institutions participated in this study, with most being enthusiastic about participation and looking forward to the results of the study. Many offered the names of deans, department chairs, and anyone else who could comment on their institution's approach to faculty diversity in hiring. I conducted the interviews between February 2019 and June 2019, interviewing 106 individuals across the thirty-six institutions—representing vast diversity in terms of public/private status, selectivity, geographical location, and group membership (i.e., Ivy League, Big Ten), and in terms of those I interviewed. My interviews included representation across various positions involved in faculty hiring at the institutions. I made sure that I had interviews with individuals who had a bird's-eye view of faculty hiring as well as interviews with those who were in the thick of faculty hiring.

Although I discussed the AAU institutions by name when talking about national data or web-based materials related to faculty diversity, I do not identify the specific AAU institutions that participated in this study or those that chose not to. I also did not identify any of the individuals with whom I spoke. I would not have been able to secure the candor that I did without protecting the identity of these individuals and the institutions. I also masked various details about the participating institutions, such as well-known events, as these would have given the participating institutions away. There are times when I talk about various pivotal events related to faculty diversity or hiring but I don't connect these to the interviews that I did. After conducting the interviews, I sent a copy of the transcript to each individual, offering the chance to review it and make any changes. Most individuals made very few changes, with the exception of correcting spelling errors made by the transcriptionists for the project.

Prior to conducting the interviews with administrators across the AAU institutions, I explored the history of the AAU as well as its current operations, mission, goals, and projects to gain a better understanding of how the institutions are gathered under the AAU umbrella. I also reviewed the membership requirements. I attempted to conduct an interview with Mary Sue Coleman, the president of the AAU, for context. She agreed to do the interview, but it was never scheduled by her assistant as requested. As this book is not about the AAU as an organization, but rather the institutions that qualify to be a part of the organization, I don't think this interview was vital to my arguments in the book.

As I was writing, I found the need to collect additional data. Many deans and provosts talked extensively about their law schools, and as a result, I wanted to know more about the student and faculty diversity within these law schools. My PhD advisee and research assistant, Daniel Blake, assisted me with pulling data on the Top 14 (T14) law schools related to their student diversity from the National Center for Educational Statistics. I also wanted to know more about the faculty diversity at the T14 law schools, given that most of the law school deans with whom I spoke told me that the majority of faculty at these institutions earn their degrees from one of three or four places—Harvard, Yale, Chicago, and Stanford. Sergio Gonzalez, a PhD student at the Claremont Graduate University and one of my research assistants, worked with me to review all of the law school faculty at T14 institutions, examining race, gender, and the institution from which they received their JD (or PhD in some cases).[1]

During my conversations with administrators from the AAU institutions, most revealed that their faculties, either by department or

1. For an interesting quantitative perspective on the law school reproduction of hierarchy, see Katz et al. (2011).

institution, tended to hire people from a limited group of institutions, that these institutions were normally in their peer group or above, and that nearly all of these institutions were members of the AAU. Curious about what AAU institutions might be missing by limiting their hiring in this way, I worked with Pearl Lo, my PhD advisee and research assistant, to pull data on those universities that produce PhDs across various disciplines at non-AAU institutions, specifically those that are in the "high research" and "very high research" categories. I was particularly interested in the diversity of PhD students at these non-AAU institutions. Andrés Castro Samayoa, an assistant professor at Boston College and my former PhD student, also assisted with data collection related to non-AAU institutions.

In addition to these data sources, I drew upon a variety of other sources, including the emails from people across the nation who read my articles in the *Washington Post* and the *Hechinger Report*. When using quotes from these emails, I anonymized them so that they could not be identified in any way. Throughout the book, I also recall conversations and situations that I was a part of throughout my career. When doing this, sometimes I mention names and other times I don't if I think that it's best not to or to protect individuals. As I wrote this book, I read the work of many others extensively, and in some cases I reached out to people who were doing research in this area for advice, guidance, and insight. These individuals included Daryl Smith, Julie Posselt, William Casey Boland, Levon Esters, Alice E. Ginsberg, and Andrés Castro Samayoa. Lastly, I reflected on my own background, motivations, and thoughts as I wrote, and in some cases these became part of the book.

A Deeper Look at Law Schools

Meera Deo recently authored *Unequal Profession: Race and Gender in Legal Academia* (2019), in which she examines the experiences of law professors of color. She engages the issue of hiring as well as that of retention, with a particular interest in women of color, who only represent 7% of all law school faculty. Her work shows that law schools continue to operate in ways that privilege and benefit White men and that they are only making moderate progress toward change. During my conversations with various law school deans across the AAU institutions, they alluded to practices and behaviors that reinforce the sameness that Deo discusses in her book. For example, the deans mentioned that "virtually all law schools" (including most outside the AAU) have hired faculty from a very small number of law schools. They told me that law schools have been insular in their hiring, more so than other disciplines. One law school dean in the Midwest explained hiring of faculty as: "Some of it is like pack dependence, 60% of the people in academia [at law schools] are probably from Harvard and Yale, and maybe now a smaller percentage is from Stanford, but basically no one at the top schools is [coming from] outside of Harvard, Yale, Stanford, University of Chicago. You might have one or two here and there, but very, very, very few." The dean told me that nearly all law school faculty members have degrees from a T14 law school—that is one of the Top 14 law schools.

Curious about the validity of this law school dean's comment, I decided to spot-check ten law schools at AAU institutions: the five most highly ranked (and T14 members) and five that are not part of the T14. I found that at the highly ranked institutions, most of the full-time tenured or tenure-track faculty earned degrees at Harvard, Yale, Chicago, and occasionally Stanford. There were a few outliers, including those coming from Fordham and Boston Universities. At those AAU institutions that were not in the T14, there was more diversity in PhD-granting institutions, but those faculty holding full professorships or endowed professorships were more likely to have graduated from a T14 institution, specifically Harvard, Yale, Chicago, and Stanford. Interestingly, the faculty of color across the T14 law schools were more likely to have earned their degrees from Harvard and Yale than any other institutions.

Based on my conversations with AAU law school deans, I decided to look more closely at the T14 law schools. These institutions, according to the most recent data available (2016) from the National Center for Educational Statistics, include Columbia University, Cornell University, Duke University, Georgetown University (non-AAU), Harvard University, New York University, Northwestern University, Stanford University, UC-Berkeley, University of Chicago, University of Michigan, University of Pennsylvania, University of Virginia, and Yale University. Among these institutions, American Indians and Alaska Natives make up less than 1% of the law school students, Asian Americans make up 10%, African Americans account for 6%, Hispanics make up 8%, Native Hawaiians and Pacific Islanders account for less than 1%, and Whites make up 56% of all students (table 17). Compared with representation among all law schools accredited by the American Bar Association, these numbers are lower for people of color with the exception of Asian Americans. Among all accredited law schools, Asians Americans make up 6% of the student body, Hispanics account for nearly 13%, and African Americans make up 8% of those students enrolled. Native Americans, Alaska Natives, Native Hawaiians, and Pacific Islanders do not fare better among this larger group of law schools as their Black and Hispanic colleagues do (Enjuris.com, 2018). Although some of the T14 law schools are becoming more diverse, some are still overwhelmingly White. For example, four of the T14 schools have student populations that are at least 60% White (Stanford University, University of Chicago, University of Michigan, and University of

Pennsylvania), and the University of Virginia's law school population is 72% White. These institutions also have very few people of color on their law school faculties—typically five individuals or fewer.

With regard to gender parity in T14 law schools, women account for the majority of students enrolled in every racial group with the exception of Whites, American Indians/Alaska Natives, and Native Hawaiian and Pacific Islander students, and there is near gender equity within the Hispanic population (National Center for Educational Statistics, 2019). The top law schools have made some progress toward diversifying their student bodies, but very little progress in the faculty ranks.

According to an AAU law school dean, "[It's been] getting a little bit better in recent years. We can now place some of our graduates in academia, a couple a year perhaps. It's diversified a little bit, but it's overwhelmingly really narrow. It's something we're thinking about a little bit." She added, "Virtually no one outside of a Top 14 school will get a tenure-track job, and I don't really see that changing. I think we are desperate to diversify along the traditional race and gender lines [overall], but I don't think there's going to be much movement really about diversifying in terms of law schools. For example, we might look at people from Duke, but you know, not a huge amount." Interestingly, this same dean discussed with me the importance of implicit bias training for the entire faculty. Of relevance, it seems that much of faculty bias is explicit and that institutions are fine with that in faculty hiring. Another law school dean claimed that not everyone on her faculty has an expansive view of quality, and there are some faculty members who would like to limit the law schools from which the institution draws faculty. Overall, however, the faculty is looking for "talented people from a diverse array of backgrounds." She elaborated, "From the committees that I've served on, it has not been a major point of conflict. I think there's a pretty good sensibility about being flexible and yes, looking for talent wherever it is."

Given the prominence, influences, and future careers of T14 graduates (from high-profile attorneys to judges to faculty to politicians to presidents), it is essential that T14 institutions cultivate a diverse faculty and student body.

Table 17 Full-time T14 Law Students by Race/Ethnicity, Fall 2016 (Percentages)

Institution	Grand Total	AIAN Total	Asian Total	Black/African American Total
Columbia University	1,240	0	14	9
Cornell University	626	1	12	6
Duke University	793	0	9	6
Georgetown University	1,745	0	2	7
Harvard University	1,787	0	12	7
New York University	1,360	0	12	5
Northwestern University	699	0	12	6
Stanford University	564	0	11	4
University of California–Berkeley	917	0	13	5
University of Chicago	603	0	10	5
University of Michigan	931	1	8	4
University of Pennsylvania	745	0	13	7
University of Virginia	894	0	8	5
Yale University	693	1	11	7
Grand total	**13,597**	**3**	**147**	**83**

Source: National Center for Educational Statistics, Integrated Postsecondary Education Data System (IPEDS), 2016.

Note: Data are collected every two years.

Hispanic Total	NHPI Total	White Total	Two or More Races Total	Unknown Total	Nonresident Total
7	0	52	1	4	12
11	0	41	0	10	20
5	0	57	1	3	20
7	0	51	0	26	6
9	0	50	3	6	12
9	0	58	3	4	8
11	0	53	3	4	11
11	0	61	8	3	2
13	0	50	9	7	2
11	0	61	3	5	4
5	0	65	5	7	6
6	0	62	1	5	5
4	0	72	4	5	1
8	0	55	3	1	13
117	**0**	**788**	**44**	**90**	**122**

ACKNOWLEDGMENTS

Typically, authors thank their family last in book acknowledgments, but in order to write and complete this book, I relied on my daughter Chloë and my mother Lilly for support. My daughter sat next to me at our dining room table doing her art or writing essays as I wrote. Often we didn't say anything to each other for hours, but having her next to me was a beautiful motivation. Given that she was in college at the time, I spent most of the time writing alone, but on the occasional weekend, on holiday breaks, and during the COVID-19 outbreak she was by my side. Seeing her create as I wrote was inspiring. I consider myself blessed in tremendous ways to be Chloë's mom. She has a joy in her heart that I have rarely seen in others and the ability to see goodness in nearly everyone. I learn from her every day, as she is patient, deeply kind, a beautiful thinker, and resilient even when she thinks she isn't.

My mother also provided support to me during my writing process. She's ninety years old and, growing up in poverty, she didn't have the good fortune of attending high school or college. Yet she is one of the wisest people I know. Some of her best advice is to "keep your friend circle small." As I grow older, I'm listening to my mom more and more.

Over the course of twenty-plus years of being a professor, I have developed strong professional relationships that have shepherded me through the mountains and valleys of the academy. These individuals range from former students to college presidents to non-profit administrators to colleagues and friends. I've worked hard to invest in these relationships, and I'm deeply loyal to them. I would stand up for them and honor their humanity and dignity. I am particularly grateful to Wanda Blanchett, David Wilson, Michael Nettles, Catherine Millett, Henry Turner, David Coleman, Andrés Castro Samayoa, Thai-Huy Nguyen, Nelson Bowman, Camille Charles, Alice Ginsberg, Jason Zisser, Wayne Bullock, Levon Esters, Matt Mayhew, Doug Christianson, Barbara Gill, Joe Castro, Don Heller, Star Sharpe, Chris Messina-Boyer, Jamal Watson, Matt Vanderburg, Caryl McFarlane, Shaun McAlmont, Dorothy Villareal, Elmira Mangum, Alvin Schexnider, Renee Booth, John Wilson, Tina Fletcher, Trina Fletcher, Ashleigh Brown Grier, Dayln Montgomery, Adriel Hilton, Rich Reddick, Victor Saenz, Susana Hernandez, Ignacio Hernandez, Luis Ponjuan, Mark Castillo, Robert Palmer, Gregory Parks, Kevin James, Ester Ra, Rashida Wellbeck, Cynthia Tyson, Judy Alston, Jessye DeSilva, Clark Chinn, Nolan Cabrera, Amy Wells, Pam Agoyo, Jim Montoya, Jason DeSousa, Jeff Martin, Robert Hoggard, Soko Starobin, Jennifer Yang, Doug Clark, Robert Leary, J. Son Arrington Rivera, Jerry Pope, Thammika Songkaeo, Lois MacNamara, Trish Williams, Andrew Lounder, Grace Kao, Jillian Fox, Noah Drezner, Oren Pizmony-Levy, Karen Dankers, A. J. Vervoort, Frank Pellicone, Menah Pratt-Clarke, Gregory Vincent, Bruce Chamberlain, Ari Betof, Nolan Peterson, Jim Alton, Anthony Hernandez, Monica Cox, William Casey Boland, Yvette Booker, Brittany Robertson, Sri Rao, Ufuoma Abiola, Mercedes Terrazas, Darryl Moran, Celia Liu, Forough Ghahramani, Ginasophia Altieri, Afsheen Shamsi, Aviva Hirschfeld Legatt, Ginger Stull, Ontario Wooden, Kim Griffin, Crystal Moore, Louis Gallian, Jonathan Zimmerman, Janelle Williams, Deborah Floyd, Chaz Howard, Abdul Qadir, John Washington, Brandy Jackson, Kevin Valentine, Tierney Bates, Ayana Lewis, Gina Nunez, David Perez, Shannon Gary, Gregory Seaton, Karen Gross, Walter Kimbrough, Michael Sorrell, Cassie Jacobs, Michael Steven Williams, Leah Hollis, Florence Hamrick, Sharon Ryan, Nichole Garcia, Saundra Thomlinson Clark, William Gipson, Tammy Smithers, Shaunna Payne Gold, Sultan Jenkins, Sergio Gonzalez, John Braxton, Lori Hultgren, Carol Sandoval, Justin Porter, Thomas Tyner, Cheron Davis, Jarrett Gupton, Maricarmen Figueroa, Caesar Thomas, Paula Langteau, Mark

Harris, Ishmail Abdus-Saboor, Deshaun Bennett, Kim Guyer, Helen Albertson, Pat Rea, Sharon Height, and Dave Stat.

I want to offer special thanks to Levon Esters, William Casey Boland, and Alice Ginsberg for reading early drafts of this manuscript and for being forthright in their constructive comments and feedback.

Although I didn't apply for funding to conduct the research and write this book, I am grateful to all those who have funded my work (and that of both the Penn and Rutgers Center for Minority Serving Institutions and the Samuel DeWitt Proctor Institute for Leadership, Equity, and Justice) in the past and currently, as I could not have written this book without their support over the years. Thank you to the Kresge Foundation, W. K. Kellogg Foundation, Leona M. and Harry B. Helmsley Charitable Trust, Andrew W. Mellon Foundation, Arthur Vining Davis Foundation, Lyle Spencer Foundation, ECMC Foundation, Lumina Foundation, USA Funds (now Strada Education Network), Greg and E. J. Milken Foundation, Educational Testing Service, National Institutes of Health, Duke Endowment, National Academy of Sciences, University of Pennsylvania, Indiana University Center on Philanthropy, Josiah H. Macey Foundation, Aspen Institute, John Smartt, Samuel DeWitt Proctor Endowment, Bright Spot Strategy, and Rockefeller Foundation. I appreciate all of the program officers, staff, and individual donors I have worked with over the years. Their support and critical feedback has been essential to my development as a scholar and professional.

I am grateful to the staff and research team members at the Samuel DeWitt Proctor Institute for Leadership, Equity, and Justice and the Rutgers Center for Minority Serving Institutions (CMSI) for their support, talent, creativity, and dedication. By name, they are Carolyn Nalewajko, Brandy Jones, Michele Coyne, Destiny Jenkins, Koor Kpogba-Thomas, Natalie Passov, and Priscilla Pierre. Some of these individuals have been with me since the CMSI opened at the University of Pennsylvania in 2014, working side by side, and others are new to the space, but they are all beautifully dedicated to the work that we do. Special thanks to the team of doctoral students

I worked with as I wrote this book: Andrew Martinez, Daniel Blake, Pearl Lo, Kemuel Benyehudah, and Sergio Gonzalez. I am grateful to all of them for believing in me, my work, and our strong relationships. It has been a pleasure to see their careers and research blossom and to support them throughout this process.

I want to thank each of the AAU administrators—across many institutions—who agreed to talk with me for this book. Some institutions turned me down, citing lack of time for or interest in the project. However, many people gave of their perspectives and energy, often sharing their passion for their work with me. I offer special thanks to Daryl Smith and Julie Posselt, who were forthcoming with their opinions and reflections, and both of whom served as a motivation for this research. Additionally, I am grateful to each person who reached out to me after reading my opinion essay "We Don't Want Them" in the *Washington Post,* which, along with the essay in the *Hechinger Report*, was the impetus for this book. Each individual had a very personal story and shared their life with me. I'm honored to hold and care for those stories.

My editor at Princeton University Press provided superb feedback that helped me to grapple with various issues in the book. Peter Dougherty is highly skilled at asking the right questions, challenging, and careful in his reading. I am also grateful to the anonymous peer reviewers of my manuscript drafts. They helped me to be more careful in my assessments and pronouncements and challenged me to write a better book.

Lastly, thank you to the *New York Times* for inviting me to speak at the annual Higher Education Forum; to the *Hechinger Report*, especially Lawrie Mifflin and Jennifer Shaw, for prompting me to write an essay on the hiring of faculty of color; and to the *Washington Post*, especially Susan Svrluga, for capturing the attention of so many by publishing my essay on faculty diversity.

REFERENCES

Almanac Staff (2011). Penn's action plan for faculty diversity and excellence. *Almanac*. https://almanac.upenn.edu/archive/volumes/v58/n02/diversityplan.html.

American Academy of Arts & Sciences (2019). *Humanities indicators*. https://www.humanitiesindicators.org/content/indicatorDoc.aspx?i=9.

American Association of University Professors (1966). *Statement on government of colleges and universities*. https://www.aaup.org/report/statement-government-colleges-and-universities.

Association of American Universities (2012). Our members. https://www.aau.edu.

Amir, R.; and Knauff, M. (2008). Ranking economics departments worldwide on the basis of PhD placement. *Review of Economic Statistics*, 90, 185–190.

Anderson, J. D. (1988). *The education of Blacks in the South, 1860–1935*. Chapel Hill: University of North Carolina Press.

—— (1993). Race, meritocracy, and the American academy during the immediate post–World War II era. *History of Education Quarterly*, 33(2), 15–175.

Andrews, K. T.; and Biggs, M. (2006). The dynamics of protest diffusion: Movement organizations, social networks, and news media in the 1960 sit-ins. *American Sociological Review*, 71(5), 752–777.

Armstrong, M. A.; and Jovanovic, J. (2017). The intersectional matrix: Rethinking institutional change for URM women in STEM. *Journal of Diversity in Higher Education*, 10(3), 216–231.

Ascoli, P. M. (2015). *Julius Rosenwald: The man who built Sears, Roebuck and advanced the cause of Black education in the American South*. Bloomington: Indiana University Press.

Associated Press (2013). University of Alabama orders sororities to end race discrimination. *Guardian*, September 17. https://www.theguardian.com/world/2013/sep/17/sorority-segregation-ended-university-alabama.

Azar, B. (2008). IAT: Fad or fabulous? Psychologists debate whether the Implicit Association Text needs more solid psychometric footing before it enters the public sphere. *Monitor on Psychology*. https://www.apa.org/monitor/2008/07-08/psychometric.

Baker, D.; Schmaling, K.; Fountain, K.; Blume, A.; and Boose, R. (2016). Defining diversity: A mixed-method analysis of terminology in faculty applications. *Social Science Journal*, 53, 60–66.

Bastedo, M.; and Bowman, N. (2010). U.S. News & World Report college rankings: Modeling institutional effects on organizational reputation. *American Journal of Education*, 116, 163–183.

Bayer, A.; and Rouse, C. E. (2016). Diversity in the economics profession: A new attack on an old problem. *Journal of Economic Perspectives*, 30(4), 221–242.

Berchini, C. (2016). How to be White: A primer. In G. David and S. F. Forbes (eds.), *What does it mean to be White in America?* (pp. 45–58). New York: 2Leaf Press.

Bertrand, M.; and Mullainathan, S. (2003). Are Emily and Greg more employable than Lakisha and Jamal? A field experiment on labor market discrimination. *National Bureau of Economic Research*. https://www.nber.org/papers/w9873.

Bhalla, N. (2019). Strategies to improve equity in faculty hiring. *Molecular Biology of the Cell*, 30, 2744–2749.

Bilimoria, D.; and Buch, K. K. (2010). The search is on: Engendering faculty diversity through more effective search and recruitment. *Change*, 42(4), 27–32.

Blackwell, L. V.; Snyder, L. A.; and Mavriplis, C. (2009). Diverse faculty in STEM fields: Attitudes, performance, and fair treatment. *Journal of Diversity in Higher Education*, 2(4), 195.

Bock, L.; and Welle, B. (2014). You don't know what you don't know: How our unconscious minds undermine the workplace. *Life at Google*. https://blog.google/topics/inside-google/you-dont-know-what-you-dont-know-how.

Bonilla-Silva, E. (2009). *Racism without racists: Color-blind racism and the persistence of racial inequality in America*. 3rd ed. Lanham, MD: Rowman and Littlefield.

Bradley, S.; Garven, J.; Law, W.; and West, J. (2018). The impact of chief diversity officers on diverse faculty hiring. NBER Working Paper no. 24969. https://www.nber.org/papers/w24969.

Brown University Steering Committee on Slavery and Justice (2006). *Slavery and justice: Report of the Brown University steering committee on slavery and justice*. Providence, RI: Brown University. https://www.brown.edu/Research/Slavery_Justice/documents/SlaveryAndJustice.pdf

Buris, V. (2004). The academic caste system: Prestige hierarchies in PhD exchange networks. *American Sociological Review*, 69, 239–264.

Butler, B. (2014). "I, too, am Harvard": Black students show they belong. *Washington Post*, March 5. https://www.washingtonpost.com/blogs/she-the-people/wp/2014/03/05/i-too-am-harvard-black-students-show-they-belong.

Butler, P. D.; Longaker, M. T.; and Britt, L. D. (2010). Addressing the paucity of underrepresented minorities in academic surgery: Can the "Rooney Rule" be applied to academic surgery? *American Journal of Surgery*, 199(2), 255–262.

Ceci, S.; and Williams, W. (2011). Understanding current causes of women's underrepresentation in science. *Proceedings of the National Academy of Sciences*, 108, 3157–3162.

Chang, M.; Milem, J.; and Antonio, A. (2005). *Making diversity work on campus: A research-based perspective*. Washington, DC: Association of American Colleges and Universities.

Chapple, L.; and Humphrey, J. E. (2014). Does board gender diversity have a financial impact? Evidence using stock portfolio performance. *Journal of Business Ethics*, 122(4), 709–723.

Chronicle of Higher Education (2018). *Faculty diversity: What colleges need to do now.* Washington, DC: Chronicle of Higher Education.

Clauset, A.; Arbesman, S.; and Larremore, D. (2015). Systemic inequality and hierarchy in faculty hiring networks. *Science Advances*, 1(1). https://advances.sciencemag.org/content/1/1/e1400005.full.

Clotfelter, C. T. (1996). *Buying the best: Cost escalation in elite higher education.* Princeton, NJ: Princeton University Press.

Collins, B. W. (2007). Tackling unconscious bias in hiring practices: The plight of the Rooney rule. *New York University Law Review*, 82, 870.

Columbia University Office of the Provost (n.d.). *Guide to best practices in faculty search and hiring.* https://provost.columbia.edu/sites/default/files/content/BestPracticesFacultySearchHiring.pdf.

Conrad, C.; and Gasman, M. (2015). *Educating a diverse nation: Lessons from Minority Serving Institutions.* Cambridge, MA: Harvard University Press.

Cooper, A. J. (1892). *A voice from the South.* Chapel Hill: University of North Carolina Press.

Cozzens, S. E. (2008). Gender issues in US science and technology policy: Equality of what? *Science and Engineering Ethics*, 14(3), 345–356.

Crenshaw, K. (1989). Demarginalizing the intersection of race and sex: A Black feminist critique of antidiscrimination doctrine, feminist theory and antiracist politics. 1989(1), article 8, http://chicagounbound.uchicago.edu/uclf/vol1989/iss1/8.

Cyranoski, D.; Gilbert, N.; Ledford, H.; Nayar, A.; and Yahia, M. (2011). The PhD factory. *Nature*, 472, 276–279.

Deo, M. (2019). *Unequal profession: Race and gender in legal academia.* Palo Alto, CA: Stanford University Press.

De Welde, K.; and Stepnick, A. (2015). *Disrupting the culture of silence: Confronting gender inequality and making change in higher education.* Sterling, VA: Stylus Publishing.

DiAngelo, R. (2018). *White fragility: Why it's so hard for White people to talk about racism.* New York: Beacon Press.

DiMaggio, P.; and Powell, W. (1983). The iron cage revisited: Institutional isomorphism and collective rationality in organizational fields. *American Sociological Review*, 48(2), 147–160.

Dobbin, F., and Kalev, A. (2007). The architecture of inclusion: Evidence from corporate diversity programs. *Harvard Journal of Law and Gender*, 30, 279.

Duckworth, A. (2018). *Grit: The power of passion and perseverance.* New York: Scribner.

Duffy, M., and Sperry, L. (2014). *Overcoming mobbing: A recovery guide for workplace agression and bullying.* New York: Oxford University Press.

Easley, J. (2018). Pilot project to test open recruitment for faculty: Searches will be by college or school, not by department. *UC Davis News*, October 30. https://www.ucdavis.edu/news/pilot-project-test-open-recruitment-faculty.

Eberhardt, J. L. (2019). *Biased: Uncovering the hidden prejudice that shapes what we see, think, and do.* New York: Viking Press.

ELI (2016). *Five real-world examples of unconscious bias.* ELI blog, March 31. https://www.eliinc.com/five-real-world-examples-of-unconscious-bias.

Ellis, L. (2019). New universities just joined the AAU: That will change their campuses in 3 ways. *Chronicle of Higher Education*, November 7. www.chronicle.com.

Enjuris.com (2018). Law school enrollment by race and ethnicity. *Law school diversity report*. https://www.enjuris.com/students/law-school-race-2018.html.

Esmieu, P. (2018). Faculty diversity at Minority Serving Institutions. In A. Castro Samayoa and M. Gasman (eds.), *Minority Serving Institutions on the landscape of higher education*. New York: Routledge Press.

Espinosa, L.; Turk, J.; Taylor, M.; and Chessman H. (2019). *Race and ethnicity in higher education*. Washington, DC: American Council on Higher Education.

Evans, S. Y. (2007). *Black women in the ivory tower, 1850–1954*. Gainsville: University Press of Florida.

Extra, N. (2018). The Black feminist who argued for intersectionality before the term existed. *Vice.com*, March 23. https://www.vice.com/en_us/article/xw7xnk/anna-julia-cooper-intersectionality-black-feminist.

Farberov, S. (2014). College fraternity under fire for throwing "racist" MLK Day party with watermelon cups, gang signs and basketball jerseys. *Daily Mail*, January 21. https://www.dailymail.co.uk/news/article-2543422/ASU-fraternity-fire-throwing-racist-MLK-Day-party-watermelon-cups-gang-signs-basketball-jerseys.html.

Finkelstein, M. J.; and Conley, V. M. (2019). *Taking the measure of faculty diversity*. Washington, DC: TIAA Institute.

Finkelstein, M. J.; Conley, V. M.; and Schuster, J. H. (2016). *The faculty factor: Reassessing the American academy in a turbulent era*. Baltimore, MD: Johns Hopkins University Press.

Flaherty, C. (2018a). Making a statement on diversity statements. *Inside Higher Education*, November 12. https://www.insidehighered.com/news/2018/11/12/former-harvard-deans-tweet-against-required-faculty-diversity-statements-sets-debate#.

——— (2018b). Open searches and diversity. *Inside Higher Education*, November 5. https://www.insidehighered.com/news/2018/11/05/uc-davis-holding-eight-faculty-searches-focused-candidates-contributions-diversity.

——— (2018c). To be in person, or not to be? *Inside Higher Education*, January 18. https://www.insidehighered.com/news/2018/01/18/first-round-faculty-job-interviews-which-once-took-place-disciplinary-meetings-are.

Fowler, J.; Grofman, B.; and Masuoka, N. (2007). Social networks in political science: Hiring and placement of PhDs, 1960–2002. *Political Science and Politics*, 40, 729–739.

Fraser, G. J.; and Hunt, D. E. (2011). Faculty diversity and search committee training: Learning from a critical incident. *National Association of Diversity Officers in Higher Education*, 4(5), 185–198.

Freeman, C. (2019). The case for cluster hires. *Chronicle of Higher Education*, October 9. https://www.chronicle.com/article/The-Case-for-Cluster-Hiring-to/247301.

Gasman, M. (2007*). Envisioning Black colleges: A history of the United Negro College Fund*. Baltimore, MD: Johns Hopkins University Press.

—— (2011). Trashing Historically Black Colleges and Universities. *Chronicle of Higher Education*, February 24. https://www.chronicle.com/blogs/innovations /trashing-historically-black-colleges-and-universities/28639.

—— (2014). Presidents in denial. *Inside Higher Education*, March 31. https://www .insidehighered.com/views/2014/03/31/essay-college-presidents-are-denial -about-state-race-relations.

—— (2016a). The five things no one will tell you about why colleges don't hire more faculty of color. *Hechinger Report*, September 20. http://hechingerreport .org/five-things-no-one-will-tell-colleges-dont-hire-faculty-color.

—— (2016b). An Ivy League professor on why colleges don't hire more faculty of color: "We don't want them." *Washington Post*, September 26. https:// www.washingtonpost.com/news/grade-point/wp/2016/09/26/an-ivy-league -professor-on-why-colleges-dont-hire-more-faculty-of-color-we-dont-want -them/.

Gasman, M.; Kim, J.; and Nguyen, T. (2011). Effectively recruiting faculty of color at highly selective institutions: A school of education case study. *Journal of Diversity in Higher Education*, 4(4), 212–222.

Geiger, R. (2004). *Knowledge and money.* Palo Alto, CA: Stanford University Press.

Gillies, A. (2016). Questions to ask to help create a diverse applicant pool. *Chronicle of Higher Education*, September 11. https://www.chronicle.com/article /Questions-to-Ask-to-Help/237747.

Golash-Boza, T. (2016). The effective diversity statement. *Inside Higher Education*, June 10. https://www.insidehighered.com/advice/2016/06/10/how-write -effective-diversity-statement-essay.

Golden, D.; and Burke, D. (2019). The unseen student victims of the "Varsity Blues" college admissions scandal. *New Yorker*, October 8. https://www.newyorker .com/books/page-turner/the-unseen-student-victims-of-the-varsity-blues -college-admissions-scandal.

Goldrick-Rab, S.; Kelchen, R.; and Houle, J. (2014). The color of student debt: Implications of federal loan program reforms for Black students and Historically Black Colleges and Universities. Wisconsin Hope Lab Discussion Paper. Madison: University of Wisconson.

Greenwald, A. G.; Banaji, M. R.; and Nosek, B. A. (2015). Statistically small effects of the implicit association test can have societally large effects. *Journal of Personality and Social Psychology*, 108, 553–561.

Griffin, K. (2019). *Redoubling our efforts: How institutions can affect faculty diversity.* Washington, DC: American Council on Education.

—— (2020). Institutional barriers, strategies, and benefits to increasing the representation of women and men of color in the professoriate. *Higher Education: Handbook of Theory and Research*, 35, 277–349.

Grimes, M. D., and Morris, J. M. (1997). *Caught in the middle: Contradictions in the lives of sociologists from working-class backgrounds.* Westport, CT: Greenwood Publishing.

Guinier, L. (2015). *The tyranny of the meritocracy: Democratizing higher education in America.* New York: Beacon Press.

Gurin, P.; Dey, E. L.; Gurin, G.; and Hurtado, S. (2004). *The educational value of diversity. Defending diversity: Affirmative action at the University of Michigan.* Ann Arbor: University of Michigan Press.

Hafsi, T., and Turgut, G. (2013). Boardroom diversity and its effect on social performance: Conceptualization and empirical evidence. *Journal of Business Ethics*, 112(3), 463–479.

Han, S. (2003). Tribal regimes in academia: A comparative analysis of market structure across disciplines. *Social Networks*, 25, 251–280.

Haney, T. J. (2015). Factory to faculty: Socioeconomic difference and the educational experiences of university professors. *Canadian Review of Sociology/ Revue Canadienne de Sociologie*, 52(2), 160–186.

Hanneman, R. (2001). The prestige of Ph.D. granting departments of sociology: A simple network approach. *Connections*, 24, 68–77.

Harvard University (2013). *Recruiting for diversity.* Cambridge, MA: Harvard University. https://hr.fas.harvard.edu/files/fas-hr/files/recruiting_for_diversity_9.17.13_0.pdf.

Henrich, F.; and Gil-White, F. (2001). The evolution of prestige: Freely conferred deference as a mechanism for enhancing the benefits of cultural transmission. *Evolutionary Human Behavior*, 22, 165–196.

Hollis, L. (2015). Bully university? The cost of workplace bullying and employee disengagement in American higher education. *Sage Open*, 5(2). https://doi.org/10.1177%2F2158244015589997.

Hruby, P. (2016). Four years a student-athlete: The racial injustice of big-time college sports. *Vice*, April 4. https://www.vice.com/en_us/article/ezexjp/four-years-a-student-athlete-the-racial-injustice-of-big-time-college-sports.

Hull, G. T.; Scott, P. B.; and Smith, B. (1993). *"But some of us are brave": All the women are White, all the Blacks are men.* New York: Feminist Press.

Hunt, V. H.; Morimoto, S.; Zajicek, A.; and Lisnic, R. (2012). Intersectionality and dismantling institutional privilege: The case of the NSF ADVANCE program. *Race, Gender & Class*, 19(1–2), 266–290.

Ifill, S. A. (2000). Racial diversity on the bench: Beyond role models and public confidence. *Washington & Lee Law Review*, 57, 405.

Jaschik, S. (2014). Snow hate. *Inside Higher Education*, January 28. https://www.insidehighered.com/news/2014/01/28/u-illinois-decision-keep-classes-going-leads-racist-and-sexist-twitter-attacks.

Johnson, A. (2007). Unintended consequences: How science professors discourage women of color. *Science Education*, 91(5), 805–821.

Jussim, L. (2017). Mandatory implicit bias training is a bad idea. *Psychology Today*, December 2. https://www.psychologytoday.com/us/blog/rabble-rouser/201712/mandatory-implicit-bias-training-is-a-bad-idea.

Kaplan, T.; Murphy, K.; and Early, D. E. (2013). San Jose State suspends students accused of tormenting black roommate. *Mercury News*, November 21. https://www.mercurynews.com/2013/11/21/san-jose-state-suspends-students-accused-of-tormenting-black-roommate/.

Katz, D.; Gubler, J.; Zelner, J.; Bommarito, M.; Provins, E.; and Ingall, E. (2011). Reproduction of hierarchy? A social network analysis of the American law professoriate. *Journal of Legal Education*, 61, 1–28.

Kelsky, K. (2014). The professor is in: Making sense of the diversity statement. *Chronicle of Higher Education*, January 13. https://tgs.unt.edu/sites/default /files/Making%20Sense%20of%20Diversity%20Statement.pdf.

Kramnick, J. (2018). What we hire in now: English by the grim numbers. *Chronicle of Higher Education*, December 9. https://www.chronicle.com/article/What -We-Hire-in-Now-English/245255.

Lamon, M. (2017). Report shows mixed results in Penn's attempt to improve faculty diversity. *Daily Pennsylvanian*, April 3. https://www.thedp.com/article /2017/04/faculty-diversity-inclusion-report.

Langefeld, R. (2018). New paper explores diversity statements in faculty hiring. *Michigan Daily,* December 4. https://www.michigandaily.com/section /administration/new-paper-explores-diversity-statements-faculty-hiring.

Lederman, D.; and Jaschik, S. (2014). Federal accountability and financial pressure: A survey of presidents. *Inside Higher Education*, March 7. https://www .insidehighered.com/news/survey/federal-accountability-and-financial -pressure-survey-presidents.

Lee, E. (2017). "Where people like me don't belong": Faculty members from low-socioeconomic-status backgrounds. *Sociology of Education*, 90(3), 197–212.

Liera, R.; and Dowd, A. C. (2018). Faculty learning at boundaries to broker racial equity. *Journal of Higher Education*, 90(3), 462–485.

Lopez, I. H. (2015). *Dog whistle politics: How coded racial appeals have reinvented racism and wrecked the middle class*. Oxford: Oxford University Press.

Malcom, L.; and Malcom, S. (2011). The double bind: The next generation. *Harvard Educational Review*, 81(2), 162–172.

Masterson, K. (2019). *Diversifying graduate schools and the faculty*. Washington, DC: Inside Higher Education Special Reports.

Matthew, P. A. (2016a). What is faculty diversity worth to a university? *Atlantic*, November 23. https://www.theatlantic.com/education/archive/2016/11/what -is-faculty-diversity-worth-to-a-university/508334/.

———(2016b). *Written/unwritten: Diversity and the hidden truths of tenure*. Chapel Hill: University of North Carolina Press.

Meyerson, D.; and Tompkins, M. (2007). Tempered radicals as institutional change agents: The case of advancing gender equity at the University of Michigan. *Harvard Journal of Law & Gender*, 30, 303.

Miller, C.; Glick, W.; and Cardinal, L. (2005). The allocation of prestigious positions in organizational science: Accumulative advantage, sponsored mobility, and contest mobility. *Journal of Organizational Behavior*, 26, 489–515.

Moody, J. A. (2012). *Faculty diversity: Removing the barriers*. New York: Routledge Press.

Mora, G. C. (2014). *Making Hispanics: How activists, bureaucrats, and media constructed a new American*. Chicago: University of Chicago Press.

Morgan, A.; Clauset A.; Larremore, D.; LaBerge, N.; and Galesic, M. (2021). Socio-economic roots of academic faculty. *SocArXiv*, March 24. https://doi.org/10.31235/osf.io/6wjxc.

Morgan, I.; and Davies, P. (2012). *From sit-ins to SNCC: The student civil rights movement in the 1960s*. Gainesville: University Press of Florida.

Morimoto, S. A.; Zajicek, A. M.; Hunt, V. H.; and Lisnic, R. (2013). Beyond binders full of women: NSF ADVANCE and initiatives for institutional transformation. *Sociological Spectrum*, 33(5), 397–415.

Moss-Racusin, C.; Dovidio, J.; Brescoll, V.; Graham, M.; and Handelsman, J. (2012). Science faculty's subtle gender biases favor male students. *Proceedings of the National Academy of Sciences*, 109, 16474–16479.

Muhs, G.; Niemann, Y.; González, C., and Harris, A. (2012). *Presumed incompetent: The intersections of race and class for women in academia*. Logan: Utah State University Press.

Muñoz, S. M.; Basile, V.; Gonzalez, J.; Birmingham, D.; Aragon, A.; Jennings, L.; and Gloeckner, G. (2017). (Counter) narratives and complexities: Critical perspectives from a university cluster hire focused on diversity, equity, and inclusion. *Journal of Critical Thought and Praxis*, 6(1), 1–21.

Musselin, C. (2018). New forms of competition in higher education. *Socio-Economic Review*, 16(3), 657–683.

Myers, B. (2016). Where are the minority professors? *Chronicle of Higher Education*, February 14, https://www.chronicle.com/interactives/where-are-the-minority-professors.

Myers, S.; Mucha, P.; and Porter, M. (2011). Mathematical genealogy and department prestige. *Chaos*, 21(4), 041104.

National Center for Educational Statistics (2019). Integrated Postsecondary Education Data System. https://nces.ed.gov/ipeds/.

National Science Foundation (2018). *2016 Doctorate recipients from U.S. universities*. Washington, DC: National Center for Science and Engineering Statistics Directorate for Social, Behavioral and Economic Sciences.

———— (2019). ADVANCE: Organizational change for gender equity in STEM academic professions. https://www.nsf.gov/funding/pgm_summ.jsp?pims_id=5383.

Nietzel, M. (2021). The well-heeled professoriate: Socioeconomic backgrounds of university faculty. *Forbes*, March 28. https://www.forbes.com/sites/michaeltnietzel/2021/03/28/the-well-heeled-professoriate-socioeconomic-backgrounds-of-university-faculty/.

Ong, M.; Wright, C.; Espinosa, L.; and Orfield, G. (2011). Inside the double bind: A synthesis of empirical research on undergraduate and graduate women of color in science, technology, engineering, and mathematics. *Harvard Educational Review*, 81(2), 172–209.

Oswald, F.; Mitchell, G.; Blanton, H.; Jaccard, J.; and Tetlock, P. (2013). Predicting ethnic and racial discrimination: A meta-analysis of IAT research. *Journal of Personality and Social Psychology*, 105(2), 171–192.

Otani, A. (2013). Black UCLA students decry lack of diversity in video. *USA Today*, November 14, https://www.usatoday.com/story/news/nation/2013/11/14/youtube-ucla-lack-diversity/3518373.

Ottaviano, G. I.; and Peri, G. (2006). The economic value of cultural diversity: evidence from US cities. *Journal of Economic Geography*, 6(1), 9–44.

Page, S. (2019). *The diversity bonus: How great teams pay off in the knowledge economy*. Princeton, NJ: Princeton University Press.

Phillips, R. (2002). Recruiting and retaining a diverse faculty. *Planning for Higher Education*, 30(2), 32–39.

Polletta, F. (1998). "It was like a fever . . .": Narrative and identity in social protest. *Social Problems*, 45(2), 137–159.

Ponjuan, L. (2011). Recruiting and retaining Latino faculty members: The missing piece to Latino student success. *Thought and Action*, 27, 99–110.

Posselt, J. (2016). *Inside graduate admissions: Merit, diversity, and faculty gatekeeping*. Cambridge, MA: Harvard University Press.

Richmond, A. S.; Boysen, G. A.; and Gurung, R. (2016). *An evidence-based guide to college and university teaching: Developing the model teacher*. New York: Routledge.

Rivera, L. A. (2015). *Pedigree: How elite students get elite jobs*. Princeton, NJ: Princeton University Press.

Roehling, M. V.; and Granberry Russell, P. (eds.) (2012). *Faculty search toolkit: A resource for search committees and administrators at Michigan State University* (NSF ADVANCE Grant #0811205). East Lansing: Michigan State University. https://www.adapp-advance.msu.edu/files_adapp-advance/content/FacultySearchToolkit-final.pdf.

Rojas, F. (2007). *From black power to black studies: How a radical social movement became an academic discipline*. Baltimore, MD: Johns Hopkins University Press.

Schick, F. (2015). University commits $50 million to faculty diversity initiative. *Yale News*, November 4. https://yaledailynews.com/blog/2015/11/04/university-commits-50-million-to-faculty-diversity-initiative.

Schmaling, K.; Baker, D.; Bluem, A.; and Trevino, A. (2019). Applicant responses to diversity selection criteria in academic staff descriptions. *Journal of Higher Education Policy and Management,* 41(2), 121–136.

Schmaling, K.; Trevino, A.; Lind, J.; Blume A.; and Baker, D. (2015). Diversity statements: How faculty applicants address diversity. *Journal of Diversity in Higher Education*, 8(4), 213–224.

Schmidt, B.; and Chingos, M. (2007). Ranking doctoral programs by placement: A new method. *Political Science and Politics*, 40, 523–529.

Schneckenberg, D. (2009). Understanding the real barriers to technology-enhanced innovation in higher education. *Educational Research*, 51(4), 411–424.

Scott-Clayton, J.; and Li, J. (2016). Black-white disparity in student loan debt more than triples after graduation. *Evidence Speaks Reports*, 2(3), 1–9.

Sensoy, Ö.; and DiAngelo, R. (2017). "We are all for diversity, but . . .": How faculty hiring committees reproduce Whiteness and practical suggestions for how they can change. *Harvard Educational Review*, 87(4), 557–580.

Singal, J. (2017). The cut: Psychology's favorite tool for measuring racism isn't up to the job. *New York Times Magazine*, https://www.thecut.com/2017/01/psychologys-racism-measuring-tool-isnt-up-to-the-job.html.

Shotton, H.; Lowe, S.; and Waterman, S. (2013). *Beyond the asterisk: Understanding Native students in higher education.* Sterling, VA: Stylus Press.

Smith, D. G. (2000). How to diversify the faculty. *Academe*, 86(5), 48–52.

——— (2020). *Diversity's promise for higher education.* Baltimore, MD: Johns Hopkins University Press.

Smith, D. G.; Turner, C. S.; Osei-Kofi, N.; and Richards, S. (2004). Successful strategies for hiring diverse faculty. *Journal of Higher Education*, 75(2), 133–160.

Smith, D. G.; Wolf, L. E.; Wolf-Wendel, L.; and Busenberg, B. E. (1996). *Achieving faculty diversity: Debunking the myths.* Washington, DC: Association of American Colleges and Universities.

Span, C. (2016). Creating the talented tenth. *Journal of Blacks in Higher Education*, June 1. https://www.jbhe.com/2016/06/creating-the-talented-tenth/.

Springer, A. (2006). How to diversify the faculty. Paper presented at American Association of University Professors Annual Meeting, San Francisco, CA, March.

Steinbaum, M.; and Vaghul, K. (2016). *How the student debt crisis affects African Americans and Latinos.* Washington, DC: Washington Center for Equitable Growth.

Stepan-Norris, J.; and Kerrissey, J. (2016). Enhancing gender equity in academia: Lessons from the ADVANCE program. *Sociological Perspectives*, 59(2), 225–245.

Survey of Earned Doctorates (2019). Alexandria, VA: National Science Foundation. https://www.nsf.gov/statistics/srvydoctorates.

Taylor, O.; Apprey, C. B.; Hill, G.; McGrann, L.; and Wang, J. (2010). Diversifying the faculty. *Academe*, 12(3). https://www.aacu.org/publications-research/periodicals/diversifying-faculty.

Teare, C. (2019). Why didn't college admissions officers catch the Varsity Blues scandal? *Forbes*, July 28. https://www.forbes.com/sites/christeare/2019/07/28/why-didnt-college-admissions-officers-catch-the-varsity-blues-scandal/.

Teranishi, R. (2013). *iCount: A data quality movement for Asian Americans and Pacific Islanders in higher education.* Los Angeles: National Commission on Asian American and Pacific Islander Research in Education.

Teranishi, R.; Nguyen, B.M.D.; and Alcantar, C. M. (2020). *Measuring race: Why disaggregating data matters for addressing educational inequality.* New York: Teachers College Press.

Thelin, J. R. (2011). *A history of higher education.* Baltimore, MD: Johns Hopkins University Press.

Thompson, C. Q. (2008). Recruitment, retention, and mentoring faculty of color: The chronicle continues. *New Directions for Higher Education*, 143, 47–54.

Tiao, A. (2006). *Access and equality: It's NOT all about the numbers. An exploratory study of Asian Pacific American aspirations for academic careers.* Unpublished

PhD dissertation, University of Pennsylvania. Dissertations available from Pro-Quest, AAI3225557.

Tierney, W. G.; and Sallee, M. W. (2008). Do organizational structures and strategies increase faculty diversity? A cultural analysis. *American Academic*, 4(1), 159–184.

Tomlinson, G.; and Freeman, S. (2018). Who really selected you? Insights into faculty selection processes in top-ranked higher education graduate programs. *Journal of Further and Higher Education*, 42(6), 855–867.

Tuitt, F. A.; Sagaria, M.A.D.; and Turner, C.S.V. (2007). Signals and strategies in hiring faculty of color. In J. C. Smart (ed.), *Higher education: Handbook of theory and research*, vol. 22, 496–535.

Turner, C. S. (2002). *Diversifying the faculty: A guidebook for search committees*. Washington, DC: Association of American Colleges and Universities.

Turner, C. S.; González, J. C.; and Wong, K. L. (2011). Faculty women of color: The critical nexus of race and gender. *Journal of Diversity in Higher Education*, 4(4), 199–211.

Turner, C. S.; González, J. C.; and Wood, L. (2008). Faculty of color in academe: What 20 years of literature tells us. *Journal of Diversity in Higher Education*, 1(3), 139–168.

Turner, C. S.; and Meyers, S. (1999). *Faculty of color in academe: Bittersweet success*. Upper Saddle River, NJ: Pearson Publishing.

Vega, T. (2014). Colorblind notion aside: Colleges grapple with racial tension. *New York Times*, February 24. https://www.nytimes.com/2014/02/25/us/colorblind-notion-aside-colleges-grapple-with-racial-tension.html.

Vloet, K. (n.d.). Being Black at U-M. *Bentley Historical Library Magazine*. https://bentley.umich.edu/news-events/magazine/being-black-at-u-m.

Wakelee, D.; and Cordeiro, W. (2006). Examining an alternative approach to hiring tenure track faculty. *Review of Business Research*, 6(3), 101–105.

Ware, L. (2000). People of color in the academy: Patterns of discrimination in faculty hiring and retention. *Boston College Third World Law Journal*, 20(1), 55–76.

Watty, K.; McKay, J.; and Ngo, L. (2016). Innovators or inhibitors? Accounting faculty resistance to new educational technologies in higher education. *Journal of Accounting Education*, 36, 1–15.

Waymer, D.; and VanSlette, S. (2016). Higher education public relations and branding: Critically interrogating universities' ranking and AAU aspirational pursuits. *Journal of School Public Relations*, 37(2), 227–248.

Weinberg, S. L. (2008). Monitoring faculty diversity: The need for a more granular approach. *Journal of Higher Education*, 79(4), 365–387.

Wilkinson, N. L. (2007). Recruiting and retaining a diverse faculty in a public university. *Yearbook of the Association of Pacific Coast Geographers*, 69, 168–172.

Williams, D. A. (2007). Examining the relation between race and student evaluations of faculty members: A literature review. *Profession*, 168–173. https://www.jstor.org/stable/25595863.

Williamson, J. (1999). In defense of themselves: The black student struggle for success and recognition at predominantly white colleges and universities. *Journal of Negro Education*, 68(1), 92–105.

Williamson-Lott, J. A. (2018). *Jim Crow Campus: Higher education and the struggle for a new southern social order*. New York: Teachers College Press.

World Population Review (2020). Houston, Texas. http://worldpopulationreview.com/us-cities/houston-population.

Wu, F. (2003). *Yellow: Race in America beyond Black and White*. New York: Basic Books.

Xia, K.; and Percy, N. (2019). Columbia has $185 million in dedicated funds: Why is hiring diverse faculty still so difficult? *Columbia Spectator*, February 1. https://www.columbiaspectator.com/news/2019/02/01/columbia-has-185-million-in-dedicated-funds-why-is-hiring-diverse-faculty-still-so-difficult-9.

Zippel, K.; and Ferree, M. M. (2019). Organizational interventions and the creation of gendered knowledge: US universities and NSF ADVANCE. *Gender, Work and Organization*, 26(6), 805–821.

SUPPLEMENTARY BIBLIOGRAPHY

Adams, K.; and Bargerhuff, M. E. (2005). Dialogue and action: Addressing recruitment of diverse faculty in one Midwestern university's college of education and human services. *Education*, 125, 539–545.

Aguirre, A. (2000a). Academic storytelling: A critical race theory story of affirmative action. *Sociological Perspectives*, 43(2), 319–339. https://doi.org/10.2307/1389799.

——— (2000b). Women and minority faculty in the academic workplace: Recruitment, retention, and academic culture. *ASHE-ERIC Higher Education Report*, 27(6).

Ahmend, S. (2012). *On being included: Racism and diversity in institutional life.* Raleigh, NC: Duke University Press.

Alger, J. R. (2000). How to recruit and promote minority faculty: Start by playing fair. *Black Issues in Higher Education*, 17, 160–163.

Allen, J.; Smith, J. L.; and Ransdell, L. B. (2019). Missing or seizing the opportunity? The effect of an opportunity hire on job offers to science faculty candidates. *Equality, Diversity and Inclusion: An International Journal*, 38(2), 160–177.

Arismendi, I.; and Penaluna, B. E. (2016). Examining diversity inequities in fisheries science: a call to action. *BioScience*, 66(7), 584–591.

Baker, D. L.; Schmaling, K.; Fountain, K. C.; Blume, A. W.; and Boose, R. (2016). Defining diversity: A mixed-method analysis of terminology in faculty applications. *The Social Science Journal*, 53(1), 60–66.

Barnett, E.; Gibson, M.; and Black, P. (2003). Proactive steps to successfully recruit, retain, and mentor minority educators: Issues in education. *Journal of Early Education and Family Review*, 10(3), 18–28.

Beattie, G.; Cohen, D.; and McGuire, L. (2013). An exploration of possible unconscious ethnic biases in higher education: The role of implicit attitudes on selection for university posts. *Semiotica*, 197, 171–201.

Beattie, G.; and Tidwell, P. (2012). Possible unconscious bias in recruitment and promotion and the need to promote equality. *Perspectives: Policy and Practice in Higher Education*, 16(1), 7–13.

Bhalla, N. (2019). Strategies to improve equity in faculty hiring. *Molecular Biology of the Cell*, 30(22), 2744–2749.

Blake, D. (2018). Motivations and paths to becoming faculty at Minority Serving Institutions. *Education Sciences*, 8(1), 30.

Bonilla-Silva, E. (2015). The invisible weight of Whiteness: The racial grammar of everyday life in contemporary America. *Ethnic and Racial Studies*, 35(2), 173–194.

Bradley, S. W.; Garven, J. R.; Law, W. W.; and West, J. E. (2018). The impact of chief diversity officers on diverse faculty hiring. NBER Working Papers no. 24969. Cambridge, MA: National Bureau of Economic Research.

Brown-Glaude, W. (Ed.) (2008). *Doing diversity in higher education: Faculty leaders share challenges and strategies*. New Brunswick, NJ: Rutgers University Press.

Buller, J. (2017). *Best practices for faculty search committees: How to review applications and interview candidates*. San Francisco: Jossey-Bass.

Carey, J. M.; Carman, K. R.; Clayton, K. P.; Horiuchi, Y.; Htun, M.; and Ortiz, B. (2018). Who wants to hire a more diverse faculty? A conjoint analysis of faculty and student preferences for gender and racial/ethnic diversity. *Politics, Groups, and Identities*, 1–19.

Carnes, M.; Devine, P. G.; Manwell, L. B.; Byars-Winston, A.; Fine, E.; Ford, C.; Forscher, P.; Isaac, C.; Katz, A.; Magua, W.; Palta, M.; and Sheridan, J. (2015). Effect of an intervention to break the gender bias habit for faculty at one institution: a cluster randomized, controlled trial. *Academic medicine: Journal of the Association of American Medical Colleges*, 90(2), 221.

Cartwright, A. D.; Avent-Harris, J. R.; Munsey, R. B.; and Lloyd-Hazlett, J. (2018). Interview experiences and diversity concerns of counselor education faculty from underrepresented groups. *Counselor Education and Supervision*, 57(2), 132–146.

Castellanos. J.; and Jones, L. (Eds.) 2003. *The Majority in the Minority: Expanding the Representation of Latina/o Faculty, Administrators and Students in Higher Education*. Herndon, VA: Stylus.

Chapman, B. G. (2001). *Minority faculty recruitment in community colleges: Commitment, attitudes, beliefs, and perceptions of chief academic officers*. Unpublished PhD dissertation, University of Texas at Austin.

Clark, R. L. (2006). *Recruitment and retention of faculty of color in Oklahoma*. Unpublished PhD dissertation, Oklahoma State University.

Cole, S.; and Barber, E. (2003). *Increasing faculty diversity: The occupational choices of high-achieving minority students*. Cambridge, MA: Harvard University Press.

Cowan, L. Y. (2006). *An examination of policies and programs used to increase ethnic and racial diversity among faculty at research universities*. Unpublished PhD dissertation, University of Illinois at Urbana-Champaign.

Deas, D.; Pisano, E. D.; Mainous, A. G., III; Johnson, N. G.; Singleton, M. H.; Gordon, L.; Taylor, W.; Hazen-Martin, D.; Burnham, W. S.; and Reves, J. G. (2012). Improving diversity through strategic planning: a 10-year (2002–2012) experience at the Medical University of South Carolina. *Academic Medicine*, 87(11), 1548–1555.

Delgado-Romero, E. A.; Manlove, A. N.; Manlove, J. D.; and Hernandez, C. A. (2007). Controversial issues in the recruitment and retention of Latino/a faculty. *Journal of Hispanic Higher Education*, 6, 34–51.

Derouse, E.; Buijsrogge, A.; Roulin, N.; and Duyck, W. (2016). Why your stigma isn't hired: A dual-process framework of interview bias. *Human Resource Management Review*, 26(2), 90–111.

Devine, P. G.; Forscher, P. S.; Cox, W. T.; Kaatz, A.; Sheridan, J.; and Carnes, M. (2017). A gender bias habit-breaking intervention led to increased hiring of female faculty in STEMM departments. *Journal of Experimental Social Psychology*, 73, 211–215.

DiAngelo, R. (2011). White fragility. *International Journal of Critical Pedagogy*, 3(3), 54–70.

DiRamio, D.; Theroux, R.; and Guarino, A. J. (2009). Faculty hiring at top-ranked higher education administration programs: An examination using social network analysis. *Innovative Higher Education*, 34(3), 149–159.

Eagan, M. K.; and Garvey, J. C. (2016). Stressing out: Connecting race, gender, and stress with faculty productivity. *Journal of Higher Education*, 86(6), 923–954.

Evans, A.; and Chun, E. B. (2007). Are the walls really down? Behavioral and organizational barriers to faculty and staff diversity. *ASHE Higher Education Report*, 33(1), 1–139.

Faria, J. R.; Loureiro, P. R.; Mixon, F. G.; and Sachsida, A. (2016). Minority faculty hiring power in academe: An economic model. *Review of Black Political Economy*, 43(3–4), 273–288.

Fernandez, E. C.; Popović, D.; and Gilmer, P. J. (2014). Recruiting women STEM faculty. In *Alliances for Advancing Academic Women* (pp. 121–145). Rotterdam: Sense Publishers.

Fine, E.; and Handelsman, J. (2012). Searching for excellence and diversity: A guide for search committee chairs. H. Handelsman (ed.). Madison: University of Wisconsin–Madison.

Fine, E.; Sheridan, J.; Carnes, M.; Handelsman, J.; Pribbenow, C.; Savoy, J.; and Wendt, A. (2014). Minimizing the influence of gender bias on the faculty search process. In *Gender Transformation in the Academy* (pp. 267–289). West Yorkshire, UK: Emerald Group Publishing.

Fleetwood, J.; and Aebersold, N. (2010). Fostering equity and diversity in faculty recruitment. *Academic Leadership*, 8(4), 26.

Fradella, H. F. (2018). Supporting strategies for equity, diversity, and inclusion in higher education faculty hiring. In *Diversity and Inclusion in Higher Education and Societal Contexts* (pp. 119–151). London: Palgrave Macmillan, Cham.

Freeman, S.; and DiRamio, D. (2016). Elitism or pragmatism? Faculty hiring at top graduate programs in higher education administration. *Journal of the Professoriate*, 8(2), 94–127.

Fujii, S. J. (2014). Diversity, communication, and leadership in the community college faculty search process. *Community College Journal of Research and Practice*, 38(10), 903–916.

Fujimoto, E. O. (2012). Hiring diverse faculty members in community colleges: A case study in ethical decision making. *Community College Review*, 40(3), 255–274.

Glass, C.; and Minnotte, K. L. (2010). Recruiting and hiring women in STEM fields. *Journal of Diversity in Higher Education*, 3(4), 218.

Greene, J.; Lewis, P. A.; Richmond, G. L.; and Stockard, J. (2011). Changing the chairs: Impact of workshop activities in assisting chemistry department chairs in achieving racial and ethnic diversity. *Journal of Chemical Education*, 88(6), 721–725.

Griffin, K. (2020). Institutional barriers, strategies, and benefits to increasing the representation of women and men of color in the professoriate. *Higher Education: Handbook of Theory & Research*, 35, 277–349.

Gutiérrez y Muhs, G.; Nieman, Y. F.; González, C. G.; and Harris, A. P. (2012). *Presumed incompetent: The intersections of race and class for women in academia.* Boulder: University Press of Colorado.

Harris, T. B.; Thomson, W. A.; Moreno, N. P.; Conrad, S.; White, S. E.; Young, G. H.; Malmberg, E. D.; Weisman, B.; and Monroe, A. D. (2018). Advancing holistic review for faculty recruitment and advancement. *Academic Medicine*, 93(11), 1658–1662.

Hasnas, J. (2018). The quest for a diverse faculty: Theory and practice. *Georgetown Journal of Law & Public Policy*, 16, 753.

Henry, A. (2015). "We especially welcome applications from members of visible minority groups": Reflections on race, gender and life at three universities. *Race, Ethnicity, and Education*, 18(5), 589–610.

Higdon, M. J. (2013). A place in the academy: Law faculty hiring and socioeconomic bias. *John's Law Review*, 87, 171.

Hopkins, N. (2007). Diversification of a university faculty: Women faculty in the MIT schools of science and engineering. *New England Journal of Public Policy*, 22(1), 11.

Hughes, A. K.; Horner, P. S.; and Ortiz, D. V. (2012). Being the diversity hire: Negotiating identity in an academic job search. *Journal of Social Work Education*, 48(3), 595–612.

Jeffcoat, K.; and Piland, W. E. (2012). Anatomy of a community college faculty diversity program. *Community College Journal of Research and Practice*, 36(6), 397–410.

Johnson, K. (2003). Encouraging the heart: How three University of California institutions responded to minority faculty recruitment after the implementation of Proposition 209. Unpublished PhD dissertation, Pepperdine University.

Johnson, K. N.; and Wiley, J. D. (2000). Analytical models for minority representation in academic departments. *Research in Higher Education*, 41(4), 481–504.

Jost, J. T.; Rudman, L. A.; Blair, I. V., Carney, D. R.; Dasgupta, N.; Glaser, J.; and Hardin, C. D. (2009). The existence of implicit bias is beyond reasonable doubt: A refutation of ideological and methodological objections and executive summary of ten studies that no manager should ignore. *Research in Organizational Behavior*, 29, 39–69.

Kaplan, S. E.; Gunn, C. M.; Kulukulualani, A. K.; Raj, A.; Freund, K. M.; and Carr, P. L. (2018). Challenges in recruiting, retaining and promoting racially and ethnically diverse faculty. *Journal of the National Medical Association*, 110(1), 58–64.

Kayes, P. E. (2006). New paradigms for diversifying faculty and staff in higher education: Uncovering cultural biases in the search and hiring process. *Multicultural Education*, 14, 65–69.

Landrum, R. E.; and Clump, M. A. (2004). Departmental search committees and the evaluation of faculty applicants. *Teaching of Psychology*, 31(1), 12–17.

Lara, L. J. (2019). Faculty of color unmask color-blind ideology in the community college faculty search process. *Community College Journal of Research and Practice*, 57(5), 1–16.

Lee, C. D. (2014). *Search committees: A comprehensive guide to successful faculty, staff, and administrative searches*. Sterling, VA: Stylus Publishing.

Li, Diyi; and Koedel, C. (2017). Representation and salary gaps by race-ethnicity and gender at selective public universities. *Educational Researcher*, 46(7), 343–354.

Lopez, I. H. (2015). *Dog whistle politics: How coded racial appeals have reinvented racism and wrecked the middle class*. Oxford: Oxford University Press.

Madera, J. M.; Hebl, M. R.; Dial, H.; Martin, R.; and Valian, V. (2018). Raising doubt in letters of recommendation for academia: Gender differences and their impact. *Journal of Business and Psychology*, 34(3). https://doi.org/10.1007/s10869-018-9541-1.

Maturana, I. M. (2005). *Factors in the search process that contribute to the recruitment and hiring of faculty of color*. Unpublished PhD dissertation, University of Massachusetts at Boston.

Mertz, N. T. (2011). Women of color faculty: Recruitment, hiring, and retention. In *Women of color in higher education: Changing directions and new perspectives* (pp. 41–71). West Yorkshire, UK: Emerald Group Publishing.

Moody, J. (2015). Rising above cognitive errors: Improving searches, evaluations, and decision-making. North Charleston, SC: CreateSpace Independent Publishing Platform.

Mora, M. T.; Qubbaj, A. R.; and Rodríguez, H. (2018). Advancing Latinas and other women in STEM through dual career hiring and other policy/climate initiatives at the University of Texas Rio Grande Valley. In M. R. McMahon, M. T. Mora, and A. R. Qubbaj (eds.), *Advancing women in academic STEM fields through dual career policies and practices* (97–114). Charlotte, NC: Information Age Publishing.

Morris, C. A. (2000). *Strategies for recruitment and retention of faculty of color in community colleges*. Unpublished PhD dissertation, University of Texas at Austin.

Morton, M. J.; Bristol, M. B.; Atherton, P. H.; Schwab, C. W.; and Sonnad, S. S. (2008). Improving the recruitment and hiring process for women faculty. *Journal of the American College of Surgeons*, 206(6), 1210–1218.

Moss, L.E.T. (2000). *Recruitment, retention, and mentoring of female and minority faculty in higher education.* Unpublished PhD dissertation, Arkansas State University.

Myers, S. L., Jr.; and Turner, C.S.V. (2001). Affirmative action retrenchment and labor market outcomes for African-American faculty. In B. Lindsay and M. J. Justiz (eds.), *The quest for equity in higher education: Toward new paradigms in an evolving affirmative action era* (pp. 63–98). Albany: State University of New York Press.

———— (2004). The effects of Ph.D. supply on minority faculty representation. *American Economic Review*, 94(2), 296–301.

O'Meara, K.; Kuvaeva, A.; Nyunt, G.; Waugaman, C.; and Jackson, R. (2017). Asked more often: Gender differences in faculty workload in research universities and the work interactions that shape them. *American Educational Research Journal*, 54(6), 1154–1186.

Onwuachi-Willig, A. (2009). Complimentary discrimination and complementary discrimination in faculty hiring. *Washington University Law Review*, 87, 763.

Ordway, D. (2017). White, male faculty earn higher salaries than women, minorities at public universities. *Journalist's Resource*, September 18. https:// journalistsresource.org/economics/faculty-college-salaries-demographics -minorities-research/.

Owino, A. Z. (2000). *An investigation of the hiring trends of women and minority faculty in institutions of higher learning.* Unpublished PhD dissertation, Pennsylvania State University.

Page, K. R.; Castillo-Page, L.; and Wright, S. M. (2011). Faculty diversity programs in US medical schools and characteristics associated with higher faculty diversity. *Academic Medicine: Journal of the Association of American Medical Colleges*, 86(10), 1221.

Peek, M. E.; Kim, K. E.; Johnson, J. K.; and Vela, M. B. (2013). "URM candidates are encouraged to apply": A national study to identify effective strategies to enhance racial and ethnic faculty diversity in academic departments of medicine. *Academic Medicine: Journal of the Association of American Medical Colleges*, 88(3), 405.

Peoples, R., III (2004). *Recruitment of minority faculty: A comparison of attitudes, beliefs, perceptions, commitments, and strategies of Texas administrators in selected community colleges.* Unpublished PhD dissertation, Baylor University.

Pew Research Center (2019). *Hispanic Trends.* https://www.pewresearch.org /hispanic/fact-sheet/latinos-in-the-2016-election-illinois/.

Price, E. G.; Gozu, A.; Kern, D. E.; Powe, N. R.; Wand, G. S.; Golden, S.; and Cooper, L. A. (2005). The role of cultural diversity climate in recruitment, promotion, and retention of faculty in academic medicine. *Journal of general internal medicine*, 20(7), 565–571.

Rai, K. B.; and Critzer, J. W. (2000). *Affirmative action and the university: Race, ethnicity, and gender in higher education employment.* Lincoln: University of Nebraska Press.

Robinson, P. A.; Byrd, D.; Louis, D. A.; and Bonner, F. A. (2013). Enhancing faculty diversity at community colleges: A practical solution for advancing the completion agenda. *FOCUS on Colleges, Universities and Schools*, 7(1).

Salvucci, C.; and Lawless, C. A. (2016). Nursing faculty diversity: Barriers and perceptions on recruitment, hiring and retention. *Journal of Cultural Diversity*, 23(2).

Schick, C. (2000). Keeping the ivory tower White: Discourses of racial domination. *Canadian Journal of Law and Society*, 15(2), 70–90.

Schmaling, K. B.; Blume, A. W.; and Baker, D. L. (2017). Characteristics of faculty position advertisements associated with applicant diversity. *Journal of Higher Education Theory and Practice*, 17(8).

Sekaquaptewa, D.; Takahashi, K.; Malley, J.; Herzog, K.; and Bliss, S. (2019). An evidence-based faculty recruitment workshop influences departmental hiring practice perceptions among university faculty. *Equality, Diversity and Inclusion: An International Journal*, 38(2), 188–210.

Sgoutas-Emch, S.; Baird, L.; Myers, P.; Camacho, M.; and Lord, S. (2016). We're not all White men: Using a cohort/cluster approach to diversify STEM faculty hiring. *Thought and Action*, 32(1), 91–107.

Sheridan, J. T.; Fine, E.; Pribbenow, C. M.; Handelsman, J.; and Carnes, M. (2010). Searching for excellence and diversity: Increasing the hiring of women faculty at one academic medical center. *Academic Medicine: Journal of the Association of American Medical Colleges*, 85(6), 999.

Smith, D. G.; Turner, C. S.; Osei-Kofi, N.; and Richards, S. (2004). Interrupting the usual: Successful strategies for hiring diverse faculty. *Journal of Higher Education*, 75(2), 133–160.

Smith, J. L.; Handley, I. M.; Zale, A. V.; Rushing, S.; and Potvin, M. A. (2015). Now hiring! Empirically testing a three-step intervention to increase faculty gender diversity in STEM. *BioScience*, 65(11), 1084–1087.

Springer, A. (2002). *How to diversify faculty: The current legal landscape*. Washington, DC: American Association of University Professors.

Stanley, J. M.; Capers, C. F.; and Berlin, L. E. (2007). Changing the face of nursing faculty: Minority faculty recruitment and retention. *Journal of Professional Nursing*, 23, 253–261.

Stewart, A. J.; Malley, J. E.; and Herzog, K. A. (2016). Increasing the representation of women faculty in STEM departments: What makes a difference? *Journal of Women and Minorities in Science and Engineering*, 22(1), 23–47.

Stewart, A. J.; and Valian, V. V. (2018). *The inclusive academy: Achieving diversity and excellence*. Cambridge, MA: MIT Press.

Subervi, F.; and Cantrell, T. H. (2007). Assessing efforts and policies related to the recruitment and retention of minority faculty at accredited and non-accredited journalism and mass communication programs. *Journalism and Mass Communication Educator*, 62(1), 27–46.

Subramaniam, M. M.; and Jaeger, P. T. (2010). Modeling inclusive practice? Attracting diverse faculty and future faculty to the information workforce. *Library Trends*, 59(1), 109–127.

Sue, D. W. (2010). *Microaggressions in everyday life: Race, gender, and sexual orientation.* Hoboken, NJ: Wiley.

Taylor, O.; Apprey, C. B.; Hill, G.; McGrann, L.; Wang, J. (2010). Diversifying the faculty. *Peer Review,* 12(3), 15.

Testy, K. Y. (2010). Best practices for hiring and retaining a diverse law faculty. *Iowa Law Review,* 96, 1707.

Turner, C.S.V. (2002). *Diversifying the faculty: A guidebook for search committees.* Washington, DC: Association of American Colleges and Universities.

——— (2003). Incorporation and marginalization in the academy: From border toward center for faculty of color? *Journal of Black Studies,* 34, 112–125.

University of Wisconsin–Madison (2008). Report of the cluster/interdisciplinary advisory committee to evaluate the cluster hiring initiative. July. http://clusters .wisc.edu/documents/ClusterReport_2008.pdf.

Urban Universities for Health (2015). Faculty cluster hiring: For diversity and institutional climate. http://urbanuniversitiesforhealth.org/media/documents /Faculty_Cluster_Hiring_Report.pdf.

Vega, W.; Yglesias, K.; and Murray, J. P. (2011). Recruiting and mentoring minority faculty members. *Hiring the Next Generation of Faculty: New Directions for Community Colleges,* 152, 49–55.

Ware, L. (2000). People of color in the academy: Patterns of discrimination in faculty hiring and retention. *British Columbia Third World Law Journal,* 20(1), 55–76.

White-Lewis, D. K. (2019). *The facade of fit and preponderance of power in faculty search processes: Facilitators and inhibitors of diversity.* PhD dissertation, UCLA.

Whitaker, M.; and Grollman, E.A. (Eds.). (2018). *Counternarratives from women of color academics: Bravery, vulnerability, and resistance.* New York: Routledge.

Williams, B. D. (2012). *A phenomenological study: Higher education search committee hiring of a diverse faculty in business departments.* Ann Arbor, MI: ProQuest.

Williams, W. M.; and Ceci, S. J. (2015). National hiring experiments reveal 2:1 faculty preference for women on STEM tenure track. *Proceedings of the National Academy of Sciences,* 112(17), 5360–5365.

Wright, C.; and Vanderford, N. (2017). What faculty hiring committees want. *Nature Biotechnology,* 35(9), 885–887.

Zajac, L. (2011). Double-loop approach: recruitment and retention of minority nursing faculty. *ABNF Journal,* 22(3), 73–77.

INDEX

academic disciplines, diversity within, 5
accountability, within leadership, 139–43, 160–61
admissions, bias within, 118–20
ADVANCE grants (NSF), 35, 42, 43, 161
affirmative action, 201–2
African Americans: accusations to, 8–9; faculty statistics of, 20, 22, 109; female faculty statistics of, 2, 42, 43–44; historical employment experiences of, 65–71; law school statistics of, 236; male faculty statistics of, 2; merit color-blindness toward, 66–70; PhD statistics of, 5, 94, 95, 102–3, 229; salaries of, 223; student statistics of, 1; tenured faculty statistics of, 32–33
American Association of Colleges and Universities (AAC&U), 16n3
American Association of Universities (AAU): authority of, 17; background of, 16; diversity lack within, 18, 18n7, 18n8; key issues of, 18n7; limiting qualified candidate pools within, 125–31; member listing of, 19; mission of, 18; regions within, 21. *See also specific universities*
American Council on Education (ACE), 16n2
American Historical Association (AHA), 154
American Indian and Alaska Natives (AIAN): faculty statistics of, 24–25, 118; female statistics of, 42–43, 101, 108; law school statistics of, 236; PhD statistics of, 94, 110–11; tenured faculty statistics of, 34–35
Anderson, James D., 22, 64–71
anthropology: African American PhD statistics within, 100, 102–3; American Indian and Alaska Natives (AIAN) PhD statistics within, 110–11; Asian American PhD statistics within, 106–7; Hispanic PhD statistics within, 104–5; Latino PhD statistics within, 101; Native Hawaiians and Pacific Islanders (NHPI) PhD statistics within, 112–13; nonresident PhD statistics within,

116–17; PhD conferrals within, 96–99; White PhD statistics within, 108, 114–15
anti-blackness, acknowledgment and confrontation of, 229–30
Arizona State University, 125, 131, 134
Asian Americans: faculty statistics of, 24, 109; female faculty statistics of, 2, 42, 44; law school statistics of, 236; male faculty statistics of, 2; PhD statistics of, 94, 101, 106–7; student statistics of, 1; tenured faculty statistics of, 34
Association of American Law Schools (AALS), 154

benchmarking, of faculty diversity, 44–45, 58
Bhalla, Needi, 200
bias training, 167–78, 180, 218–19
Bieniasz, Paul, 188
Big Ten Alliance, 227
biological and biomedical sciences: African American PhD statistics within, 102–3; American Indian and Alaska Natives (AIAN) PhD statistics within, 110–11; Asian American PhD statistics within, 101, 106–7; Hispanic PhD statistics within, 104–5; Latino PhD statistics within, 100; Native Hawaiians and Pacific Islanders (NHPI) PhD statistics within, 112–13; nonresident PhD statistics within, 116–17; PhD conferrals within, 96–99; White PhD statistics within, 108, 114–15
Bivort, Benjamin de, 188
#BlackintheIvory, 7n
board of trustees, leadership role of, 135
Boston University: AAU membership of, 19; Asian American faculty statistics of, 34; faculty racial and ethnic diversity statistics of, 26–27; female faculty statistics of, 46–47, 52–53; tenured faculty racial and ethnic diversity statistics of, 36–37

Boudaie, Arya, 189

Brandeis University: AAU membership of, 19; African American faculty statistics of, 22; Asian American faculty statistics of, 24, 34; faculty racial and ethnic diversity statistics of, 26–27; female faculty statistics of, 46–47, 52–53; tenured faculty racial and ethnic diversity statistics of, 36–37

Brown University: AAU membership of, 19; African American degree holders from, 68; African American faculty statistics of, 20; faculty racial and ethnic diversity statistics of, 26–27; female faculty statistics of, 46–47, 52–53; Hispanic faculty statistics of, 23; strategic plan of, 45, 58; tenured faculty racial and ethnic diversity statistics of, 36–37

budgeting, 135

California Institute of Technology (Cal Tech): AAU membership of, 19; African American faculty statistics of, 22, 33; faculty racial and ethnic diversity statistics of, 26–27; female faculty statistics of, 46–47, 52–53; strategic plan of, 45n18; tenured faculty racial and ethnic diversity statistics of, 36–37; White faculty statistics of, 25

candidate fit, 204–5

Carnegie Mellon University: AAU membership of, 19; African American faculty statistics of, 22, 33; faculty racial and ethnic diversity statistics of, 26–27; female faculty statistics of, 46–47, 52–53; Hispanic faculty statistics of, 33; tenured faculty racial and ethnic diversity statistics of, 36–37

Carolina Post-Doctoral Program, 23

Case Western Reserve University: AAU membership of, 19; Asian American faculty statistics of, 24; faculty racial and ethnic diversity statistics of, 26–27; female faculty statistics of, 46–47, 52–53; Hispanic faculty statistics of, 33; tenured faculty racial and ethnic diversity statistics of, 36–37

checklists, for quality, 75

chief diversity officers, 158–62

Clotfelter, Charles, 80

cluster hires, 200–202

Columbia University: AAU membership of, 19; African American degree holders from, 68; diversity funding within, 134; diversity statistics within, 236; faculty racial and ethnic diversity statistics of, 26–27; female faculty statistics of, 46–47, 52–53; handbook from, 179; law school student statistics of, 238–39; student diversity within, 2; tenured faculty racial and ethnic diversity statistics of, 36–37

competition, 82–83, 208, 222–23

consultants, outside, 213–14

Cooker, Siobhan, 189

Cornell University: AAU membership of, 19; American Indian and Alaska Native (AIAN) faculty statistics of, 34; diversity funding within, 134; diversity statistics within, 236; faculty racial and ethnic diversity statistics of, 26–27; female faculty statistics of, 46–47, 52–53; law school student statistics of, 238–39; tenured faculty racial and ethnic diversity statistics of, 36–37

Crow, Michael, 125

CUNY Graduate School and University Center, 131

curriculum, diversity within, 153

CVs, pedigree link within, 76–77

Dartmouth College, 17n4

Davis, Shardé, 7n

Davis, William Boyd Allison, 66

deans: accountability of, 141, 142, 143; hiring role of, 151–52, 153–54; incentivizing, 144–45; influence and strategy of, 145–47; leadership role of, 135, 138, 141–42; shared governance of, 139–40

degree attainment rates, knowledge within, 119–20

Deo, Meera, 235

Deutsch, Monroe, 67

disciplines, quality variances within, 71–73

Diversifying the Faculty: A Guidebook for Search Committees (Turner), 11

diversity: accountability within, 139–43; benefits of, 211; communication of, 212; of curriculum, 153; data sharing regarding, 220–21; excellence and, 10–11, 91–92; funding for, 134; geographical excuses for, 205–9; importance of, 10; incentivizing, 144–45; within job descriptions, 163–67

diversity representative, 158–62

Diversity's Promise for Higher Education (Smith), 10

diversity statements, 185–93, 227

Duckworth, Angela, 178

Duke University: AAU membership of, 19; diversity statistics within, 236; faculty racial and ethnic diversity statistics of, 26–27; female faculty statistics of, 46–47,

52–53; law school student statistics of, 238–39; tenured faculty racial and ethnic diversity statistics of, 36–37; White faculty statistics of, 25

Eberhardt, Jennifer, 168
economics: African American PhD statistics within, 95, 100, 102–3; American Indian and Alaska Natives (AIAN) PhD statistics within, 110–11; Asian American PhD statistics within, 106–7; Hispanic PhD statistics within, 104–5; Latino PhD statistics within, 101; Native Hawaiians and Pacific Islanders (NHPI) PhD statistics within, 112–13; nonresident PhD statistics within, 116–17; nonresidents within, 108; PhD conferrals within, 96–99; White PhD statistics within, 108, 114–15
ELI, 168–69
elites/elitism: control of, 63; within job descriptions, 163–64; merit of, 217; old boys' network and, 90; ratings/rankings within, 84
Emory University: AAU membership of, 16–17, 19; African American faculty statistics of, 20; African American women faculty statistics of, 43–44; faculty racial and ethnic diversity statistics of, 26–27; female faculty statistics of, 46–47, 52–53; Hispanic faculty statistics of, 33; tenured faculty racial and ethnic diversity statistics of, 36–37
engineering: African American PhD statistics within, 102–3; American Indian and Alaska Natives (AIAN) PhD statistics within, 110–11; Asian American PhD statistics within, 106–7; Hispanic PhD statistics within, 104–5; Latino PhD statistics within, 100; Native Hawaiians and Pacific Islanders (NHPI) PhD statistics within, 112–13; nonresident PhD statistics within, 116–17; nonresidents within, 108; PhD conferrals within, 96–99; White PhD statistics within, 108, 114–15
English language and literature discipline: African American PhD statistics within, 95, 102–3; American Indian and Alaska Natives (AIAN) PhD statistics within, 110–11; Asian American PhD statistics within, 101, 106–7; Hispanic PhD statistics within, 104–5; Latino PhD statistics within, 100; Native Hawaiians and Pacific Islanders (NHPI) PhD statistics within, 112–13; nonresident PhD statistics within,

116–17; PhD conferrals within, 96–99; White PhD statistics within, 108, 114–15
enrollment, statistics of, 1–2
equity, embracing, 211
ethnic and cultural studies: African American PhD statistics within, 95, 102–3; American Indian and Alaska Natives (AIAN) PhD statistics within, 110–11; Asian American PhD statistics within, 106–7; Hispanic PhD statistics within, 104–5; Latino PhD statistics within, 100; Native Hawaiians and Pacific Islanders (NHPI) PhD statistics within, 108, 112–13; nonresident PhD statistics within, 116–17; White PhD statistics within, 108, 114–15
excellence in diversity, 10–11, 91–92
exceptions, examples of, 198–200
excuses, confrontation of, 198–200, 221–23
exercise, metaphor of, 9, 72, 208–9, 215
extraneous assumption, 221

faculty: bias within, 166–67; diversity statistics within, 2; incentivizing, 144–45; leadership role of, 137–39; placement strategies of, 215–16; shared governance of, 139. See also specific universities
Faculty of Color in Academe: Bittersweet Success (Turner and Meyers), 11
faculty of color series, 138
Faculty Search Toolkit (Michigan State University), 179
fit, defined, 204–5
Flier, Jeffrey, 187–88
foreign language and linguistics: African American PhD statistics within, 95, 102–3; American Indian and Alaska Natives (AIAN) PhD statistics within, 110–11; Asian American PhD statistics within, 106–7; Hispanic PhD statistics within, 104–5; Latino PhD statistics within, 100; Native Hawaiians and Pacific Islanders (NHPI) PhD statistics within, 112–13; nonresident PhD statistics within, 116–17; PhD conferrals within, 96–99; White PhD statistics within, 114–15
funding: diversity, 134; for hiring, 140, 141; incentivizing through, 144; inequities within, 205; leadership and, 135

gender, 35, 42–44, 148
geographical excuses, 205–9
Georgetown University, 236, 238–39

Georgia Institute of Technology (Georgia Tech): AAU membership of, 19; faculty racial and ethnic diversity statistics of, 26–27; female faculty statistics of, 46–47, 52–53; tenured faculty racial and ethnic diversity statistics of, 36–37; White faculty statistics of, 25

Gildersleeve, Virginia, 69

Golash-Boza, Tanya, 186

González, Carmen, 12

graduate schools, admissions bias within, 118–20

Guide to Best Practices in Faculty Search and Hiring (Columbia University), 179

handbook, for faculty hiring, 175, 178–81

Hannah-Jones, Nikole, 4, 23n13

Harris, Angela, 12

Harvard University: AAU membership of, 19; African American degree holders from, 68; Asian American faculty statistics of, 34; diversity statistics of, 236; faculty racial and ethnic diversity statistics of, 26–27; female faculty statistics of, 46–47, 52–53; handbook from, 179–80; hiring competition with, 82–83; Implicit Bias Assessment from, 180–81; law school student statistics of, 238–39; racial incident at, 133; tenured faculty racial and ethnic diversity statistics of, 36–37

hate, justification for, 8

hiring: benefits and design within, 211, 213; cluster, 200–202; competition within, 82–83; conferences for, 154; cost factor within, 81; faculty weaknesses within, 85; funding for, 140, 141; handbook for, 175, 178–81; hierarchical structure of, 61–62; learning promotion within, 220–21; legalities within, 182; networks for, 88–91; pack dependence within law schools, 235; process of, 151–54; ranking process within, 77; replication within, 85–86; targets of opportunity within, 151. *See also* search committees

Hispanics: doctorate statistics of, 5; faculty statistics of, 23–24, 118; female faculty statistics of, 2, 42, 44; law school statistics of, 236; male faculty statistics of, 2; PhD statistics of, 94, 100–101, 104–5; salaries of, 223; student statistics of, 1; tenured faculty statistics of, 33

Hispanic Serving Institutions (HSIs), 125, 220

Hispanic Serving Institutions: Pathways to the Professoriate program, 227

Historically Black Colleges and Universities (HBCUs), 2n, 82, 125, 220

history: African American PhD statistics within, 95, 102–3; American Indian and Alaska Natives (AIAN) PhD statistics within, 110–11; Asian American PhD statistics within, 101, 106–7; Hispanic PhD statistics within, 104–5; Native Hawaiians and Pacific Islanders (NHPI) PhD statistics within, 112–13; nonresident PhD statistics within, 116–17; PhD conferrals within, 96–99; White PhD statistics within, 108, 114–15

humanities, hiring conferences within, 154

Implicit Bias Assessment/Test, 180–81, 218

implicit bias training, 167–78, 218–19

incentivizing, within diversity hiring, 144–45

inclusive excellence, 2–3

Indiana University: AAU membership of, 19; Asian American faculty statistics of, 34; female faculty statistics of, 46–47, 52–53; strategic plan of, 45; tenured faculty racial and ethnic diversity statistics of, 36–37; White faculty statistics of, 25

Indiana University-Bloomington, 26–27

inequity, color-blind policies and, 66–67

Institute for the Recruitment of Teachers, 227

institutional racism, 65

Integrated Postsecondary Education Data System (IPEDS), 146

Interfolio, 145–46

intersectionality, 42

interviews: of African American candidates, 69; diversity statements within, 191–93; within hiring conferences, 154; NFL requirements for, 143; preliminary, 176–77; standard questions within, 173

Iowa State University: AAU membership of, 19; Asian American faculty statistics of, 34; faculty racial and ethnic diversity statistics of, 26–27; female faculty statistics of, 46–47, 52–53; tenured faculty racial and ethnic diversity statistics of, 36–37

job description, crafting of, 163–67, 227

Johns Hopkins University: AAU membership of, 19; African American faculty statistics of, 20; African American women faculty statistics of, 43; Asian American faculty statistics of, 24; Asian American women faculty statistics of, 44; faculty diversity approach within, 33–34; faculty racial and ethnic diversity statistics of, 26–27;

female faculty statistics of, 46–47, 52–53; tenured faculty racial and ethnic diversity statistics of, 36–37
Johnson, Jim, 188–89
Josephson, Clarence, 70
Julius Rosenwald Fund, 66n4

Kelsky, Karen, 185–86

Lach, Denise, 163
law schools, 235–39
leadership: within AAU institutions, 135; accountability within, 139–43; commitment from, 136–39; criticism to, 212; diversity communication by, 212; necessity of leading within, 212–13; structure of, 135
Leadership Alliance, 227
Lewis, Julian H., 66n3
Liberal Arts Diversity Council, 227
low-income rates, faculty factors within, 25, 32

Massachusetts Institute of Technology (MIT): AAU membership of, 19; African American degree holders from, 68; faculty racial and ethnic diversity statistics of, 26–27; female faculty statistics of, 46–47, 52–53; tenured faculty racial and ethnic diversity statistics of, 36–37
mathematics and statistics: African American PhD statistics within, 95, 102–3; American Indian and Alaska Natives (AIAN) PhD statistics within, 110–11; Asian American PhD statistics within, 106–7; Hispanic PhD statistics within, 104–5; Latino PhD statistics within, 100; Native Hawaiians and Pacific Islanders (NHPI) PhD statistics within, 112–13; nonresident PhD statistics within, 108, 116–17; PhD conferrals within, 96–99; White PhD statistics within, 108, 114–15
Matthew, Patricia, 12
McNair Scholars Program, 227
Mellon Mays Undergraduate Fellowship, 227
men, faculty diversity statistics of, 2, 151n1
merit, 59n1, 62–63, 65, 66–70, 217. See also quality
Meyers, Samuel, 11
Michigan State University: AAU membership of, 19; American Indian and Alaska Native (AIAN) faculty statistics of, 34; faculty racial and ethnic diversity statistics of, 26–27; female faculty statistics of, 46–47, 52–53; handbook from, 179; Native

Hawaiians and Pacific Islanders (NHPI) faculty statistics of, 24; tenured faculty racial and ethnic diversity statistics of, 36–37
Mifflin, Lawrie, 4
Moody, JoAnn, 11, 221
Muhs, Gabriella, 12

National Science Foundation (NSF), 35, 42
Native Americans, 1, 2
Native Hawaiians and Pacific Islanders (NHPIs): enrollment statistics of, 1; faculty statistics of, 24, 118; female faculty statistics of, 43, 44; law school statistics of, 236; PhD statistics of, 108, 112–13; tenured faculty statistics of, 35
networks, 88–91, 215
New York University (NYU): AAU membership of, 19; diversity statistics within, 236; faculty racial and ethnic diversity statistics of, 26–27; female faculty statistics of, 46–47, 52–53; law school student statistics of, 238–39; strategic plan of, 45n18; student diversity within, 2; tenured faculty racial and ethnic diversity statistics of, 36–37
NFL, Rooney rule within, 143
Niemann, Yolanda, 12
nonresidents, 108, 109, 116–17
Northwestern University: AAU membership of, 19; diversity statistics within, 236; faculty racial and ethnic diversity statistics of, 26–27; female faculty statistics of, 46–47, 52–53; student diversity within, 2; tenured faculty racial and ethnic diversity statistics of, 36–37

objective data, 73–78
Ohio State University: AAU membership of, 19; faculty racial and ethnic diversity statistics of, 26–27; female faculty statistics of, 48–49, 54–55; tenured faculty racial and ethnic diversity statistics of, 38–39
old boys' network, 88–91

pathways, creating and tapping, 227–28
pedigree: within CVs, 76–77; influence of, 78–88; institutional, 80–82, 86–87; manifestations of, 63–64; measures of, 60; old boys' network and, 88–91; privileging within, 79, 195–97; research institutional, 87–88

Pell Grant-eligible students, 2n
Pennsylvania State University: AAU membership of, 19; faculty racial and ethnic diversity statistics of, 28–29; female faculty statistics of, 48–49, 54–55; tenured faculty racial and ethnic diversity statistics of, 38–39; White faculty statistics of, 25
personal character, 62
PhDs: admissions bias within, 118–20; limiting qualified candidate pools within, 125–31; nonresidents within, 108; recruitment of, 226–27; statistics of, 94, 229; within STEM fields, 79. *See also specific universities*
philosophy and religious studies: African American PhD statistics within, 95, 102–3; American Indian and Alaska Natives (AIAN) PhD statistics within, 110–11; Asian American PhD statistics within, 106–7; Hispanic PhD statistics within, 104–5; Latino PhD statistics within, 100–101; Native Hawaiians and Pacific Islanders (NHPI) PhD statistics within, 112–13; nonresident PhD statistics within, 116–17; PhD conferrals within, 96–99; White PhD statistics within, 108, 114–15
physical sciences: African American PhD statistics within, 95, 102–3; American Indian and Alaska Natives (AIAN) PhD statistics within, 110–11; Asian American PhD statistics within, 106–7; Hispanic PhD statistics within, 104–5; Latino PhD statistics within, 100; Native Hawaiians and Pacific Islanders (NHPI) PhD statistics within, 112–13; nonresident PhD statistics of, 108, 116–17; PhD conferrals within, 96–99; White PhD statistics within, 114–15
pipeline, 93–94, 121–24, 227–28
placement rates, 120
political science and government: African American PhD statistics within, 100, 102–3; American Indian and Alaska Natives (AIAN) PhD statistics within, 110–11; Asian American PhD statistics within, 106–7; Hispanic PhD statistics within, 104–5; Latino PhD statistics within, 101; Native Hawaiians and Pacific Islanders (NHPI) PhD statistics within, 112–13; nonresident PhD statistics within, 116–17; PhD conferrals within, 96–99; White PhD statistics within, 108, 114–15
Porter, Andy, 138
Posselt, Julie, 87–88, 118–20

preliminary interviews, 176–77
presidents, leadership role of, 135
Presumed Incompetent: The Intersections of Race and Class for Women in Academia (Muhs et al.), 12
Princeton University: AAU membership of, 19; Asian American faculty statistics of, 24, 34; faculty racial and ethnic diversity statistics of, 28–29; female faculty statistics of, 48–49, 54–55; tenured faculty racial and ethnic diversity statistics of, 38–39
privileging, 63–64, 195–97
protests, 170, 214–15
provosts: accountability of, 141, 142; incentive funds from, 144; influence and strategy of, 145–47; leadership role of, 135, 136, 137, 141; race of, 147–49; shared governance of, 139–40
psychology: African American PhD statistics within, 95, 102–3; American Indian and Alaska Natives (AIAN) PhD statistics within, 110–11; Asian American PhD statistics within, 101, 106–7; Hispanic PhD statistics within, 104–5; Latino PhD statistics within, 101; nonresident PhD statistics within, 116–17; White PhD statistics within, 108, 114–15
publishing, hiring regarding, 203–4
Purdue University: AAU membership of, 19; Asian American faculty statistics of, 24, 34; Asian American women faculty statistics of, 44; faculty racial and ethnic diversity statistics of, 28–29; female faculty statistics of, 48–49, 54–55; tenured faculty racial and ethnic diversity statistics of, 38–39

qualifications, as discriminatory, 61
quality: characteristics within, 75–76; checklists for, 75; defined, 59n1; by disciplines, 71–73; diversity and excellence within, 91–92; guidance for, 86; measures for, 60; old boys' network and, 88–91; questioning, 59–60, 216–18; ranking process within, 77. *See also* merit

racism, 8, 65, 133–34
ranking, 84
ratings, within elitism, 84
Recruiting for Diversity (Harvard University), 179–80
recruitment, faculty, 11–12, 224–27
rejection, examples of, 5–9
research institutions, 87–88, 126–30

resumes, bias within, 168–69

retention, 228–29

Rice University: AAU membership of, 19; African American faculty statistics of, 33; faculty racial and ethnic diversity statistics of, 28–29; female faculty statistics of, 48–49, 54–55; Hispanic faculty statistics of, 23; tenured faculty racial and ethnic diversity statistics of, 38–39

Rivera, Lauren, 72, 78, 151, 178, 211, 217

Rooney rule, 143

Roosevelt College, 70

Rutgers University: AAU membership of, 19; faculty racial and ethnic diversity statistics of, 28–29; female faculty statistics of, 48–49, 54–55; strategic plan of, 45; tenured faculty racial and ethnic diversity statistics of, 38–39; White faculty statistics of, 25

salaries, excuses for, 207, 222, 223

San Jose State University, 133

science, technology, engineering, and math (STEM) fields, 35, 42, 79

search committees: composition and work of, 155–58; considerations for, 216–17; diversity representative within, 158–62; diversity statements and, 191–93; diversity within, 156–57; excuses within, 221; faculty hiring process of, 151–54; handbooks for, 175, 178–81; job description crafting by, 163–67, 227; leadership within, 219; overview of, 150–51; patterns of, 181–84; quality consideration within, 216–18; recruitment process of, 224–27; rethinking, 219–20; service responsibility challenges within, 157–58; training for, 167–78, 218–19

search processes, dismantling and reconstruction within, 213–16

shared governance, 139

Shibley, Robert, 188

Simmons, Ruth, 20, 22, 58

Smith, Daryl: exercise analogy of, 9, 72, 208–9, 215; quote of, 10, 14, 15, 35, 42, 45, 190, 215, 222; story of, 9–10

social sciences: African American PhD statistics within, 95, 102–3; American Indian and Alaska Natives (AIAN) PhD statistics within, 110–11; Asian American PhD statistics within, 106–7; Hispanic PhD statistics within, 104–5; Latino PhD statistics within, 101; Native Hawaiians and Pacific Islanders (NHPI) PhD statistics

within, 112–13; nonresident PhD statistics within, 116–17; PhD conferrals within, 96–99; White PhD statistics within, 114–15

sociology: African American PhD statistics within, 100, 102–3; American Indian and Alaska Natives (AIAN) PhD statistics within, 110–11; Asian American PhD statistics within, 106–7; Hispanic PhD statistics within, 104–5; Latino PhD statistics within, 101; Native Hawaiians and Pacific Islanders (NHPI) PhD statistics within, 112–13; nonresident PhD statistics within, 116–17; PhD conferrals within, 96–99; White PhD statistics within, 108, 114–15

Southwestern College, 70

Span, Chris, 22

special lines for diversity, hiring within, 198–200

Springer, Ann, 144

Sproul, Robert, 68

Stanford University: AAU membership of, 19; diversity statistics within, 236; faculty racial and ethnic diversity statistics of, 28–29; female faculty statistics of, 48–49, 54–55; law school student statistics of, 238–39; student diversity within, 2; tenured faculty racial and ethnic diversity statistics of, 38–39; Varsity Blues scandal within, 74; White law school population statistics of, 236

Sterling College, 70

Stony Brook University: AAU membership of, 19; faculty racial and ethnic diversity statistics of, 28–29; female faculty statistics of, 48–49, 54–55; tenured faculty racial and ethnic diversity statistics of, 38–39

Suppes, Lexi, 189

Survey of Earned Doctorates, 123

systemic racism, 65, 195–97

targets of opportunity, 151, 198–200

technology, bias within, 168

Texas A&M University: AAU membership of, 16–17, 19; faculty racial and ethnic diversity statistics of, 28–29; female faculty statistics of, 48–49, 54–55; Hispanic faculty statistics of, 33; tenured faculty racial and ethnic diversity statistics of, 38–39

theater-based training, 170–71

Thelin, John, 16

top-down strategy for diversification, 152–53

training, 167–78, 218–19

Trent, William, 22

Tulane University: AAU membership of, 19; American Indian and Alaska Native (AIAN) faculty statistics of, 34; faculty racial and ethnic diversity statistics of, 30–31; female faculty statistics of, 48–49, 54–55; tenured faculty racial and ethnic diversity statistics of, 38–39
Turner, Caroline Sotello, 11

UC-Berkeley: AAU membership of, 20; diversity statistics within, 236; faculty racial and ethnic diversity statistics of, 28–29; female faculty statistics of, 48–49, 54–55; law school student statistics of, 238–39; student diversity within, 2; tenured faculty racial and ethnic diversity statistics of, 38–39; White faculty statistics of, 25
UC-Davis: AAU membership of, 19–20; African American faculty statistics of, 33; Asian American women faculty statistics of, 44; faculty racial and ethnic diversity statistics of, 28–29; female faculty statistics of, 48–49, 54–55; Hispanic women faculty statistics of, 44; tenured faculty racial and ethnic diversity statistics of, 38–39; top-down strategy for diversification within, 152–53
UC-Irvine: AAU membership of, 20; Asian American faculty statistics of, 24, 34; Asian American women faculty statistics of, 44; faculty racial and ethnic diversity statistics of, 28–29; female faculty statistics of, 48–49, 54–55; Native Hawaiians and Pacific Islanders (NHPI) faculty statistics of, 24; tenured faculty racial and ethnic diversity statistics of, 38–39
UCLA: AAU membership of, 20; American Indian and Alaska Native (AIAN) faculty statistics of, 34; Asian American faculty statistics of, 34; Asian American women faculty statistics of, 44; faculty racial and ethnic diversity statistics of, 28–29; female faculty statistics of, 48–49, 54–55; Hispanic faculty statistics of, 23, 33; Native Hawaiians and Pacific Islanders (NHPI) women faculty statistics of, 44; racial incident at, 133; student diversity within, 2; tenured faculty racial and ethnic diversity statistics of, 38–39
UC-San Diego: AAU membership of, 20; faculty racial and ethnic diversity statistics of, 28–29; female faculty statistics of, 48–49, 54–55; Hispanic faculty statistics of, 23, 33; Hispanic women faculty statistics of, 44; tenured faculty racial and ethnic diversity statistics of, 38–39
UC-Santa Barbara: AAU membership of, 20; American Indian and Alaska Native (AIAN) faculty statistics of, 24–25, 34; American Indian and Alaska Native (AIAN) women faculty statistics of, 44; faculty racial and ethnic diversity statistics of, 28–29; female faculty statistics of, 48–49, 54–55; Hispanic faculty statistics of, 23, 33; Hispanic women faculty statistics of, 44; tenured faculty racial and ethnic diversity statistics of, 38–39
UC-Santa Cruz, 17n4
University of Alabama, 133
University of Arizona: AAU membership of, 19; African American faculty statistics of, 33; American Indian and Alaska Native (AIAN) faculty statistics of, 34; American Indian and Alaska Native (AIAN) women faculty statistics of, 44; faculty racial and ethnic diversity statistics of, 28–29; female faculty statistics of, 48–49, 54–55; Hispanic faculty statistics of, 23, 33; Hispanic women faculty statistics of, 44; tenured faculty racial and ethnic diversity statistics of, 38–39
University of Buffalo: AAU membership of, 19; American Indian and Alaska Native (AIAN) faculty statistics of, 34; American Indian and Alaska Native (AIAN) women faculty statistics of, 44; Asian American faculty statistics of, 34; faculty racial and ethnic diversity statistics of, 28–29; female faculty statistics of, 48–49, 54–55; tenured faculty racial and ethnic diversity statistics of, 38–39
University of Chicago: AAU membership of, 20; African American degree holders from, 68; diversity statistics within, 236; faculty racial and ethnic diversity statistics of, 28–29; female faculty statistics of, 48–49, 54–55; law school student statistics of, 238–39; student diversity within, 2; tenured faculty racial and ethnic diversity statistics of, 38–39; White law school population statistics of, 236
University of Colorado-Boulder: AAU membership of, 20; African American faculty statistics of, 22, 33; American Indian and Alaska Native (AIAN) faculty statistics of, 34; faculty racial and ethnic diversity statistics of, 28–29; female faculty statistics

of, 48–49, 54–55; Native Hawaiians and Pacific Islanders faculty statistics of, 24; tenured faculty racial and ethnic diversity statistics of, 38–39

University of Florida: AAU membership of, 16–17, 20; faculty racial and ethnic diversity statistics of, 28–29; female faculty statistics within, 48–49, 54–55; tenured faculty racial and ethnic diversity statistics of, 38–39

University of Illinois: AAU membership of, 20; African American faculty statistics of, 20, 22, 32; faculty racial and ethnic diversity statistics of, 28–29; female faculty statistics of, 50–51, 56–57; Hispanic faculty statistics of, 23; racial incident at, 133–34; tenured faculty racial and ethnic diversity statistics of, 40–41

University of Iowa: AAU membership of, 20; faculty racial and ethnic diversity statistics of, 28–29; female faculty statistics of, 50–51, 56–57; tenured faculty racial and ethnic diversity statistics of, 40–41

University of Kansas: AAU membership of, 20; American Indian and Alaska Native (AIAN) faculty statistics of, 34; faculty racial and ethnic diversity statistics of, 30–31; female faculty statistics of, 50–51, 56–57; tenured faculty racial and ethnic diversity statistics of, 40–41

University of Maryland: AAU membership of, 20; faculty racial and ethnic diversity statistics of, 30–31; female faculty statistics of, 50–51, 56–57; White faculty statistics of, 25

University of Michigan: AAU membership of, 20; African American degree holders from, 68; African American faculty statistics of, 32; description of, 17–18; diversity statistics within, 236; female faculty statistics of, 50–51, 56–57; law school student statistics of, 238–39; racial incident at, 134; tenured faculty racial and ethnic diversity statistics of, 40–41; White law school population statistics of, 236

University of Minnesota: AAU membership of, 20; faculty racial and ethnic diversity statistics of, 30–31; female faculty statistics of, 50–51, 56–57; tenured faculty racial and ethnic diversity statistics of, 40–41

University of Missouri: AAU membership of, 20; faculty racial and ethnic diversity statistics of, 30–31; tenured faculty racial and ethnic diversity statistics of, 40–41

University of North Carolina-Chapel Hill: AAU membership of, 20; African American faculty statistics of, 20, 32; African American women faculty statistics of, 43; Asian American faculty statistics of, 24, 34; faculty racial and ethnic diversity statistics of, 30–31; female faculty statistics of, 50–51, 56–57; Hispanic faculty statistics of, 23; tenured faculty racial and ethnic diversity statistics of, 40–41

University of Oregon: AAU membership of, 20; African American faculty statistics of, 33; Asian American faculty statistics of, 24, 34; faculty racial and ethnic diversity statistics of, 30–31; female faculty statistics of, 50–51, 56–57; tenured faculty racial and ethnic diversity statistics of, 40–41

University of Pennsylvania: AAU membership of, 20; African American degree holders from, 68; description of, 17; diversity funding within, 134; diversity statistics within, 236; faculty racial and ethnic diversity statistics of, 30–31; female faculty statistics of, 50–51, 56–57; law school student statistics of, 238–39; tenured faculty racial and ethnic diversity statistics of, 40–41; White law school population statistics of, 236–37

University of Pittsburgh: AAU membership of, 20; Asian American faculty statistics of, 24; Asian American women faculty statistics of, 44; faculty racial and ethnic diversity statistics of, 30–31; female faculty statistics of, 50–51, 56–57; Native Hawaiians and Pacific Islanders (NHPI) faculty statistics of, 24, 35; tenured faculty racial and ethnic diversity statistics of, 40–41

University of Rochester: AAU membership of, 20; African American faculty statistics of, 33; Asian American faculty statistics of, 34; faculty racial and ethnic diversity statistics of, 30–31; female faculty statistics of, 50–51, 56–57; Hispanic faculty statistics of, 33; tenured faculty racial and ethnic diversity statistics of, 40–41; White faculty statistics of, 25

University of Southern California: AAU membership of, 20; faculty racial and ethnic diversity statistics of, 30–31; female faculty statistics of, 50–51, 56–57; tenured faculty racial and ethnic diversity statistics of, 40–41; Varsity Blues scandal within, 74

University of Texas-Austin: AAU membership of, 20; faculty racial and ethnic diversity statistics of, 30–31; female faculty statistics of, 50–51, 56–57; Hispanic faculty statistics of, 23; Hispanic women faculty statistics of, 44; tenured faculty racial and ethnic diversity statistics of, 40–41

University of Utah, 17n4

University of Virginia: AAU membership of, 20; African American faculty statistics of, 20, 32; Asian American faculty statistics of, 24, 34; diversity statistics within, 236; faculty racial and ethnic diversity statistics of, 30–31; female faculty statistics of, 50–51, 56–57; law school student statistics of, 238–39; tenured faculty racial and ethnic diversity statistics of, 40–41; White faculty statistics of, 25; White law school population statistics of, 237

University of Washington: AAU membership of, 20; African American faculty statistics of, 22; American Indian and Alaska Native (AIAN) faculty statistics of, 34; American Indian and Alaska Native (AIAN) women faculty statistics of, 44; faculty racial and ethnic diversity statistics of, 30–31; female faculty statistics of, 50–51, 56–57; tenured faculty racial and ethnic diversity statistics of, 40–41

University of Wisconsin: AAU membership of, 20; African American degree holders from, 68; faculty racial and ethnic diversity statistics of, 30–31; female faculty statistics of, 50–51, 56–57

Vanderbilt University: AAU membership of, 20; African American faculty statistics of, 32; African American women faculty statistics of, 43–44; Asian American faculty statistics of, 24, 34; faculty racial and ethnic diversity statistics of, 30–31; tenured faculty racial and ethnic diversity statistics of, 40–41

Varsity Blues scandal, 74–75

Wale, Fred, 66–70

Washington University (St. Louis): AAU membership of, 20; African American women faculty statistics of, 43; faculty racial and ethnic diversity statistics of, 30–31; female faculty statistics of, 50–51, 56–57; Hispanic faculty statistics of, 33; tenured faculty racial and ethnic diversity statistics of, 40–41

Whiteness, reproduction of, 61

Whites: ADVANCE grants for, 42; exceptions for, 195–97, 198–200; faculty statistics of, 25, 109; female faculty statistics of, 2, 43; law school statistics of, 236; male faculty statistics of, 2; passes for, 202–5; PhD statistics of, 94, 108, 114–15; salaries of, 223; service responsibilities of, 157; tenured faculty statistics of, 35

William Penn College, 70

women, statistics of, 2, 46–57, 237

Woods, Joy Melody, 7n

Written/Unwritten: Diversity and the Hidden Truths of Tenure (Matthews), 12

Yale University: AAU membership of, 20; Asian American faculty statistics of, 34; diversity funding within, 134; diversity statistics within, 236; faculty racial and ethnic diversity statistics of, 30–31; female faculty statistics of, 50–51, 56–57; Hispanic faculty statistics of, 33; law school student statistics of, 238–39; Native Hawaiians and Pacific Islanders (NHPI) faculty statistics of, 24; Native Hawaiians and Pacific Islanders (NHPI) women faculty statistics of, 44; strategic plan of, 45n18; tenured faculty racial and ethnic diversity statistics of, 40–41

YouTube, technology bias within, 168